THE
LEAN CEO

THE
LEAN CEO

BUILDING WORLD-CLASS ORGANIZATIONS, ONE STEP AT A TIME

JACOB STOLLER

New York   Chicago   San Francisco   Lisbon   London   Madrid   Mexico City
Milan   New Delhi   San Juan   Seoul   Singapore   Sydney   Toronto

1 2 3 4 5 6 7 8 9 0   DOC/DOC   1 2 0 9 8 7 6 5

ISBN: 978-0-07-183306-6
MHID: 0-07-183306-4

e-ISBN: 978-0-07-183307-2
e-MHID: 0-07-183307-3

Library of Congress Cataloging-in-Publication Data
Stoller, Jacob.
  The lean CEO : building world-class organizations, one step at a time / Jacob Stoller.
    pages cm
  ISBN 978-0-07-183306-6 (alk. paper) — ISBN 0-07-183306-4 (alk. paper)   1. Chief executive officers—Case studies.   2. Leadership—Case studies.   3. Cost control—Case studies.
4. Lean manufacturing—Case studies.   5. Organizational effectiveness—Case studies.
6. Leadership—Case studies.   I. Title.
  HD38.2.S764 2015
  658.4'2—dc23
                                                                                2015001205

McGraw-Hill Education books are available at special quantity discounts to use as premiums and sales promotions, or for use in corporate training programs. To contact a representative, please visit the Contact Us page at www.mhprofessional.com.

CONTENTS

FOREWORD   BY DANNEL P. MALLOY   vii

ACKNOWLEDGMENTS   xi

PREFACE   xv

Chapter 1   **How Waste Became Business as Usual**   **1**

Chapter 2   **Lean: A Radical New Approach to Production**   **21**

Chapter 3   **West Meets East and the Unbelievable**   **47**

Chapter 4   **A New Way Out of Financial Crisis**   **71**

Chapter 5   **Capacity Without Capital Expenditure**   **107**

Chapter 6   **A Realistic Approach to Worker Motivation**   **127**

Chapter 7   **Building Collaborative Management Teams**   **141**

Chapter 8   **Putting People First**   **159**

Chapter 9   **Building the Learning Organization**   **187**

Chapter 10   **Integrating a Diversified Corporation**   **217**

Chapter 11   **Reducing Dependence on the CEO**   **235**

Chapter 12 **Solving the Cost/Quality Conundrum in Healthcare** 251

Chapter 13 **Defining and Delivering Value in Government** 283

Chapter 14 **Conclusions** 305

NOTES 317

READING LIST 321

INDEX 323

FOREWORD

by Dannel P. Malloy,
Governor, State of Connecticut

When I finished law school in 1980 and began my career as a district attorney, the Lean movement was just starting to reach public consciousness in the United States. The wake-up call for many of us was NBC's documentary *If Japan Can, Why Can't We?* which chronicled how Japan, led by Toyota, was overtaking the United States as an industrial power. Although the management philosophy was not identified as Lean until a decade later, it was clear that there was a systematic approach behind Japan's commercial success that was radically different from what the business community was practicing in the United States.

Those watching the broadcast were probably surprised to learn that many of Japan's "secrets" came from W. Edwards Deming, an American who had been all but ignored in this country. Deming had traveled to Japan as a consultant, assisting Douglas MacArthur's post–World War II reconstruction efforts, and by the 1960s he was a national hero there.

Throughout the 1980s, signs of Lean management began surfacing in our industrial sector, including the use of methods such as Total Quality Management (TQM) and Just-in-Time (JIT).

By the 1990s, a small group of American companies had begun to use the Toyota Production System (TPS), which became the prototype for Lean. What many didn't realize was that this new approach was much more than a set of shop floor methods: it represented a reinvention of the way companies manage all their operations. This meant that Lean could, and soon would, be applied to service industries, healthcare, and government.

As governor of Connecticut, I am also effectively the state's CEO and can draw parallels between my role and those of my counterparts in the private sector. As we strive to make state government leaner and more cost-effective in the face of a tough budget and a challenging economy, it is clear that government is not exempt from the same belt-tightening measures being made in corporations and households across the country. Simply put, we know we must find ways to do more with less while still being responsive to taxpayers.

When I took office, I directed all executive branch agencies to implement Lean methods to get routine activities functioning smoothly and consistently and to free up staff members' time so they could focus on higher-value tasks that are more directly linked to meeting the needs of citizens. Connecticut is not alone. We are one of 15 states that have embraced the Lean approach, and we regularly share resources and compare notes with our colleagues in other states and in the federal government and with our partners in the private sector.

Since implementing Lean methods, we have seen significant and encouraging progress in our efforts to attain a smaller, more efficient executive branch, efforts that to date have saved over $2 billion in taxpayer dollars. For example, our Department of Energy and Environmental Protection cut the approval time for coastal projects by half and reduced processing time for 12 of its permits by 74 percent.

Another Lean team streamlined processes at our Department of Revenue Services by reducing the levels of management at the agency, eliminating two stand-alone business units, and cutting annual operational costs by $8.25 million—all done without laying people off.

Although the implementation of Lean at our state agencies is being led by the commissioners, much of the change and improvement we have achieved stems from the input of many hardworking frontline state employees. This is important to note because Lean was founded on a profound respect for people and the understanding that when workers are consulted, they become more engaged, enthusiastic, and innovative. In fact, the improvements that allowed Toyota to multiply its productivity were not designed in engineering offices but right on the shop floor by frontline workers. The underlying assumption here is that the deepest understanding of how to improve a process does not come from management but from the workers who go through those processes day in and day out.

Although we have made great strides to modernize state government, achieve quantifiable savings, and streamline various state agency processes, we still have more work to do. This is only the beginning of an ongoing, expansive, and fundamental transformation of Connecticut's state government.

As we continue on our path to enhance the effectiveness, efficiency, and timeliness of the processes we use every day in state government, we are proud to have some great role models to look to right here in Connecticut. This includes one of the most successful Lean companies in the world: United Technologies Corporation. Two Hartford-area companies whose stories are told in this book were among the first North American companies to bring in Lean experts from Japan. Both of these companies achieved extraordinary results, and in the ensuing decades they served as mentors for a select group of American companies.

Lean, however, comes with a caveat. As with most new ideas, there is a tendency to adopt it superficially as another flavor of the month.

Even worse, if it is implemented purely as a cost-cutting measure, it will lead to alienation of workers and unsustainable results. The good news is that Lean uses simple conceptual tools. Although it doesn't take a large investment to get started, successfully implementing Lean requires sustained and determined leadership spearheading a disciplined and continuous improvement program to ultimately change the culture throughout an organization.

The pages you are about to read feature narratives from CEOs in various sectors who personally championed Lean. Their experience provides solid evidence that our factories can compete globally; our healthcare system can be affordable, sustainable, and safe; and all levels of our governments can provide the efficient high-quality services that citizens deserve. By empowering our people to improve the processes that define their workplace, we can tap a powerful force that will lead the way to a stronger, more prosperous world.

ACKNOWLEDGMENTS

An unusual number of people provided input for this book, so there's a lot to acknowledge.

Let's start with Jon Miller, author and leading authority on Lean and CEO of the Kaizen Institute, who provided feedback and expert guidance at virtually every stage of the planning and creation this book.

I also have special gratitude for Masaaki Imai, founder of the Kaizen Institute, who has shaped my thinking about the true meaning of Lean.

Many others provided advice and encouragement. They are Mark Graban of Kai Nexus, Karen Martin of The Karen Martin Group, Cliff Ransom of Ransom Research Inc., Larry Grasso of Central Connecticut State University, Gareth Morgan of York University, Chet Marchwinski of the Lean Enterprise Institute, Rocky Dwyer and Tim Nerenz of Athabasca University, and Larry Coté of Lean Advisors, who first introduced me to Lean. Special thanks to Alberto Bastos of the Kaizen Institute Portugal, Carlo Ratto of the Kaizen Institute Italy, Dan Alexander of the Kaizen Institute UK, Julien Bratu of the Kaizen Institute Romania, Brian Maskell of BMA Inc., and Jean Cunningham of Jean Cunningham Consulting, who introduced me to their Lean CEO clients.

I'd like to thank my personal friends Tessa Marquis and Mike Brown of the New Standard Institute who provided inspiration, advice, and introductions. Author Bill Freeman first encouraged me to write this book and coached me through the proposal. My sister Tia Stoller of Stoller Design Group provided the initial cover design. My friend Jerry Shiner provided helpful feedback on the manuscript.

I'd also like to thank my sons, Mark, Jonathan, and Benjamin, for their thoughts and inspiration, and to extend a very special thank you to my wonderful wife Susan for her encouragement, counsel, and unwavering support.

A special thank you to my editor Knox Huston, senior editor at McGraw-Hill, for his expert help and encouragement; to Mary Glenn, associate publisher, for her support; and to senior editor Judy Bass, who first read my proposal and forwarded it to Knox Huston.

Thanks finally to the Lean CEOs and their accomplices for sharing their knowledge, experiences, and insights. They include George Koenigsaecker of Lean Investments LLC, Orest Fiume of Lean Accounting Management Institute, Arthur Byrne of J.W. Childs Associates, Pat Lancaster of Lantech, Jim Lancaster of Lantech, Dan Ariens of Ariens Inc., Steve Brenneman of Aluminum Trailer Company (ATC), Paul Steffes and Joe Rothschiller of Steffes Corporation, Mary Andringa of Vermeer Corporation, Brian Walker and Matt Long of Herman Miller Inc., Jorge Pinto of CaetanoBus, Pierluigi Tosato of Acqua Minerale San Benedetto, Ed Byczynski of PLZ Aeroscience, Bob Chapman, Jerry Solomon, and Dick Ryan of Barry-Wehmiller, Tom Everill and Mike Quinn of Northwest Center, Jim Martin of Goodwill Industries, Kevin Meyer of Gemba Academy, Mark Richards and Jason Schulist of Appvion, Eric Ries of The Lean Startup, Chris McBean of E-Leather, Mike Lamach and Dan McDonnell of Ingersoll Rand, Karl Wadensten and Linda Kleineberg of Vibco Vibrators, Hugo Levente Bara of Supremia

Grup, Dr. John Toussaint of ThedaCare Center for Healthcare Value, Dr. Gary Kaplan of Virginia Mason Medical Center, Bob Brody and Joe Swartz of Franciscan St. Francis Health, Jay Inslee, Darrell Damron, Wendy Korthuis-Smith, and Hollie Jensen of the State of Washington, Dannel P. Malloy and Alison Newman Fisher of the State of Connecticut, Dan Florizone of the Province of Saskatchewan, Canada, and John Shook of the Lean Enterprise Institute.

PREFACE

One of the most promising developments in modern business history has been the emergence of the global Lean movement, which was founded on the practices that vaulted Japan to manufacturing stardom in the late 1970s. Today, the Lean approach has a remarkable track record for helping organizations do more with less and it is rapidly gaining ground in nonindustrial sectors such as healthcare, government, and financial services.

Most people, however, see Lean as merely a set of tactical methods, and most organizations that practice Lean do so superficially. Typically, a company might undertake a series of Lean projects to reduce costs, cut down on defects, or solve a bottleneck in a manufacturing process. These isolated attempts rarely result in real change, and invariably lead to the abandonment of Lean for the next flavor of the month.

Lean's true potential to build world-class performance depends on a commitment to continuous improvement that involves every worker in the organization and requires uncommon discipline and persistence. The basic tenets of Lean, moreover, challenge many aspects of traditional management theory and call for a mindset that is foreign to most executives.

Lean is therefore a tough sell in the boardroom, and CEOs who actively lead Lean transformations are the exception rather than the rule. A popular rule of thumb in the Lean community is that 95 percent of Lean transformations fail from lack of senior management support.

The successes of the remaining 5 percent, however, are often stunning. Lean organizations routinely achieve results such as the doubling of capacity with existing resources, the reduction of lead times to a fraction of what they were, or a dramatic rise to leadership in their sector. In many cases, these gains lead to a complete financial turnaround.

But this isn't just about making numbers. Lean empowers employees, builds closer bonds with customers and suppliers, removes silos, creates transparency, and helps build a sustainable future. To evoke a popular cliché, Lean builds great companies.

THE LEAN CEOs

The 28 Lean CEOs you are about to hear from speak from a remarkable vantage point. Together, they represent a brain trust of leaders from a variety of backgrounds and organizations who share a common experience: they have followed a path that diverges from convention, and they have done so with considerable success.

Accordingly, their insights provide a fresh perspective on the challenges facing businesses today. Absent are the timeworn formulas, the corporate-speak, and the empty phrases. Their narratives are all about execution and reflect a realism that is all too rare in the business world.

These Lean CEOs openly challenge many common business practices, such as standard cost accounting, top-down management, emphasis on batch sizes and economies of scale, and our modern obsession with data and computers. Their criticism carries the authority of practical leaders who have walked the talk.

MANY STARTING POINTS, ONE JOURNEY

Taiichi Ohno, one of the founding fathers of Lean, began his work in the almost impossible circumstances of post–World War II Japan.

> "I strongly believe that 'necessity is the mother of invention,'" he said in his book *The Toyota Production System*. "Even today, improvements at Toyota plants are made based on need. The key to progress in production improvement, I feel, is letting the plant people feel the need."[1]

Ohno's belief is borne out by the CEO experiences in this book: in each case Lean was adopted in response to a pressing business need. The burning platforms, as we call them, are highly diverse, demonstrating Lean's applicability to a wide range of business problems.

The core content of the book is organized according to the following burning platforms:

- A New Way out of Financial Crisis
- Capacity Without Capital Expenditure
- A Realistic Approach to Worker Motivation
- Building Collaborative Management Teams
- Putting People First
- Building the Learning Organization
- Integrating a Diversified Corporation
- Reducing Dependence on the CEO
- Solving the Cost/Quality Conundrum in Healthcare
- Defining and Delivering Value in Government

These categorizations come with an important caveat: they are by no means mutually exclusive. The desire to increase capacity, for example, does not preclude the desire to create a learning organization, nor does a need to reduce costs preclude people-centric leadership. Lean is a holistic undertaking that works to address these issues simultaneously. The Lean CEOs profiled in this book had broad objectives and beliefs that went far beyond the addressing the circumstances they faced at the outset of their Lean journeys.

HOW TO USE THIS BOOK

This book is concerned with the CEO role. Therefore, there is particular interest in boardroom conversations, relationships between workers and managers, company finances, engagement with customers and business partners, change management, and the way a CEO approaches the general topic of leadership. In other words, how do the traditional challenges that leaders face play out within the context of Lean?

My role as author has been to provide structure and context for the CEO narratives that form the core content of this book. I think readers will agree that the messages coming from the CEOs are extremely powerful in their own right. Therefore, I have tried to step back and let the CEOs speak for themselves.

Those new to Lean should be advised that this is not a Lean primer. Although the early chapters give a cursory overview of Lean to provide context for the stories, they do not address the huge extent of the work involved in a Lean transformation. It is suggested, therefore, that those unfamiliar with Lean acquire at least one book from the Reading List to use as a reference guide or to read in parallel. These books are, by the way, first-rate.

Books, however, don't tell the full story about Lean, and as anybody in the Lean world will confirm, going to *gemba*, the workplace where customer value is actually created, is essential. I therefore urge the reader who has not done so to visit at least one Lean organization. Finding one is not difficult; there is a vibrant global community built around the sharing of Lean ideas, and organizations such as the Association for Manufacturing Excellence (AME) and the Lean Enterprise Institute (LEI) organize frequent tours.

It is very much in the spirit of Lean to ask why repeatedly, and I would urge the reader to approach this material with a few questions in mind. Here are several suggestions:

> What skills, methods, and personal attributes do CEOs need to effectively lead a Lean transformation?
>
> How, in conventional terms, do Lean transformations change companies for the better?
>
> What are the implications for our organization?

I hope the reader will add many more.

One important note: although Lean is often discussed in conjunction with Six Sigma, there is no discussion of Six Sigma in this book. The reason is that it rarely came up in my research. I recognize that Six Sigma is widely practiced, and I will leave it to other authors to explore that subject and its relationship with Lean.

One final exhortation: some will be tempted to jump right into the stories that involve their sector and ignore the rest. I would urge the reader to do the opposite. As CEOs say over and over in the book, their most important learnings often came from other industries. Thus, if you're going to read selectively, leave your own sector for last.

Now let's get on with our story.

CHAPTER 1

❖

HOW WASTE BECAME
BUSINESS AS USUAL

Take a look at the following three scenarios:

- A recreational trailer manufacturer was forced into bankruptcy after revenues dropped 60 percent during the 2009 recession.
- A medium-size hospital closed its doors amid rising costs, quality concerns, and growing competition from larger providers.
- A manufacturer of diesel engine components, dogged by chronic delivery problems, poor labor relations, and the loss of a key patent, shut down its plant and sold its assets to a large automotive manufacturer.

Scenarios like these are, sadly, not unusual. Layoffs, plant closings, downsizings, cutbacks, and offshoring are so common that they no longer have any shock value; there's a certain air of inevitability to it all. We just say "too bad" and move on. In the meantime, millions of lives are thrown into turmoil.

There's a twist to the three scenarios above, however: they never happened. In each case, the CEO defied the odds after discovering and adopting Lean.

The results were astonishing. The organizations excelled not only in terms of financial performance but also in areas such as employee engagement, customer satisfaction, and influence in the business community. You will meet these Lean CEOs and many others in the pages ahead.

The CEOs, however, did not just apply a method. They adopted a way of thinking that is fundamentally different from what is taught in business schools.

Through this new set of glasses, they began to see their situations very differently. Instead of viewing their challenges as circumstances beyond their control, they saw how their organizations were laboring under a heavy burden of wasteful processes. We're not talking about losses of a few percentage points here or there. This is waste on a monumental scale, enough to sink a company.

Waste as seen through the Lean lens is not something that can be eradicated with the stroke of a pen. Instead, it is distributed throughout the organization, often in small, barely visible increments. It takes enormous discipline to see it, more to eliminate it, and constant vigilance to prevent it from creeping back in. Waste removal, as will be shown, is an activity that requires the participation of every employee in the organization and a corporatewide commitment to continuous improvement that never ends.

To see the waste, the Lean CEOs turned much of their attention to an aspect of the organization that is neglected in modern business theory, so much so that we don't have a name for it. The Japanese, however, do have a word: *gemba*, which means "the real place." In the Lean context, this means the place where people create a product or service that customers pay for.

In an automotive factory, for example, *gemba* is the shop floor where people make cars. In a school, *gemba* is the classroom where teachers help students learn. In a hospital, *gemba* is found wherever doctors, nurses, or support staff members are providing care to patients. Through the Lean lens, everything else—administration, finance, human resources, sales, and even senior management—is there to support *gemba*.

Respect for the people who spend their days in *gemba* is one of the cornerstones of Lean. It is through their initiative that the breakthrough gains that characterize successful Lean transformations are achieved.

To empower this kind of participation, managers need to quickly rid themselves of the illusion that they know all the answers. On the contrary, Lean CEOs must be constantly inquiring and must do so openly.

All this goes against the grain of conventional management thinking. Managers are taught that by applying the professional skills they learned in business school, they can control what happens in *gemba* without actually being there. *Gemba* is something to be delegated, outsourced, managed from a distance. Furthermore, the employees in *gemba* are seen to be dispensable cogs rather than strategic assets.

Yet *gemba* is the aspect of any organization that has the most direct impact on the value that customers pay for. A customer can't buy a great product design, a go-to-market strategy, or a powerful brand. In the end, the company has to deliver, and the work that makes this possible is ultimately the purpose and the livelihood of the organization. This work happens in *gemba*.

Neglect of *gemba* and the people who work in it is behind many of the failures we hear about in the news. It's why North America has the best healthcare resources in the world but is struggling to deliver an affordable healthcare system. It's why U.S. automotive manufacturers filed for bankruptcy in 2008.

To understand how managers lost sight of something as fundamental as *gemba* and became blind to the widespread waste in modern organizations, we have to go back a century or so.

THE MIRACLE OF MASS PRODUCTION

The American industrial golden age, which was to end in the 1970s, began when Henry Ford opened his first factory in 1908. Like his mentor Thomas Alva Edison, Ford was an impassioned experimenter. He loved machinery and the art of fabrication and developed the Model T with his own hands. *Gemba* was near and dear to him.

Ford was always convinced that there was a better way. When he designed his first factory, Ford believed that he could make cars faster, cheaper, and of better quality than the manufacturers of that day. He was certain that the key to doing this was eliminating waste.

Ford had watched workers in other plants very closely and had noticed that they spent perhaps half their time transporting parts, retrieving tools, and waiting for workpieces to arrive—activities that did nothing to directly improve the product that would eventually be owned by a customer. If an activity didn't involve the worker having his or her hands on the product, Ford saw this as a waste, and he believed he could make great strides in efficiency by reducing such waste.

Much of this wasted human effort resulted from the way machinery was located on the plant floor. Machine tools got their power from huge steam-propelled line shafts that ran through the facilities, and layouts were determined by the most efficient way to deliver power to the equipment. Because those configurations were inflexible and had little to do with work flow, almost half of plant workers were hired solely to move materials around the plant.

Electricity changed all this. When Ford built the company's iconic Highland Park facility in 1908, manufacturers were beginning to use electrically powered tools that could be located anywhere in the plant and factory planners were beginning to pay more attention to the optimum location of a machine in relation to the work flow. The Edison Illuminating Company of Detroit was a leading proponent of the electrical revolution, and Ford's close connection with that company put him right on top of this trend.

"The electrification of the assembly line at Ford Motor Company's Highland Park plant radically altered the U.S. automobile industry," wrote Canadian economist Bernard C. Beaudreau. "The relationship between inputs and outputs was changed forever, moreover, work would never be the same."[1]

This innovation made possible what is considered the company's greatest accomplishment: the moving assembly line. The system was developed by Charles E. Sorensen, a pattern maker from Denmark who had joined the company in 1905. Sorensen quickly became a principal with no particular title; his job was simply to invent a production system that would reduce waste to the absolute minimum.

Sorensen, who tells his story in one of the definitive accounts of the company's rise, *My Forty Years with Ford*, inherited a system whereby the vehicle was stationary and workers and parts traveled to the workpiece successively until it was completed and could be driven out of the plant. Sorensen began to experiment with something completely different:

> What was worked out at Ford was the practice of moving the work from one worker to another until it became a complete unity, then arranging the flow of these units at the right time and the right place to a moving final assembly line from which came a finished product.[2]

Sorensen arrived at the moving assembly line through a series of weekend experiments conducted with the assistance of Charles Lewis, another Ford executive:

> The idea occurred to me that assembly would be easier, simpler, and faster if we moved the chassis along, beginning at one end of the plant with a frame and adding the axles and the wheels; then moving it past the stockroom, instead of moving the stockroom to the chassis. I had Lewis arrange the materials on the floor so that what was needed at the

start of assembly would be at that end of the building and the other parts would be along the line as we moved the chassis along. We spent every Sunday during July planning this. Then one Sunday morning, after the stock was laid out in this fashion, Lewis and I and a couple of helpers put together the first car, I'm sure, that was ever built on a moving line.[3]

The new production system that grew out of these experiments entailed far more than a reconfigured floor plan; equally important was the set of principles by which the factory was run. Ford recognized that high productivity was not a matter of telling workers to work harder but of designing work processes in a way that would enable workers to be as productive as possible.

"The thing is to keep everything in motion and take the work to the man and not the man to the work," Ford said in his book *Today and Tomorrow*. "That is the real principle of our production, and conveyors are only one of the means to an end."[4]

The system was continually improved to achieve this. Tool counters were eliminated, and tools were brought to workers instead. Even the extra motion of picking up the workpiece from the floor was a target for elimination:

Stooping to the floor to pick up a tool or a part is not productive labor—therefore, all material is delivered waist high.[5]

Waste of materials was also targeted. Ford, noting that the company's salvage department was reclaiming upward of $20 million a year in materials, wondered why all that material had been wasted in the first place:

As that department grew and became more important and more strikingly valuable, we began to ask ourselves: "Why should we have so much to salvage? Are we not giving more attention to reclaiming than to not wasting?" And with that in mind, we have to examine all of our processes.[6]

It took several years to perfect the production system, but by the time it was fully operational, the Ford Motor Company was producing cars 10 times as fast as its competitors, and costs were declining rapidly. Figure 1-1 illustrates one of the most phenomenal technical achievements in human history.

Ford remained a true believer in the manufacturer as a contributor to the public good. He decried the influence of outside investors, who he felt would downgrade the business from contributing to society to simply making money:

> When the chief function of any industry is to produce dividends rather than goods for use, the emphasis is fundamentally wrong. The face of the business is bowed toward the

Figure 1-1   Ford production vs. price, 1909–1916.

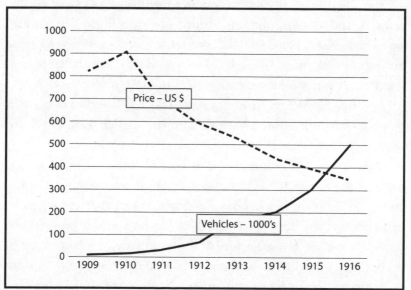

Data compiled by R. E. Houston, Ford Production Department, 1927.

stockholder and not toward the consumer, and this means the denial of the primary purpose of industry.[7]

Ford eventually sold 15 million Model T's, all of them black. The Ford juggernaut seemed unstoppable in 1920, and Ford believed that as long as his company maintained its commanding technical leadership, its place in the market was assured. This was not the case, however, and Ford was soon up against a CEO who played by very different rules.

FUNCTION TAKES A BACKSEAT

In 1920, the General Motors Corporation enlisted Alfred Sloan, a young engineer and businessman, to craft a strategy to overtake Ford. At the time, GM was a loose confederation of automakers that held a 12 percent share of the market compared with Ford's 60 percent.

Sloan had made his reputation and fortune as a bearing manufacturer, and although he was trained as an engineer, his business savvy had already played a much greater role in his success than had his technical abilities. In stark contrast to Ford, Sloan believed that the primary purpose of a company was to make money.

In 1916, he merged his company, Hyatt Roller Bearing, with others to form the United Motors Company, which soon afterward became part of General Motors.

Sloan knew that he couldn't beat Ford in technical prowess, and so he set out to attack Ford's weaknesses. Ford believed that customers would settle for black, boxy-looking cars and that as long as he had a cheaper and better product, there was no need for sales pitches. Ford also had little respect for his dealers, many of whom came to despise him when he forced them to take on inventory in the 1920s.

Sloan consequently set out to beat Ford on the dealer's lot. The watershed moment was the introduction of the 1923 Chevrolet, which GM hoped could compete with the still-dominant Model T. The original plan had been to stage an innovative coup with a copper-cooled engine. Development was slow, however, and Sloan ordered it scrapped, claiming that this emphasis on engineering undermined the "commercial-mindedness of our strategic plan."[8]

Instead, GM released a dressed-up version of a model that was essentially nine years old. The more stylish-looking car, deftly marketed through GM's superior dealer network, was a huge success, and a new era in the automobile industry was launched.

As Sloan was to reflect later,

> Mr. Ford, who had had so many brilliant insights in earlier years, seemed never to understand how completely his market had changed from the one in which he had made his name and to which he was accustomed.[9]

When he became CEO in 1923, Sloan devoted much of his energy to building and supporting his dealers, often visiting as many as 10 a day on road trips in a private railcar. GM's market share grew steadily, and in 1927 Sloan reached his goal of overtaking Ford.

Ford fought back that year with the more stylish Model A, but by then the game had changed and GM had become the master. In the same year, Sloan hired the industry's first stylist, Harley Earl from Hollywood, who created the first automotive style department. Earl's first accomplishment was the 1927 Cadillac La Salle.

Sloan's plan to dominate the market was based on offering a range of brands—Chevrolet, Pontiac, Oldsmobile, Buick, and Cadillac—to suit every budget. He then consolidated the production of those brands using interchangeable parts wherever possible, which included not only the obvious—wheels, transmissions, engine parts—but the basic foundations for the bodies. This allowed for extraordinary economies of scale.

To complement this, Sloan successfully introduced the idea of the yearly model change, reflecting an accurate assessment of the age of consumerism that was dawning. Companies were learning that selling to people's emotions as opposed to their functional needs was good business: people bought whether or not there was a real need. This took the pressure off quality; if a car was fashionable and a status symbol, people wouldn't mind the occasional trip to the repair shop.

Sloan's victory over Ford went far beyond car sales. Ultimately, it was his vision, not Ford's, that set the paradigm for the archetypal American corporation. Throughout the twentieth century, Sloan became the ultimate proponent of concepts such as divisional autonomy, formalized marketing and public relations, operational planning and reporting, financial controls, and the use of monetary incentives.

"How could we exercise permanent control over the whole corporation in a way consistent with the decentralized scheme of organization?"[10] he mused in *My Years with General Motors*.

The short answer was that Silent Sloan, as he came to be called, was to manage from behind the scenes, guided by the growing discipline of management theory.

THE "ONE BEST WAY"

The leading figure in industrial management in the 1920s was an American engineer named Frederick Taylor whose work defined the field for much of the twentieth century. Famous for walking plant floors with a stopwatch, he developed the first time and motion studies, which measured the duration of each step of production down to several decimal places. This obsession with micromanagement extended to his personal life as well to the extent that he budgeted his time for all activities in minute detail, including his leisure walks.

Taylor's main preoccupation was cost reduction, and his reputation as a cost cutter became legendary. Taylor believed that for every task, there was "one best way" and promised that managers who applied his theories could determine this and "scientifically" supply all the intelligence needed to run an organization.

The key tool for cutting costs was a concept called division of labor, which had been famously documented in Adam Smith's description of a pin factory in his 1776 treatise *Wealth of Nations*. The idea is to subdivide work into simple repetitive tasks, each of which can be performed by a worker with minimal education. Thus, an organization can assign work to the lowest-paid workers. In the nineteenth century, this idea was widely used to create opportunities to employ child labor, which could be procured at a fraction of the cost of skilled artisans.

Taylor was a strong proponent of the idea that all the thinking should be done by managers. "You are not supposed to think," he is alleged to have told workers. "There are other people paid for thinking around here." Workers were treated like interchangeable cogs in a machine whose only interest was their paychecks.

In the style of management that evolved from this thinking, the foreman knew better than the workers, the section supervisor knew better than the foreman, the department managers knew better than the section supervisors, and so on, all the way up the line. By practicing the science of management, a company president could direct thousands of workers so that they would complete their work in the best possible way.

In this way of thinking, the machine was the ideal worker. Machines are bigger and stronger than humans, they don't complain or make mistakes, and they work around the clock. Accordingly, companies sought to automate their processes wherever possible.

The paradigm of the organization that developed with the help of Taylor's contribution is described in the hierarchical organization chart that began to appear in the early twentieth century. The CEO ruled from the top of the heap by applying the science of management to command and control the various entities in the organization. The primary means for achieving this control was the purse strings.

THE FINE ART OF MAKING THE NUMBERS

While engineers were busy building bigger production facilities, accountants worked on methods to measure and control costs. The trick was divining, from a great variety of expenses, the actual cost of manufacturing an individual product.

Part of this was easy: compiling the readily available cost data for the materials and labor that contributed directly to an individual product, which became known as direct labor and direct materials. This could be calculated with a great degree of precision.

The hard part was overhead: fixed costs that couldn't be directly attributed to a product. This included facility costs, equipment costs, maintenance, management, and other functions whose utility was spread throughout the output of a plant. To quantify the contribution of overhead to the total cost of the product, accountants developed a series of methods to estimate the amount of overhead that could be reasonably assigned to the product, a concept that became known as absorption.

A common approach used by Taylor and others was to add up the total cost of overhead for the entire facility and then assign a portion of it to each product in direct proportion to the direct labor involved, sort of like a tax.

As machinery took over more and more of the workload, the correlation between direct labor and real product costs diminished. Consequently, some companies began to use machine hours as a determinant. However, as indirect costs took a growing share of the pie, determination of costs became increasingly dependent on calculations as opposed to direct measurement.

The early practice had been to apply overhead equally to all operations within a plant. Some industrial processes, however, might have higher overhead than others. For example, a plating department might have higher maintenance and servicing costs than a grinding department. As a result, manufacturers began to establish separate overhead rates for each department.

As manufacturing environments got more complex, accountants developed more rules for standardizing costs for individual products, and this became standard cost accounting as we know it today. The central idea was to predict costs by calculation and then correct the numbers after the fact by using actual data.

Typically, cost accountants would calculate their actual costs at the end of a reporting period, identify how they diverged from the standard costs (divergences here are called variances), find explanations for the variances, and report them to management, which would either adjust its targets or take measures to reduce costs.

These methods worked reasonably well for generating financial reports but created a number of problems when they were used for operational decisions. First of all, they were based on past data, and so they were often irrelevant by the time they were discussed. The identification of variances also became a blame game in which managers were penalized for shortfalls that had already occurred. Also, apportioning overhead to various departments pitted managers against one another.

Traditional cost accounting also supported the creation of functional silos within the organization. Managers were rewarded for achieving targets that were narrowly defined according to the apparent efficiency of a department, and absorption of overhead was often a determining factor.

A machining department, for example, was considered to be performing well if its equipment was running and producing product a high percentage of the time, essentially absorbing its fixed costs in the products it was producing. Whether the output was sold and produced revenue was considered somebody else's problem, as the costs of maintaining inventory showed up elsewhere.

The numbers game was further reinforced by the growing use of information technology. During the 1960s and 1970s financial numbers became readily available in large corporations, encouraging managers to run their operations from a distance.

The upshot of management by numbers was that CEOs were getting more and more out of touch with the real drivers of sustainable profitability. Thomas Johnson and Robert Kaplan summed up these concerns about traditional accounting in their seminal 1987 book *Relevance Lost: The Rise and Fall of Management Accounting*:

> Management accounting reports are of little help to operating managers as they attempt to reduce costs and improve productivity. . . . By not providing timely and detailed information on process efficiencies or by focusing on inputs such as direct labor that are relatively insignificant in today's production environment, the management accounting system not only fails to provide relevant information to managers, but it also distracts their attention from factors that are critical for production efficiencies.[11]

A MECHANISTIC VIEW OF PEOPLE

There was, however, a much more serious problem: workers were being managed as if they were machines. Worker motivation was seen as dependent only on the paycheck, and the idea that workers could provide creative input to make production more efficient was not even on the table.

Nowhere was this more prominent than at GM, as Peter Drucker observed in his authorized profile of the company, *Concept of the Corporation*:

> For the great majority of automobile workers, the only meaning of the job is in the pay check, not in anything connected

with the work or the product. Work appears as something unnatural, a disagreeable, meaningless and stultifying condition of getting the pay check, devoid of dignity as well as of importance. No wonder that this results in an unhappy and discontented worker—because a pay check is not enough to base one's self-respect on.[12]

Drucker felt there was a better way, and as evidence he cited GM's experience in supporting U.S. efforts in World War II. GM had adapted its production facilities to produce tanks, aircraft engines, and other equipment with which it had no experience. Since much of the seasoned workforce was fighting overseas, all this had to be accomplished with unskilled workers.

What might have looked like a recipe for disaster turned out to be the exact opposite: productivity and morale were high, and workers showed phenomenal creativity in solving problems and finding ways to improve efficiency. A contributing factor was a government-sponsored program called Training Within Industry (TWI), an innovative training and work improvement program that placed supervisors in a mentoring role and gave workers an active role in improving their work processes. TWI was employed with great success in 6,000 factories during the war.

Drucker was so impressed with the results that he suggested it was time to question some of the narrowly defined practices employed by GM and others over the past decades:

The war showed that this type of assembly line is neither the only application of the [mass production] concept, nor in all circumstances the best. It showed further that the concept of human contribution to production as a minor appurtenance to the machine that was inherent in the orthodox assembly line, is neither the only possible concept, nor always the best.[13]

Drucker went on to challenge the accepted principles of mass production:

> I was struck again and again by the need for a new theory of mass-production technology, more or less a complement to Frederick Taylor's famous studies but with the focus on the individual worker rather than on the individual manipulation.[14]

In other words, Drucker was telling Alfred Sloan that there really is no one best way and that the tacit knowledge and creativity of workers could pave the way for a new era in mass production. Sloan wasn't amused, however, and although the book was highly complimentary about GM in other areas, Sloan forbade his managers to read it and GM quickly reverted to its old style of management.

The U.S. government canceled the TWI program in 1945. Although Drucker was to soon become a major influence on corporate management, his criticism of traditional mass production attracted little interest, that is, except in Japan.

THE RUDE AWAKENING

Throughout the twentieth century, industrial machinery got bigger and more sophisticated and allowed companies to mass-produce manufactured goods in quantities not dreamed of a century before. The prices of automobiles, appliances, furniture, office equipment, toys, and other commodities plummeted, and North American lifestyles improved dramatically.

In 1970, America was on a roll. The industrial sector had been steaming ahead at full capacity for over two decades. Factories were buying bigger and better machines and rapidly expanding their operations globally. The perfect corporate machine seemed to be unshakable.

However, all this had occurred under ideal conditions. Families were growing rapidly in the post–World War II period, buying power was up, people were purchasing houses, and natural resources, including energy, were plentiful and cheap. Furthermore, World War II had destroyed much of the global competition for U.S. manufacturers.

Everything began to change in the early 1970s, when the U.S. economy was hit by a series of body blows. The OPEC oil embargo of 1973 resulted in long lines at gas stations, quadrupled prices, and stimulated a growing realization that the days of cheap energy that had fueled the boom years were gone forever. Other industrial countries were beginning to catch up with the United States, and so the balance of trade suffered. The national debt soared, in part as a result of the high cost of the Vietnam War, and when the vets came home looking for work, unemployment jumped to nearly 8 percent. To make matters even worse, rising inflation began to eat into Americans' standard of living.

These circumstances were devastating for the U.S. automotive industry. In the wake of the oil crisis, production dropped by almost 22 percent. Faced with high inventories, Chrysler shut down five of its plants in 1974. Utility rather than status became the order of the day, and consumers began to forsake the gas-guzzling cars that had been so profitable for U.S. car makers in favor of high-quality fuel-efficient cars from Japan. At the end of the decade, Ford and GM were losing money, Chrysler had declared insolvency, and the money-losing American Motors was sold to the government-owned French carmaker Renault.

"I TAUGHT THEM TO WORK SMARTER, NOT HARDER"

In late 1979, Clare Crawford-Mason, an NBC-TV producer based in Washington, D.C., knocked on the basement door at the home of an 80-year-old statistics professor who was virtually unknown in the United States. Her assignment was unusual for a journalist who had spent much of the previous decade covering the White House: find answers to the question in executive producer Reuven Frank's working title, *What Ever Happened to Good Old Yankee Ingenuity?* The obvious sources weren't providing answers, and Crawford-Mason, who was beginning to doubt that there was even a story, had gotten the unlikely lead from Herbert Streiner, dean of the business school at American University.

It was an election year, and the domestic decline in manufacturing had become an issue on the campaign trail. "There is one domestic problem that all 1980 presidential contenders, including the incumbent, preach against: the disturbing decline in U.S. productivity," wrote Crawford-Mason in *People* magazine.[15] "Not surprisingly, Japan, with its annual productivity growth rate of 11 percent, is held up as a shining example of 're-industrialization'— already a bipartisan buzzword for Campaign '80."

Japan's turnaround seemed almost unbelievable for a country that rose out of the ashes of World War II and whose manufacturing sector was the butt of many jokes in the 1960s. Japan's manufacturers succeeded with very little money, with few natural resources, and without the benefit of the high-volume domestic market that U.S. manufacturers enjoyed. NBC hoped to find the secret sauce behind this miracle.

The interview got off to a rough start. The gentleman was dismissive of many of Crawford-Mason's questions, and his answers sounded either cryptic or overly technical—certainly not the kinds of sound bites suitable for a general news audience. After two hours, when Crawford-Mason was beginning to suspect that there must have been some mistake, her subject walked over to a cabinet and produced some magazine articles documenting his work in Japan and a medal he had received from that nation's emperor.

When Crawford-Mason asked him what he had taught the Japanese, the response, which is now a household phrase, gave her hope that she might be on to something: "I taught the Japanese to work smarter, not harder."

After the interview, Crawford-Mason got in touch with NBC in Tokyo. As it turned out, her source, W. Edwards Deming, was a national celebrity in Japan; the only better-known American there was General Douglas MacArthur.

The show aired in June 1980 under the title *If Japan Can, Why Can't We?* According to Crawford-Mason, it was one of the most successful news documentaries in the history of television, with thousands of calls coming in afterward for transcripts. Deming was featured on the show for the last 12 minutes and spent much of that time discussing the work with his sole American client, the Nashua Corporation, which had found Deming through its association with the Japanese electronics manufacturer Ricoh. In what was perhaps the clincher, Nashua's CEO, William E. Conway, appeared on the program, relating how Deming's approach had saved his company millions of dollars.

Deming's grandson Kevin Edwards Cahill, who now heads the W. Edwards Deming Institute, was staying with Deming at the time and was given the task of making sure his grandfather, not much of a TV watcher, saw the show. Cahill was close to Deming and knew of his many trips to Japan but had no idea of the impact he had had.

"I was in awe," says Cahill. "I just looked at my grandfather and said 'That's you—you've done all this?'"

For the rest of the summer, Deming was approached by dozens of companies hoping to learn the secrets of Japanese success. Deming, hard of hearing, kept his speaker phone at high volume, and Cahill recalls standing at the top of the basement stairs with his grandmother, listening to calls coming in from the likes of Lee Iacocca of Chrysler, Donald Petersen of Ford, and David Kearns of Xerox. "It was quite a summer—it changed my life," says Cahill.

Deming, however, had warned that there were no magic bullets. "I think that people here expect miracles," he told show host Lloyd Dobyns. "American management thinks that they can just copy from Japan—but they don't know what to copy!"[16]

PUTTING QUALITY IN ITS PLACE

The buzz following the show kick-started a flurry of activity in the West that became known as the quality movement. Organizations established or grew their quality departments, consultants began to package and teach statistical quality control methods, and production techniques from Japan, complete with Japanese terminology, became the latest fashion.

Formalized programs and standards soon followed. In 1985, the U.S. Navy published its Total Quality Management (TQM) program for improving quality throughout organizations. The British Standards Association (BSA) developed the prototype for ISO 9000, which was published in 1987. That same year, the U.S. government established the Malcolm Baldrige Award for quality. Six Sigma, Motorola's tool set for improving processes, became popular after that company won the award in 1988.

What emerged was a robust knowledge community, replete with training programs, assessments, certifications, and even martial arts–style colored belts. The movement was highly successful in many respects. Defect rates for manufactured products dropped significantly, workplaces were made safer, quality entered the service industries, and eventually organizations began to pursue certifications for environmental performance.

Deming had warned, however, that the road to industrial leadership would demand a lot more than add-ons to existing management practices. His definition of total quality, in fact, called for no less than a fundamental overhaul of the way companies managed people.

"I ask people in management what proportion of this [productivity] problem arises from your production worker," he told Lloyd Dobyn on the show, "and the answer is always, 'All of it!' That's absolutely wrong! There's nobody that comes out of a school of business that knows what management is or what its deficiencies are. There's no one coming out of a school of business that ever heard of the answers that I'm giving your questions—or probably even thought of the questions."

◆

CHAPTER 2

LEAN: A RADICAL NEW APPROACH TO PRODUCTION

By the end of World War II, Allied bombing had systematically destroyed much of Japan's industrial capability, forcing many manufacturers, including the Toyota Motor Corporation, to suspend operations. It was under those dire circumstances that Kiichiro Toyoda, Toyota's founding CEO, issued his most famous directive.

"Catch up with America in three years," he said, "or the automobile industry in Japan will not survive."

The dream of becoming a major player in the U.S.-dominated industry had come from Kiichiro's father, Sakichi Toyoda, inventor and founder of Toyoda Loom Works. The elder Toyoda believed that the textile industry belonged to a bygone era and wanted his son to set out in a bold new direction. Before he died in 1930, he sold the patent for his flagship automatic loom to Platt Brothers, a textile company in the United Kingdom, and designated the proceeds as seed money for the new enterprise.

"Kiichiro, I have worked hard for many years with my looms," he told his son. "Now it's your turn. Go do the same with the automobile."

Kiichiro started the Toyota Motor Corporation in 1933 as a division of Toyoda Loom Works. What he had inherited was not just seed money and a mandate but a set of deeply held values. Central to those values were the duty to serve the people of Japan and a sense of obligation to employees, which included a philosophy of lifetime employment.

Even before the war, Kiichiro Toyoda was not naive about the challenges that lay ahead. In the 1930s, it had been estimated that productivity per worker was nine times higher in the United States than it was in Japan. GM, Ford, and Chrysler, of course, had large, well-equipped factories, phenomenal production engineering skills, an abundance of natural resources, and a huge market.

Undeterred, Toyoda began to work on the first prototype, using several U.S.-made cars as reference points and incorporating what he believed to be their best features. He and his engineers also decided to use common parts that were compatible with the American-made cars that were common in Japan.

Toyoda also began to study American methods and took a special interest in the writings of Peter Drucker and Henry Ford. He admired Ford's determination to reduce waste, and was greatly inspired by the continuous flow established in Ford's assembly lines, whereby all materials, labor, and production equipment converged on the workpiece exactly when they were needed. Toyoda coined the term "Just-in-Time" (JIT) to describe this ideal state, and this became one of the pillars of his company and the Lean movement that followed.

In 1935 the Toyota Motor Company had its first prototype, and in 1936 it began production of its Model AA, which resembled the fashionable Chrysler DeSoto. Toyoda soon decided, however, that the most promising future was in smaller cars. They were better suited to Japan's high fuel prices and scarcity of natural resources and had been neglected by American manufacturers. In 1939, way ahead of its time, the company began to study the technology for battery-powered vehicles.

The war changed everything. Materials were very difficult to acquire, and by the time the war ended in 1945, much of the Toyota manufacturing capability had been destroyed. When Toyoda gave his famous directive to catch up with the United States, he had to rebuild the company first.

Japan's recovery from the war, however, did not initially go as well as hoped. In 1949, the country was still struggling and experienced a severe economic slump. The Toyota Motor Company, having badly miscalculated demand, wound up with an inventory of unsold cars and ran out of cash. A strike in 1949 caused its financial situation to deteriorate further, and in 1950, after fighting hard to maintain its commitment to lifetime employment, the company was forced to lay off 1,600 employees. Kiichiro felt that he had broken a sacred trust and resigned along with his entire senior management team.

SEEING MASS PRODUCTION IN REVERSE

One employee who took Toyoda's mandate to heart was a young engineer named Taiichi Ohno. Ohno had begun to experiment with ways to improve productivity at Toyoda Loom Works and had experienced early success by moving looms closer together and into a configuration that would allow a single worker to operate several looms at a time. Ohno had been transferred to the automotive business in 1943.

Following Kiichiro Toyoda's directive, Ohno began to reflect on what it would actually take to catch up with the United States. As he saw it, there were two problems. First, he had to increase productivity per worker by a factor of 10, but without sophisticated American technology. He was convinced, however, that there was no reason a

Japanese worker couldn't learn to be as productive as an American worker:

> Could an American really exert ten times more physical effort? Surely, Japanese people were wasting something. If we could eliminate the waste, productivity should rise by a factor of ten.[1]

Like his boss, Ohno recognized the accomplishments of Ford, and he believed that if he could find a way to create perfect flow, waste such as excessive inventory could be reduced to the absolute minimum:

> Just-in-time means that, in a flow process, the right parts needed in assembly reach the assembly line at the time they are needed and only in the amount needed. A company establishing this flow throughout can approach zero inventory.
>
> From the standpoint of production management, this is an ideal state. However, with a product made of thousands of parts, like the automobile, the number of processes involved is enormous. Obviously, it is extremely difficult to apply just-in-time to the production plan of every process in an orderly way.[2]

Pursuing this ideal state, Ohno realized, could serve as a powerful guiding principle for reducing waste. Each time a barrier to continuous flow was removed, waste would be automatically eliminated along with it, and efficiency would therefore be improved.

Ohno's definition of waste—*muda* in Japanese—was by Western standards very broad, and he had extremely high expectations about reducing it. Waste here includes any outlay or activity that is extraneous to the physical improvement of the product. For example, if a worker is physically attaching a bumper to a vehicle, this work adds value because the final product is improved as a result. If that worker walks across the plant to find a screwdriver, this is considered waste because the workpiece is not improved while this activity takes place.

In the Toyota Production System, Ohno put waste in the spotlight with the following formula:[3]

Present capacity = work + waste

He went on to list seven categories of waste, which became known in the Lean world as the Seven Wastes:

1. *Overproduction:* Producing more than required by the next downstream process or the customer. Ohno saw this as the cardinal sin of waste because essentially it forces all the other wastes.
2. *Time on hand (waiting):* Workers standing idle awaiting what is required for their next work.
3. *Transportation:* Excessive movement of the workpiece or parts.
4. *Overprocessing:* More than the necessary amount of work being done on the workpiece, perhaps because of poor process design or defective tools.
5. *Inventory:* More finished goods, works in process, parts, or raw materials than required by customer demand.
6. *Movement:* Unnecessary movements by workers, including bending, straining, and walking to procure tools or parts.
7. *Defects:* Fabrication of a defective workpiece that will later require correction.

Ohno sensed that there was an enormous amount of waste in any manufacturing system: perhaps 50 percent or more. He also suspected that this might be the key to catching up with American automakers.

However, there was another major problem: economies of scale. Even in the early days of mass production, Ford was making 1 million cars a year, far more than the Japanese market could sustain. The Toyota Motor Company would have to find ways to create flow in much smaller quantities.

Ohno began to ponder how this could be done:

> I am fond of thinking about a problem over and over. I kept thinking about how to supply the number of parts needed just-in-time. The flow of production is the transfer of materials. The conventional way was to supply materials from an earlier process to a later process. So, I tried thinking about the transfer of materials in the reverse direction.[4]

What Ohno envisioned was a pull system, whereby production is triggered by a "pull signal" each time a product is withdrawn from the end of the assembly line. The signal initiates a chain reaction whereby each stage informs the previous stage that new materials are required. Only the quantities called for are provided and at the exact time when they are needed. Therefore, the entire production system is driven by customer demand.

In this ideal state, there is no excess inventory: all that is made is exactly what has been ordered. A pull system therefore prevents work in process (WIP) from building up between stages in the assembly process. If there is no demand from the downstream process, the upstream process simply stops producing.

This challenged much of the conventional wisdom about economies of scale. Conventional production systems were designed to accommodate large batches in every aspect of production, including ordering of materials, stocking of parts, allowable amounts of WIP between stages of production, and finished goods inventory.

However, because of the costs that these batches entailed, such as storage, deterioration, maintenance, inventory management, and scrap, Ohno suspected that bigger was not necessarily better.

Ohno began his efforts to improve the production system by continuing his experiments with machinery layouts:

> As an experiment, I arranged the various machines in the sequence of machining processes. This was a radical change

from the conventional system in which a large quantity of the same part was machined in one process and then forwarded to the next process.

In 1947, we arranged machines in parallel lines or in an L-shape and tried having one worker operate three or four machines along the processing route.[5]

The new configurations required workers to complete multiple tasks. For example, a machinist might be required to do some welding. In his early experiments this caused considerable resistance from workers.

In 1950, shortly after Kiichiro Toyoda's resignation, the Korean War began, and the U.S. Army began to order trucks from Toyota. The growing demand gave the company some breathing room and a chance to develop its production techniques. Also, the conditions of Toyota's bank loans did not allow it to hire additional workers to meet the growing demand, and so the pressure was on for the company to meet growing demand with the workers it had.

Ohno in the meantime had been promoted and now had the authority to pursue his experiments more forcefully. He also had an important ally: senior executive and future CEO Eiji Toyoda, whom Ohno credited with having the foresight to support his activities in spite of considerable opposition.

Moving equipment around, however, was only the beginning as Ohno set about his work; there were many more problems to be solved. Continuous flow with no inventory requires a finely tuned sequence of interdependent actions. Ohno used to compare this with a biological organism. In fact, when one considers all the potential barriers to creating continuous flow in small quantities, what Ohno and his people were able to achieve is truly remarkable.

What follows is a very brief overview that will provide context for the CEO conversations in the following chapters. Readers are urged to refer to the Reading List to gain a more comprehensive understanding of Lean principles.

Redefining Work and Management

As mentioned above, the new work environment called for workers to exercise multiple skills. With that added responsibility, however, came respect; Ohno had great faith in the ability of workers not only to complete tasks but to provide input for improving them. Furthermore, he did not believe that managers had all the answers.

"Just-in-Time" called for an uncommon level of teamwork and discipline. To prevent inventory from building up between processes or avoid having a later process have to wait for an earlier process, all steps had to be synchronized. Ohno used a metric called *takt* time—the frequency at which customer orders can be expected—to determine the ideal timing for the respective steps.

To establish this, each work step had to be precisely defined, and an important role for workers was to create and maintain standards: concise documents that spelled out their work. Those documents were posted in clear view of the workstation and specified the following:

- The time required to complete the work
- The sequence of steps involved
- The materials required

Supervisors became coaches who removed barriers and helped workers understand and improve their work processes. As an underlying method, Toyota adopted the Training Within Industry (TWI) program that had been used so effectively by American industry during the war. The program included job instruction techniques, a procedure for breaking a job into components and optimizing them, and measures for improving the human relations aspects of a job.

Toyota also encouraged worker suggestions through a program called the Creative Idea Suggestion System, which was launched in 1951. Unlike many organizations, Toyota took this program very seriously, and participation was significant.

The broader role of workers also included maintaining their own equipment through a process that is now called autonomous maintenance, a pillar of Toyota's comprehensive Total Productive Maintenance (TPM) program.

Another aspect of worker autonomy came through a concept called *jidoka*, which Ohno brought over from Toyoda Loom Works. This idea was based on a feature of Sakichi Toyoda's automatic loom that automatically stopped the machine if a thread broke, preventing a defective fabric from being processed any further.

Ohno extended this idea to human work processes. If circumstances prevented a worker from completing standard work within the allotted time or if there was a safety issue, it was the worker's responsibility to ensure that the problem was resolved on the spot. This was initiated by pulling the *andon* (Japanese for "lantern"), a cord or lever that activated a signal light that instantly escalated the problem to a supervisor. If the problem was not resolved immediately, the supervisor pulled the *andon*, directing all others on the line to cease work.

Shutting down an entire line to resolve an incident might sound like an extreme measure, but it forced the organization to build quality into the process so that work was completed correctly the first time. This was a radical departure from the traditional approach to catching defects, which is based on inspection.

Jidoka was considered so important that Ohno named it as one of the two pillars of the Toyota Production System, with "Just-in-Time" being the other.

The Power of Visual Information

To manage the environment so that everything was synchronized and regulated, Ohno used a series of visual methods that gave workers instant cues about relevant activity in their environment. This low-tech approach might seem rudimentary, but as the Lean experience proves, visual information is immediate and extremely powerful.

At the heart of this was a communication system called *kanban*, derived from two Japanese characters: *kan* ("to see") and *ban* ("card"). *Kanban* relayed the pull signal, or the trigger to produce, sequentially to all the production stages, starting with the final process and progressing back to the first. The signal was sent by means of *kanban* cards, which resemble the stock-out cards used in the retail environment. The card specified the exact quantity of materials needed and the exact time they were required.

Variants on the card included triangle-shaped metal tags, empty bins, and empty carts. In a production environment, a *kanban* could be used to signal the need for raw materials, finished parts, or a workpiece.

Implementing *kanban* throughout the Toyota facilities was a huge undertaking that took years to complete, and its development was marked with difficulties. Through Ohno's persistence and his management's support, *kanban* became, in Ohno's words, the "central nervous system" of the Toyota Production System, and for many in the early decades of study of Toyota's success, TPS became erroneously known as the *Kanban* System.

Other visual information was provided by whiteboards, color coding (for example, posting a metric in red when there was a problem), lights, and the visibility of related processes.

To support visual management, Ohno enforced measures to create an orderly, clutter-free environment where visual cues could remain clear and unobstructed. For example, tools were placed for easy access and visibility, sight lines were cleared so that workers could see adjoining processes, and storage areas were color coded for easy identification. Today, Lean companies use a conceptual tool called 5S to create such an environment.

An orderly visual environment also made it easier to see problems and waste. Ohno instilled a high level of vigilance among his workers not only to see problems but to inquire relentlessly to determine their root cause. His method was simply to ask why five times, as in the following example:

1. *Why* did the machine stop? There was an overload and the fuse blew.
2. *Why* was there an overload? The bearing was not sufficiently lubricated.
3. *Why* was it not lubricated sufficiently? The lubrication pump was not pumping sufficiently.
4. *Why* was it not pumping sufficiently? The shaft of the pump was worn and rattling.
5. *Why* was the shaft worn out? There was no strainer attached and metal scrap got in.[6]

Often Ohno would instruct a manager to stand in a circle and watch production for a period and take note of any problems. If the manager had the temerity to suggest that there weren't any problems, Ohno would reply, often quite forcefully, that there were always problems and anybody who didn't realize this had not learned to see. Legend has it that he would occasionally leave a manager in the circle for an entire day.

Days Reduced to Minutes

To produce multiple models in low volumes, Toyota needed to change lines quickly from one model to the next. Large stamping presses used to make body sections were the biggest challenge; they were huge machines, and the dies had to be lifted in place by a crane and positioned manually within strict tolerances. The process could take as long as three days.

To solve this, Ohno used an ingenious method that breaks down the changeover process into small components and redesigns them so that as much of the work as possible can be completed while the equipment is still running. This method was later codified by Shigeo Shingo, a consultant who had worked with Toyota, who named it Single-Minute Exchange of Dies (SMED) in reference to the objective of completing changeovers in single-digit durations, that is, in less than 10 minutes.

As the name suggests, the results derived from SMED were phenomenal: processes that took many hours were routinely reduced to minutes. Consequently, SMED became an essential technique for producing many models in low volumes.

Suppliers as Production Partners

When Toyota started cutting back on inventory and got rid of warehouses and storage areas, this meant that it could no longer receive large orders from suppliers. Suppliers therefore had to deliver "Just-in-Time" in smaller batches, and this sometimes required considerable adjustments on their part. Toyota soon began to play an active role in helping suppliers conform to "Just-in-Time" and eventually began to help them adopt the Toyota Production System.

"Just-in-Time" affected sales as well. Traditional automotive manufacturers, with their emphasis on inventory, tended to overproduce and flood their dealer networks with unsold cars. Toyota was interested in maintaining a steady flow of orders that was compatible with continuous flow.

Production from 30,000 Feet

One of the best ways to get an overview of the kind of production environment Ohno was creating is to use a concept called the Lean value stream: an end-to-end representation of all the steps required to fulfill a customer need. The value stream accomplishes what a traditional organizational model cannot: it depicts how diverse entities within the organization combine to create value.

The Lean value stream is a powerful metaphor for focusing the entire organization on customer value. When employees understand the value stream, for example, they can see how their work relates to the processes of all their coworkers and, accordingly, their role in creating value for the customer.

Many Lean organizations organize their resources, their reporting structures, and even their finances around value streams, supplementing or replacing the traditional functional groupings.

The value stream is also used to eliminate waste through a formal process called value stream mapping (VSM), which was introduced to the West through the Lean Enterprise Institute handbook *Learning to See* by Mike Rother and John Shook. Typically, a cross-functional team creates a graphical depiction of an entire value stream on a wall with sticky notes. Then, systematically, steps that are unnecessary and represent waste are labeled and then targeted for elimination. This is typically followed up with a future state map that shows the ideal waste-free process. The differences between actual and ideal are then attacked through a series of improvement projects.

An important feature of VSM is that it includes both material flow and information flow, reflecting the reality that a problem with information flow can be just as disruptive to production as a bottleneck in the material flow.

A sample VSM is shown in Figure 2-1.

Sustaining the High-Wire Act

If all that has been described here—"Just-in-Time," standard work, *kanban,* Single-Minute Exchange of Dies—sounds like an impossible high-wire act, then you have understood it correctly. Perfecting a working environment that follows the Toyota Production System takes years of hard work, much of it trial and error, and calls for extraordinary discipline from every manager, engineer, supervisor, and worker. This is an all-hands-on-deck journey that never ends.

Figure 2-1 Current state maps like this one are used to identify waste, which usually occurs between processes. In this case, excessive production lead time might be caused by the workpiece being transported to another building, waiting for equipment to finish a large batch, or poor management of materials. Improving the processes might make it unnecessary for production control to send information to each stage of production.

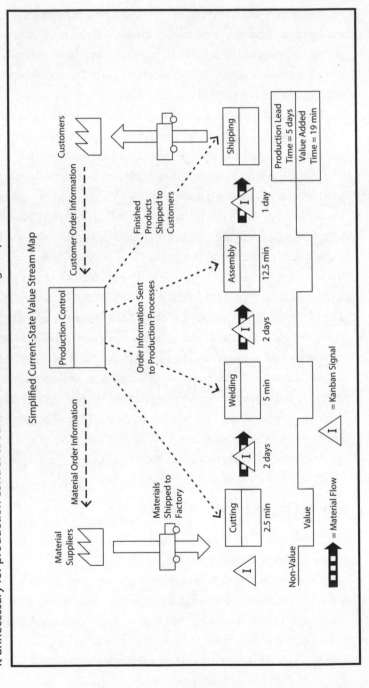

This delicate balance, furthermore, is highly susceptible to circumstances outside the plant. If they are not on board, suppliers, sales, accounting, and other functions can all disrupt the delicate balance of continuous flow.

As the Toyota Production System developed and the company grew, the senior leadership team began to see the need for a comprehensive management approach that could support companywide continuous improvement. As it turned out, a movement was flourishing in Japan that was soon to become instrumental in Toyota's enterprise management strategy.

THE UNSTOPPABLE DRIVE TO IMPROVE

In the late 1940s, General Douglas MacArthur, commander of the U.S. occupying forces in Japan, had a public relations problem. The word on the street was that U.S. efforts to reconstruct Japan were in fact intended to exploit the Japanese people, and the messages coming from communist China were not helping. MacArthur needed a way to communicate with the general public, but Japanese radios were of such poor quality that the message was not getting through.

It was decided, therefore, that the U.S. forces should help the Japanese improve their electronics industry so that the Japanese people would have working radios. The task fell to an engineer from MIT named Homer Sarasohn, who headed an entity called the Civil Communications Section (CCS). What the Japanese firms needed, he determined, was instruction in statistical quality control. The statistician he brought in to teach them was one of the leading authorities on the subject, W. Edwards Deming.

Deming, who had made an earlier trip to Japan to help with that country's census, gave a series of lectures to the electronics manufacturers. The sessions were so successful that Deming's unique abilities as a teacher came to the attention of Ichiro Ishikawa, a highly influential business leader who was busy setting up an industry-funded association called the Union of Japanese Scientists and Engineers (JUSE).

In 1950, Deming was invited to give a weeklong JUSE-sponsored course in statistical quality control. Five hundred engineers attended. Deming was, unlike some of his compatriots, respectful of the Japanese and also was personable and kind. At the conclusion of the sessions, he was invited to return; in the envelope with the invitation were a check and an airline ticket.

Deming was to make numerous visits, with thousands attending his lectures and courses, which were funded without government assistance. The content, however, was about a lot more than producing defect-free radios. Deming's definition of quality encompassed all aspects of making a good product, and this included everything from concept and design to manufacturing, delivery, and customer support. As it turned out, this definition was already widely accepted in Japan.

This viewpoint was reinforced by another thought leader, Joseph Juran, who gave talks on management methods that reflected the same holistic approach to quality.

Deming reflected on the subject in his article "What Happened in Japan?" published in 1967:

> Management must assume the responsibility to optimize the use of statistical methods in all stages of manufacture, and to understand the statistical control of quality as a never-ending cycle of improved methods of manufacture, test, consumer research, and re-design of product.[7]

As a result of these events, JUSE flourished, signing up hundreds of companies, and, using Deming's and Juran's methods, created a quality standard called Total Quality Control (TQC) that spearheaded a quality movement across Japan. In 1951, JUSE established the Deming Prize, to be awarded to a company that achieved excellence in TQC. The Deming Prize became highly coveted; soon

Japanese companies were engaging in massive multiyear improvement programs in their quests to win it.

TQC was immediately applied by Japanese companies to a wide range of targets, such as improved productivity, savings on energy and materials, and reduction of rework. However, the most salient feature of TQC was its focus on developing people, as Masaaki Imai explained in his groundbreaking book *Kaizen*.

> When speaking of "quality," one tends to think first in terms of product quality. Nothing could be further from the truth. In TQC, the first and foremost concern is with the quality of people. Instilling quality into people has always been fundamental to TQC. A company able to build quality into its people is already halfway toward producing quality products.[8]

This philosophy challenged the basic tenet of Taylorism that for every process there was "one best way" that could be determined by an engineer and then dictated to workers. Deming believed that processes are subject to a never-ending cycle of continuous improvement and that this cycle depends on wide input from the people who work directly with the processes.

Deming's statistical methods, furthermore, were not long drawn-out calculations for engineers but simple conceptual tools that were easily learned and applied in the workplace. At the core was a method developed by Deming's mentor, Walter Shewhart, which became known as PDCA, an acronym for plan-do-check-act, as shown in Figure 2-2.

PDCA was central to a JUSE-initiated program called quality control circles (QC circles) that was launched in 1962. The JUSE website provides the following definition:

> A QC Circle is a small group consisting of first-line employees who continually control and improve the quality of their network, products and services.[9]

Figure 2-2   The PDCA (Plan, Do, Check, Act) circle illustrates the steps in the continuous improvement process introduced by Deming. Many prefer to call it PDS, with "Study" used instead of "Check."

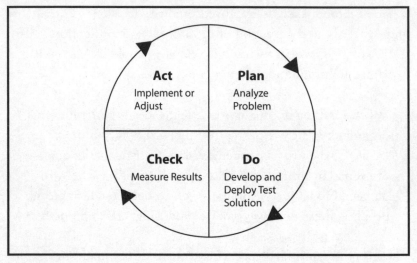

Through the program, workers form autonomous groups of 3 to 10 volunteers in the workplace to meet on a regular basis to discuss and initiate improvements in that workplace. QC circles quickly became a Japan-wide phenomenon that eventually involved millions of people. The program is alive and well today.

Although QC circles have considerable latitude in selecting problems, they approach this task methodically by using graphs, Pareto diagrams, histograms, and other statistical tools and then apply the PDCA cycle to continuously improving the process. Improvements may range from creating a layout of the working environment, to eliminating wasteful steps in a process, to building cooperation between departments.

Management maintains a central role in promoting wide participation in QC circles by providing training, guidance, and support for QC activities; showing respect for the creative input of employees; and maintaining a clear vision of the company's improvement goals.

According to Deming, the success of QC circles was due in part to a tradition in Japan of continuous improvement:

Workers in Japan always had the privilege not only of making suggestions, but of trying them out. For example, a suggestion on a change in sequence of operations could be tried out in an autonomous group.[10]

Behind this attitude of improvement is a Japanese concept called *kaizen*, which is derived from two words: *kai* meaning "change" and *zen* meaning "good." The idea is that everything can be improved and that it is the responsibility of every worker to contribute to improvement.

As Imai explains, Deming's scientific methods and the *kaizen* philosophy were a perfect fit.

Kaizen strategists believe that standards are by nature tentative, akin to stepping stones, with one standard leading to another as continuing improvement efforts are made. This is the reason why QC Circles no sooner solve one problem than they move on to tackle a new problem. This is also the reason why the so-called PDCA (Plan-Do-Check-Act) cycle receives so much emphasis in Japan's TQC movement.[11]

QC circles, however, are not merely an end but a vehicle to develop people and create a culture in the organization whereby everybody embraces the spirit of continuous improvement. *Kaizen* is everywhere: in daily improvements, in the pursuit of goals and individual improvements, and in target projects from autonomous study groups. Often the results are intangible.

Imai summed this up on the Kaizen Institute website:

Kaizen is everybody improvement, every day improvement, everywhere improvement.[12]

One of the most successful adopters of both the spirit and the practice of continuous improvement, it turned out, was Toyota.

The Five-Day Kaizen

In North America, the term *kaizen* is most commonly associated with the five-day *kaizen* event, or *kaizen* blitz, in which a cross-functional team participates in an intensive weeklong improvement targeted at a particular problem. Although this is the de facto standard in North America, this approach was never used by Japanese companies, says leading Lean authority Jon Miller in the book *Kaizen Culture*, of which he is a coauthor.

"The kaizen event, in its popular five-day format, is an American innovation on a Japanese process," he says, noting that the format was adopted to suit the schedule of traveling consultants.[13]

Toyota Becomes a Global Force

In 1955, Toyota introduced its first successful passenger car, the Crown, and the company began to experience significant growth. Within five years, production had grown sevenfold and personnel had doubled. The company, however, was experiencing growing pains. Inadequate training, inexperienced managers, and poor communication were taking their toll, and quality was suffering. Furthermore, Toyota's competitors were improving their quality, raising consumers' expectations.

In 1961, the company began a comprehensive project to adopt TQC throughout the enterprise and, as a goal, to pursue the coveted Deming Prize. Interestingly, the 1960 winner was Toyota's competitor Nissan.

Eiji Toyoda, who would become president of Toyota in 1967, reflected later on the objectives of the company's QC efforts:

> We realized that what was needed was firstly for top management to set clearer quality targets and ensure these were thoroughly

transmitted to employees, and secondly to put in place a system to improve functional cooperation between departments.

Having identified these two shortcomings, we resolved to expand our regular quality control activities to a company-wide initiative.[14]

The criteria for the prize, as the breadth of TQC suggests, were all-encompassing in terms of establishing excellence. In addition to some of the more familiar aspects of quality, they encompassed management's vision, the ability to communicate that vision to employees, cost control, research and development, development of personnel, and customer satisfaction.

The challenge was not taken lightly. The company laid out a four-year plan to win the prize in 1965 that involved all the divisions of the company. Through a series of companywide audits conducted by senior management, problem areas were identified and corrective plans were mapped out.

As part of the preparation process, two important initiatives were launched to address the goals that Eiji Toyoda had outlined, both of which were to become central components of Toyota's management system. To improve how efficiently management's vision was executed, a system for policy deployment, or *hoshin kanri*, was developed. This included a scorecard-like structure for codifying and communicating goals and aligning activity in the workplace with those goals.

To improve cross-functional cooperation, the company adopted a matrix management structure that allows key functions such as quality control and cost control to be managed across different departments, such as product design, manufacturing, and sales. Significantly, this allowed the exercising of authority throughout the value stream. For example, the chief engineer of a product line could ensure end-to-end quality of the product from concept and design through production and delivery.

The overall effects of the effort far outstripped the prestige of winning the prize. Quality improved, and warranty claims were drastically reduced. During that period, Toyota introduced the Corolla, the first model to crack the U.S. market. Finally, Toyota was able to reduce its production costs significantly.

However, as the managing director at that time, Shoichiro Toyoda, who had been one of the leaders of the QC efforts, commented, Toyota had become a different company:

> [T]he initiative also dramatically improved our corporate makeup. One example of this is that managers learned management methods, and another is that human relations across the company improved. TQC provided a framework for everyone from suppliers to Toyota Motor Sales [Co., Ltd.] to cooperate toward a common goal, and by clarifying who was responsible for which duties and who held what authority, people were able to hold frank discussions. As a result, processes were standardized as quality assurance rules and cost control rules, establishing a set management system.
>
> Our employees are now aware that QC is beneficial and are keen to continue with QC initiatives in the future.[15]

The company had, in addition to its many quantifiable accomplishments, created a culture of continuous improvement throughout the organization that was to prove essential over the next decades.

Toyota, however, was determined not to rest on its laurels. The companywide audits continued, and Toyota continued to make improvements. The drive to improve led to the winning of the newly established Japan Quality Control Prize in 1970 and to continuing efforts to refine TQC throughout all aspects of its operations:

The Toyota we know today would not exist if TQC had been a one-time affair. Introducing TQC and winning the Deming Prize was only a starting point. Toyota has been diligently continuing and expanding TQC-related activities right up to the present.[16]

The combination of TPS and TQC became what we now call Lean. TPS provides the tools and the model for production, and TQC provides the framework for continuous improvement, culture, and overall management. Both are essential components of Lean.

Letting the Cat Out of the Bag

One of the criticisms by the prize committee was that Toyota needed to establish better cooperation with suppliers, and the company set out immediately to address that issue. As part of that effort, it began in 1966 to actively encourage vendors to adopt TQC methods and provided assistance for their efforts.

That fall they held an event called the All Toyota Quality Control Conference, which included presentations and panel discussions on quality issues. Seventy vendors attended, one of whom won the Deming Prize in 1967. Toyota introduced the Toyota Quality Control Award in 1969 to further strengthen the initiative.

In the meantime, Taiichi Ohno had established the Operations Management Consulting Division (OMCD), an internal group of consultants dedicated to studying the Toyota Production System and teaching it to its supplier network. The group began providing hands-on assistance to suppliers, helping them solve problems and of course helping them meet Toyota's "Just-in-Time" requirements.

The cat was out of the bag, and it was only a matter of time before the secrets of Toyota would become available to companies outside of Toyota's network. The question was, would anybody be listening?

Terms and Concepts Introduced in This Chapter

The following terms and concepts were discussed in this chapter:

Andon: Literally "lantern": the signal light that is activated by a worker to indicate a problem and, if the problem is not resolved immediately, stop the line.

Autonomous maintenance: The practice of having workers maintain their own equipment.

Cell: A work area where equipment is arranged, typically in an L- or U-shaped pattern, to allow a worker to conduct multiple functions.

5S: The modern term for systematically creating a tidy and orderly work environment. The five S's are Sort, Straighten, Shine, Standardize, and Sustain.

Five Whys: The process of asking "why?" five consecutive times to get to the root of a problem.

Flow: The ideal condition in which the product progresses through production without interruption. Often referred to as continuous flow or one-piece flow.

Gemba: Literally "the real place": the workplace where value is created.

Genchi genbutsu: Literally "go and see": the practice of direct observation.

Hoshin kanri: Literally "policy management": consists of goal setting and deployment through a set of conceptual management tools.

Jidoka: The principle that a machine or a process must stop immediately if a defect or safety issue occurs that cannot be resolved on the spot. Also called autonomation.

Just-in-Time: The provision of parts and processes at the exact time and only in the exact quantity that are needed in production.

Kaizen: Literally *kai* ("change"), and *zen* ("good"), this term describes the concept of continuous improvement. In North America, the term is used to describe rapid improvement events known as five-day *kaizens*, or *kaizen* blitzes.

Kanban: Literally *kan* ("see") and *ban* ("card"): the manual system of signaling demand from later to earlier processes by using cards, tags, bins, and other visual indicators.

Muda: Japanese for "waste": includes work or outlay that is extraneous to production. Often codified as the Seven Wastes.

PDCA: A conceptual tool for managing improvement projects. The acronym stands for plan-do-check-act. Many prefer "study" to "check." The tool was popularized by W. Edwards Deming and became a central pillar of continuous improvement.

Pull: The idea of triggering production by customer demand, as opposed to a "push" signal from a scheduling system or an internally determined production target. The pull signal moves upstream from later processes to earlier processes, that is, in the opposite direction of material flow.

SMED: Acronym for Single-Minute Exchange of Dies; refers to a methodology for rapidly changing over equipment to accommodate a low-volume/high-mix production environment.

Takt **time:** Based on the German word *Takzeit* ("meter"), the metric for ideal production timing that is based on the required speed of production to meet customer demand.

TQC: Acronym for Total Quality Control; the name given to the quality standard developed in Japan in the 1950s. Today this is called TQM, with "Control" having been changed to "Management." The standard was central to the quality circle movement that began in Japan in the 1960s.

TWI: Acronym for Training Within Industry, the training and job improvement methodology introduced by the U.S.

government and used extensively in American factories to improve production capabilities during World War II.

Value stream: The conceptual representation of the entire production process from receipt of materials from suppliers to shipment to the customer. Value stream mapping (VSM) uses the value stream to map material and information flows to first identify waste and then design improvements to eliminate it.

CHAPTER 3

❖

WEST MEETS EAST AND THE UNBELIEVABLE

The quality revolution in Japan resulted in a complete change of direction for Masaaki Imai.

As a recent graduate in international relations at the University of Tokyo, Imai had begun his career in the late 1950s at the Japan Productivity Center, arranging tours of American factories for Japanese executives. He was keenly interested in helping Japanese companies and, like many of his compatriots, felt that the United States was the role model to aspire to.

By the 1980s, the roles had reversed: American manufacturers were struggling, and Japan had become the shining model. Imai, who was by then widely known as a management consultant and executive recruiter, began to arrange study tours of Japanese factories for American executives.

To prepare, he visited a number of Deming Prize winners, including Toyota. One of his requirements was to get supporting information to help explain the companies' success to their visitors. As it turned out, the companies had submitted extensive documentation in their Deming Prize applications, and Imai offered to translate them into English. The companies happily obliged, and Imai found that he had a mountain of information.

> *Masaaki Imai:* In those days, Japanese executives felt great honor that foreigners were coming to visit them, so they more than welcomed my request. So I received tons of documents that they had prepared. When I saw what these companies had been doing, this was a real eye-opener. And I think at that time, I probably had more materials in my office about what was going on with these companies than any other library. So I thought, Why don't I write a book about what I am finding out?

The result was his groundbreaking book *Kaizen: The Key to Japan's Competitive Success,*[1] which came out in 1986.

Imai conducted many tours and later founded the Kaizen Institute, which was to become one of the most important global consulting firms promoting the new methods. He also began to organize conferences on Japanese management throughout the industrialized world. In the process, he got to know many industry leaders, including Shoichiro Toyoda, who later became chairman of Toyota; Taiichi Ohno; and Yoshiki Iwata, one of Ohno's most important disciples.

Iwata had been designated by Ohno to conduct TPS training events for Toyota's suppliers. The format was to begin with an introduction of basic principles and then conduct hands-on work directed at a particular problem in a supplier's production environment. The duration would range from several days to a week. The work, Imai explained, was very intense and went on, often until after midnight, until the problem was completely solved.

In the late 1980s, Iwata and several colleagues from the Toyota group retired and formed Shingijutsu, a consulting firm dedicated to bringing TPS methods to other companies. Imai had brought Iwata with him on talks and hired him for his first consulting engagement outside Japan. The approach, Imai explained, was unusual:

> Normally when experts go to consult, they give lectures, and that's the end of the story. But Toyota's way was very little lecture—most of it was about making things happen and guiding the change.

In 1988, as *kaizen* was beginning to have an impact in North America, Imai organized a weeklong training event at the Hartford graduate center of Rensselaer Polytechnic Institute. The presenters included Iwata and two of his Shingijutsu colleagues, Akira Takenaka and Chihiro Nakao.

One of the workshop attendees was George Koenigsaecker, president of nearby Jake Brake, the nickname for Jacob's Vehicle Equipment Company.

"THIS IS THE WORST FACTORY I'VE EVER SEEN"

Koenigsaecker's first encounter with "Just-in-Time" had come in the late 1970s, when as an executive at John Deere he became the lead on a joint venture with the Japanese company Yanmar Diesel. On a visit to Japan, he toured plants, met dealers, and generally went through the normal paces of getting acquainted with the new partner. Then he attended a presentation that changed everything.

> *George Koenigsaecker:* At one point we had a meeting with the executive committee of the corporation. They gave us a presentation—sort of a corporate overview—and at one point they started talking about their improvement work. It was only one or two slides, but it showed some amazing numbers—productivity on a revenue-per-person basis had gone up a little over 100 percent during the prior three years,

and improvements in quality and lead time were huge. At the same time they were doing that, they'd increased their product range fourfold, trying to grow out of the early 1970s oil crisis in Japan.

At first I thought that I'd misunderstood. The presentation was in English, but I figured that maybe they had mistranslated. So I probed it three or four different ways, and it turned out that yes, this is what they really intended to say and what had been happening.

It turns out they were a part of the Toyota family of companies, if a distant cousin. Taiichi Ohno had visited and told them about the Toyota Production System, but they hadn't really started listening until the oil crisis. They then went through a forced march transformation with a couple of his guys who were spending their weeks at Toyota, and then spending weekends at Yanmar teaching teams how to transform their work processes.

At this point, I think it was 1977, they had three years of results. For me that became kind of a flag—this was serious stuff. At Deere, we were spending $300 million a year on capital investment, and a big target of that was to grow productivity. We thought 3 percent improvement every year would be really good. But this place was growing their productivity in the range of 20 to 30 percent a year.

Excited by the possibilities, Koenigsaecker, with the help of Jim Abegglen, a Westerner who had been working with those techniques in Japan, presented his findings to Deere's senior management team. The reception was lukewarm: the executives found the results interesting but couldn't see themselves taking on "that Japanese stuff."

Expecting that people in the automotive industry would be sure to be interested in the Japanese approach, Koenigsaecker accepted a job offer at Rockwell International's automotive group, which was making heavy truck components. Although it turned out to have little awareness of or interest in this new approach, the company allowed Koenigsaecker to set up a team to benchmark best practices in manufacturing throughout the world. This allowed him not only to visit companies practicing "Just-in-Time" but to compare them with other leading companies.

The team visited some of the top performing factories in the world, looking for best practices.

George Koenigsaecker: There were some great organizations in Europe and in the United States too that had developed a deep expertise in some process technology or product range. But when you looked at the way they operated, it wasn't fundamentally different from what we were already doing.

In Japan, however, we began to see some companies whose operating metrics were radically different. It was difficult to benchmark in terms of dollars, because the yen was undervalued, so we tried to look at how many man-hours it took to make a truck axle and numbers like their quality rate, lead time, inventory turns, and other core metrics that were in some sense independent of currency valuations.

What we began to realize is that a subset of Japanese companies—about 15 percent of the firms that we visited—were using the Toyota Production System and were achieving on average four times our enterprise productivity. Here we were, number one and number two global market share in all our businesses, and yet we were finding businesses that had multiples of our enterprise productivity.

So that was kind of earth-shattering. We'd learned about setup reduction and some of those kinds of things. We were applying the pieces that we'd picked up back at Rockwell—how to reduce setup times and how to get some flow going—but had a very small picture of the total.

The amazing thing about these companies was that it wasn't just shop labor that was four times as productive—so were the salary numbers. If you looked at the business and how many truck axles they made a year and did the ratios, we would have four times as many salaried and indirect people per axle as they did. And those productivity differences in the plant held through to all of the administrative processes as well. We benchmarked how many people these companies had in accounting, HR, and other departments versus our equivalent. Obviously there were variations, but the average turned out to be fourfold in all of the indirect areas as well.

When Koenigsaecker reported all this to Rockwell's senior management team, the numbers sounded, for somebody who hadn't actually been there, too good to believe, so they were not believed. Koenigsaecker and Bob Pentland, his production engineer, continued to learn about Lean wherever they could, applying ideas such as flow and setup reduction in the plants on an experimental basis. Two years later, Koenigsaecker left Rockwell to become president of Jake Brake.

Jake Brake had made its name with a patented product for using heavy diesel engines to slow, or brake, a truck, and its customers included the major diesel manufacturers Cummins Engine, Caterpillar Diesel, and Detroit Diesel. However, orders were typically late, the product was considered overpriced, and customer relations were poor. Shortly before Koenigsaecker came on board, the patents expired, and the company was soon thrown into crisis.

George Koenigsaecker: It was all hitting at once. I said the only thing that might save us would be a conversion to a Toyota system. I thought we might be able to do this well enough that something would work out. So we started on a Lean transformation path, and in the midst of all this we became the first significant acquisition for Danaher Corporation.

I had brought over Bob Pentland from Rockwell. Initially, we did everything we knew how to do from my days at Deere and Rockwell, and we acted quickly. Only about six months into this, we had already moved probably every machine twice to refine the flow of the cells and that sort of thing.

But we were implementing only what we knew, and we realized that there was a lot we didn't know. We hadn't quite run out of ideas yet, but we were a little concerned, because we were pretty sure we didn't really know where we were going.

Then, in early 1988, Koenigsaecker and Pentland saw the announcement for a four-day workshop that Masaaki Imai had organized with the Shingijutsu group in Hartford. When he read the announcement, Koenigsaecker realized that the presenters—Iwata, Takenaka, and Nakao—were the people who had led the transformation at Yanmar Diesel.

George Koenigsaecker: I said to Bob, "These are the guys." They were from the production engineering department at Toyota under Ohno. Obviously we were going to go, so Bob and I went to this thing.

In the course of the event, we learned that the presenters had planned to do some work at a local plant, but the local plant leadership wouldn't allow them to make the kinds of changes that they expected to be able to do. So they needed a plant, and I was determined that it would be ours.

Three or four days into the workshop, we finally convinced them to have a look at Jake Brake. We told them that it was about 15 minutes away and that we'd take them to dinner first.

After dinner we took off—the time to get there was actually about 45 minutes, not 15—and we walked into the plant at about 11 p.m., which was pretty unusual. This was a UAW plant, and there had been a strike that had been more than a year long somewhere back in Jacob's history. So labor relations were not good, and people weren't too receptive about Lean either.

So it was Bob and me and a couple of our night superintendents, with three Japanese consultants and three translators in tow. Iwata, who was highly revered in the Lean world of the time, was the lead guy and did the talking.

So we started walking through the facility, and the first thing he threw out through the translator was, "Interesting warehouse, but where is your factory?" We were in the middle of the factory, but admittedly there were boxes of inventory everywhere.

I wasn't quite sure where this was going, but I desperately wanted to work with these guys to learn from them. I'd been trying to learn about this stuff for about 10 years, and these were the guys.

So we walked a little farther, and he stopped and said, "This is a very bad factory." I'm sure my guys were thinking, "I wonder where this is going." We walked a little farther and he stopped again, and he said through the translator, "I think this is the worst factory I have seen in my whole life."

Then, he said, "This is so bad, I think you should be fired immediately." Fortunately there was nobody there who could fire me.

Eventually we got to what was our best component cell, where they made a component called a cross head, which is a high-value component of an engine brake. We had 16 machines arranged in a sequence of operation, and this was our best stuff.

Iwata spoke to the interpreter, who then said to me, "Iwata-san wants to know if you want to fix this cell."

When I said "Yes," there was more talk, and then, "Iwata-san wants to know if you want to fix it immediately."

I realized that they were testing us, and this was my chance. So I pulled over my night superintendent, who was a really good guy, and said, "Are you up for this?"

And he said, "Yeah, sure."

Then I told him, "Well you better find every maintenance guy, and every forklift, and every piece of equipment, because we are going to be overwhelmed."

And so he took off, and I turned back to Iwata and said, "Okay, we would like to do that." He said, "Okay."

Iwata and his people began with the Ohno circle, where they stood and just watched the operation in the cell. This was probably only five minutes, but it seemed like forever.

Then, Iwata finally turned back and said, "Well, for one thing, the cell is backward."

And I said, "Well what does that mean?"

He explained that though it's second nature to do things clockwise, you should always build a cell counterclockwise, because most people are right-handed. This way you can increase overall productivity by 3 percent because the strong, better-coordinated side faces the work.

So we start moving 100 percent of the equipment in the cell, completely reversing the order, and then while they were doing that, they were looking at some machines we'd set up and making jigs out of wood blocks so we could simulate the setup reduction work.

Then the night shift superintendent from the UAW, who was a really huge guy who had strong memories of fighting against the Japanese in World War II, came storming up with a couple of his guys, and he was just ballistic. He had gone completely off the deep end, and you can kind of imagine why. In the first place they thought that this was their plant, not Danaher's plant.

So this guy was literally ready to punch Iwata out. I was no great athlete, but I'd been a high school wrestler and that sort of thing, so I'm doing a wrestling move trying to block my guy from punching out my new friend over here and trying to talk to them and say, "They're here to help. They'll make this a lot better; they know how to do this stuff."

It almost didn't matter, because I'm sure he wasn't hearing anything.

Eventually, he realized that in order to punch out this Japanese guy, he's going to have to punch out the president of the company, so eventually he said, "Well, we'll see about this," and stormed off.

Koenigsaecker had a lot of apologizing and convincing to do the next day. The union had many divisions, and so there were numerous conversations. The point he drove home was that the company was about to go bankrupt and the people from Japan had special knowledge that could help turn around the company.

Then there was the task of persuading the Shingijutsu consultants to come to the United States to work with Jake Brake. Koenigsaecker got some help from his group president, Art Byrne, who had been exposed to Lean through his work at General Electric (GE). Byrne was, like Koenigsaecker, very determined and very persuasive. After two months of back-and-forth, Byrne met Iwata over dinner in Tokyo and persuaded him to come in the fall to work with Jake Brake and a sister Danaher company, Jacob's Chuck. This was Shingijutsu's first engagement in North America.

George Koenigsaecker: After a lot of persuading, we were able to hire the Shingijutsu folks as our Lean senseis, and we became their first clients in North America. Over a two-year period, they did a lot of hands-on work with us in the shop floor, led weeklong *kaizen* events, taught us how to use Lean tools, and helped us build a culture of continuous improvement throughout the organization. Lead times eventually dropped from 30 days to 1 day, and enterprisewide productivity grew 86 percent, which was achieved by meeting our 2 percent target each month.

In the evenings, we wrote up what we had learned in the form of standards, teaching materials, and our production system, which eventually evolved into the Danaher Business System.

For the next four years, Byrne's Danaher companies remained Shingijutsu's only North American clients. As the results started to turn heads, the pressure was on to spread the initiative to all the other plants. Shingijutsu, however, had only three consultants at the time, and they were reluctant to spread themselves too thin; as they put it, Jake Brake and Jacob's Chuck were in such bad shape that they needed to fix them first.

To respond to the need, Byrne created something they called President's Kaizens. To kick it off, they brought the 13 company presidents to Japan to visit various Shingijutsu clients. Each president was ordered to participate in a three-day *kaizen* event every six weeks. Workshop materials from Shingijutusu were used, and Byrne and Koenigsaecker led many of the events.

Art Byrne: We just got fantastic results with these President's Kaizens, and everybody really opened their eyes, like, "Wow, that's incredible." For example, we went with one process from 14 people down to 3 to do the same amount of work—or maybe a little bit more—in a three-day *kaizen*. If you're running a company and you're CEO of a company, it's pretty hard to go home and say, "Well I don't want to do that." We made a lot of progress with Danaher, Jacob's Engine Brake turned out to be very good, and Jacob's Chuck got to be very good.

In September 1991, Byrne left Danaher to assume the role of CEO of Wiremold, an electrical components manufacturer outside of Harford, Connecticut.

DISPELLING THE MYTHS OF PRODUCTION

When Byrne arrived at Wiremold, he found an ally who had been considering many of the same problems he and Koenigsaecker had wrestled with at Danaher. The individual was the company's vice president of finance, Orest Fiume.

Orest Fiume: In 1988, after I'd been at Wiremold for 10 years, we started trying to change how we did business, not because we were in trouble but because we could see foreign competition coming. Although we were still the market leaders and making a lot of money, we felt that we needed to improve. This was around the time of Total Quality and Deming. I had seen the NBC white paper *If Japan Can, Why Can't We?* and had shown the video to our employees.

So we started down this improvement path without really knowing what we were doing and made every mistake you could possibly conceive of. For example, we tried to implement "Just-in-Time" and a new MRP [manufacturing resource planning] system simultaneously, not realizing they were incompatible. We did nothing to reduce setup time but reduced production batch sizes, thus chewing up all of our time with more frequent but long setups. From 1987 to 1990, our operating income went down 82 percent, so there wasn't a lot left. When I looked to our standard cost financial statements to try to figure out what was going on, I realized they were absolutely useless.

So I started experimenting with other ideas to try to uncover what was really happening in the business. I began by putting some numbers on a spreadsheet. We didn't even have Excel at the time—I believe we were using Lotus 1-2-3. I'd send the spreadsheet out maybe a week after the regular financial statements to the management group, and I'd say, "We're trying something new; I'd like your feedback."

What evolved was an alternative to the financial reports that managers were used to seeing: a profit and loss (P&L) statement that gave managers the information they needed to run the business without the financial gobbledygook. Although it was only supplemental, it gave managers a better look into what was happening with the business.

This turned out to be the perfect setup for the Lean transformation that was to follow.

Orest Fiume: When Art Byrne became the new CEO in 1991, he said in one of our first conversations that the standard cost approach was terrible, and it had to go. So I pulled out one of our plain-English P&L reports and said, "Is this what you're looking for?" and he said, "Yeah, that works." And that's what we used from then on. Standard cost accounting went away, and from that day on we only looked at our actual costs.

The problem Byrne and Fiume had with standard cost accounting is that it drives decisions on the basis of past information, the proverbial managing through the rearview mirror approach. Furthermore, because it is driven by algorithms rather than real data, it often instills the wrong kind of thinking and, even worse, the wrong kind of action.

Art Byrne: Standard cost accounting drives companies to make things in big batches, and they absorb the overhead based on either the hours of the machines or the man-hours. And so what you find in most of those companies is near the end of the month or near the end of the quarter, people will be running machines that they don't need to run at all. They don't have any orders for the product, but that product has the most absorption hours in it and they want to make the financial month, and they'll do things like that all the time. And so the fact is that by running them, all you are doing is building up inventory.

This kind of formulaic thinking has very little connection with customer value.

Art Byrne: If you walk out on a shop floor, you can't tell if you're ahead or behind. The customer is never present in a traditional manufacturing company. Instead of the customer being present, you have a forecast for the end of the month. So people spend their time trying to make the forecast even though it is not correct most of the time.

Byrne wanted to create an environment where his managers could monitor their real costs on a weekly or even a daily basis and make timely decisions that were based on how they could best help the bottom line of the company.

Art Byrne: You're trying to improve the business moving forward. So when you want to establish targets, I think the most important thing is to try to pick those things that are going to have the most impact on changing the results going forward. Then run the business based on those targets. Don't run the business based on last month's results, or last quarter's results, or things like that. Last month's results already happened— you can't do anything about them. And so what's the point in spending a lot of time on it?

Keeping Score with Real Numbers

Working with goals and targets that were straightforward and devoid of extraneous information was the cornerstone of Byrne's management strategy. Byrne ran the Wiremold business using the following five metrics:

- *Customer service percentage:* the proportion of orders that were shipped on time
- *Productivity:* the ratio of sales to worker hours
- *Quality:* the total reduction in defects compared with the previous period
- *Inventory turns:* the ratio of cost of sales to average value of inventory
- *Visual control:* defined by the rules of 5S and judged by a quality team

Art Byrne: We ran Wiremold off these five measurements. Of course, we had to close the books every month and we had a look at the numbers, but we really never had any meetings about that—we never had a big review meeting at the end of the month looking at those numbers. If there were some problems, I would talk separately with the individual or the people involved.

We had broken everything into value streams, and we had a value stream manager for each. The value stream in our case was like a product family, a fairly big product family, and so we had six product families of value streams, and the manager of that value stream honed these five measurements.

Every week we would get together, myself, the staff, and the value stream managers, and they each had 10 minutes to present on how they were doing on the five measurements. We had a big digital clock, and they had to stand up in front of everybody and present how they were doing. And if they went over the 10 minutes, everybody would boo them, so they would stay pretty much on time.

We just used these five measurements. We didn't spend much time on past results, because that had already happened. If it takes the finance group three weeks to close the books at the end of the month, now you're looking back seven weeks to see what happened, and by then something new has come along. So we said, "That's a waste of time."

The Lean metrics Byrne was using differ from what many managers are used to in that they apply to value streams, not to internal entities within the company, and specifically target waste in those value streams. Increasing inventory turns, for example, reduces the wasteful expense of holding inventory, thus improving the efficiency achieved in a value stream. Raising the utilization percentage of the equipment in a machining department, in contrast, may appear to create efficiency, but if the result is unsold inventory, this could result in weaker performance in relation to that value stream.

In a nutshell, a Lean metric such as customer service percentage has a direct impact on bottom-line results.

Art Byrne: If you buy from me and three other guys, and I deliver 100 percent on time all the time and the other guys are spotty—sometimes they're okay, sometimes they're two weeks late—over time, people are going to start to drop them and just buy from me, because I'm really easy to deal with. I'm very reliable.

Lean metrics also make sense to all employees, not just a few accountants. It's pretty hard for the average employee to have a direct impact on indicators such as return on assets and cash ratio, but customer service percentage posted on the wall has real meaning to every worker. Participation in shared measurable goals energizes workers for the continuous improvement activity that will drive the company forward. It also removes tedious administrative tasks that managers hate.

Art Byrne: The plant manager asked, "Does this mean I don't have to write a 25-page plan report every month?" I said, "You can write it if you want, but I can guarantee you that we're not going to read it. We'd much rather you spend your time fixing the mess in the plant than writing some stupid report."

"We're at Three and We Have to Go to Twenty?"

The clarity of goals had an important counterpart. The targets Byrne set for his teams were extremely aggressive; in fact, they could be achieved only if people radically changed their behavior, which was precisely what Byrne was looking for in this Lean transformation.

Initially, of course, his management team was stunned.

Art Byrne: When I began the process at Wiremold, I told the management team that the target for inventory turns was 20. They said, "Wait a minute. We're at 3 turns, and we have to go to 20?" This was a shocking thing.

Byrne explained the rationale for his approach:

These kinds of targets not only help you drive value to the customer, they also change the conversation and the style if you will—it changes the internal culture of the company tremendously. It's an aspirational goal. We're going after a bigger goal. It's like saying, "Let's start the season and all agree that our only goal is to win the Super Bowl."

So we're not trying to go from three times inventory to four. We're trying to go to 20. If you can get everybody focused on that and everybody talking about working toward those goals, you're going to move forward much faster than the company that's looking over its shoulder and saying, "Gee, we've only done three. What would be a good goal for next

year? Can we say three and a half?" And we make three and
a half, and we say great.

Byrne's target for reducing defects was equally aggressive. As he
pointed out, even if employees missed the goal, the results would
lead to a competitive advantage:

> Our target for reduction in defects was 50 percent. I think we
> had 50 percent in only one year, but we were in the 40s a lot.
> If my target is 50 percent and I miss it but I'm in the 40s and
> your target is a 5 percent reduction and you beat that every
> year by 9 percent, I'm going to beat you to death.

The True Meaning of Respect

The setting of stretch goals was really about trust and empowerment.
Byrne believed in his people and believed that they were capable of
accomplishing far more than had been demanded of them in the past:

> Most people want to have an argument about stretch goals.
> They say people will quit. I think that's a foolish way to look
> at it and disrespectful of your people. What you're really say-
> ing is, "I don't think my people can achieve such a thing."

This wasn't just about managers making numbers, however.
Byrne recognized that if a company was to improve, the real action
would take place on the shop floor, and to act quickly and decisively, workers had to be free of any procedural restrictions. Byrne
empowered his workers to act by giving them a degree of latitude
that sometimes surprised them.

> *Art Byrne:* Early on at Wiremold we were trying to create one
> of the initial cells in order to make the product complete. This

meant combining equipment from two different departments. The team responsible—I think they were maintenance workers or electricians—came and found me in the plant at around eight-thirty at night.

These teams were empowered to take the necessary steps—we didn't require them to fill out requisitions or any of that nonsense. Well, these guys were frustrated, because the rolling mill was 90 or 100 feet long and didn't fit where we wanted it.

I asked, "What are your options?" They said, "Well, we could make it fit if you would let us cut a big hole in the wall—we could just run it through the wall." So I said, "Go ahead." And they just stared at me: "You mean just like that?" I answered, "Yeah. I asked you what you need to do, so go ahead."

So they went off and chopped a hole through the wall, and they got this thing done, and it stayed like that for years. But it worked. And the workers were excited because they could see that they were really changing the company. Before people would have just talked about it.

The trust that the employees had in Byrne was reinforced by a decree that he issued at the beginning of his tenure. In the Toyota tradition, he announced that no employee would be laid off as a consequence of the savings generated from Lean.

Another factor in building this trust was the continuation of a profit-sharing plan that directly reflected the improvements the company was making as a result of the employees' efforts.

Art Byrne: I think you can go a long way in Lean without workers' incentives, but I think you're way better off if you have it. There's only one that I like, and that's profit sharing.

You have to make sure to keep the finance guys out of it, because they're going to want to create some really complicated thing, and then they want to move the goal posts all the time. If you want to profit share, you do it off of dollar one. And don't change the plan every year—just make it a simple plan and keep it the same forever.

If you make a dollar, you share a dollar. If you make a hundred dollars, you share a hundred dollars. If you lose fifty dollars, you don't go and claw it back. And that way everybody understands that you're all in the same boat. And everybody in the business should be on the profit-sharing plan—the CEO down to the janitor.

Acquisition with a Twist

As the Lean transformation took hold and the company started to make progress on its goals, Wiremold began to generate a significant amount of cash. Soon Byrne began to look for companies to acquire. It was a foregone conclusion that he would make these companies Lean.

In his tenure as CEO, Byrne oversaw 21 acquisitions and developed a standard process for introducing Lean to new companies. Byrne would show up on the first day, introduce Wiremold, and then deliver a two-hour overview of Lean concepts. After lunch, he would personally lead the first *kaizen* session. The action would begin immediately: equipment would be moved, cells would be created, and anything extraneous would be eliminated.

> *Art Byrne:* So people were kind of shocked by this. But if you get the CEO of your new company down on the shop floor for the rest of the week doing *kaizen*, helping you move the equipment around, and improving things, it leaves quite an impression on most people.

The Lean transformation was so successful that the first five acquisitions, according to Fiume, were financed solely with the cash that the company had freed up by eliminating inventory. In Byrne's tenure, operating income increased by 14.4 times and gross profit went from 38 percent to 51 percent, plus the valuation of the company increased from $30 million to $770 million.

Leading on the Front Lines

Being a hands-on CEO should, according to Byrne, come with the territory. The members of the Toyoda family in Japan all knew how to build cars. In contrast, the traditional CEO who relies on financial information that flows up the management ranks is essentially flying blind.

> *Art Byrne:* You have the CEO at the top and you have the value-adding people at the bottom, and it should be the other way around. Trying to get the right information to filter up through all the layers to the CEO to tell him that there are any problems and that there are any opportunities is pretty difficult. They don't really know in a lot of cases how bad they are; they don't really understand what the opportunities are in their own company. So they don't really understand what you can do and what things you can improve.

Byrne is also adamant that the Lean transformation has to be led from the top. One reason is that the change required is so fundamental that some things simply have to be decreed. Consulting with management on a suitable target for inventory turns, for example, could take weeks or months.

> *Art Byrne:* If you have consultation, you're going to lose that fight. They would tell you why you can't do it, they would give you a big list, etc. So you have to have enough confidence in yourself as a CEO to say, "I don't care. We're doing it anyway; we're going to do it over time."

Also, it often takes the clout of the CEO to get everybody in the company on the same page.

Art Byrne: If you are asking your factories to remove waste from their value streams, and on the other side you're asking your sales force to bring in huge orders at the end of the quarter or offer huge volume discounts to drive big batches, you are working against yourself. Or you tell the manufacturing guy to get the inventory turns up, and then you tell the purchasing guy to shave every cent he can from all the raw material costs, and he does that by brute force by buying six months' worth, then you're not going to increase your inventory turns; you're going against yourself. But people don't understand that—they can't seem to think of this as a strategy where everybody has to work together.

Finally, the CEO needs to be the champion of the Lean transformation, clearly articulating the direction and removing the many barriers that inevitably come up.

Art Byrne: If you think about Lean simplistically and say this is the strategy, you say I'm trying to deliver more value to my customer, and in order to do that I have to change from batching to an organization where things flow. So all we were ever really trying to do was go from batch to flow. You could always see what you needed to do.

There's nothing hard about understanding that you're going from batch to flow. What's hard is understanding how you're going to do that. What are the things you have to do specifically to make that occur? Then you have to overcome all the reasons why everybody says it can't be done.

"BRING YOUR CEO..."

By the late 1990s, Wiremold's success was widely reported, and many companies were showing interest in following suit. Byrne, recognizing how he and his team had learned from visiting other factories, began to host tours of Wiremold for companies interested in adopting Lean.

Lean was by then being widely used as a toolkit to solve specific production problems, and adopted by departments as opposed to organizations. Many plant visitors apparently hoped they could achieve Wiremold's results without any fundamental change to their existing management practices.

This was, of course, not the kind of change that Byrne was talking about. When he became inundated with tour requests, he decided to draw the line. "We wanted to help," he later told Masaaki Imai, "but we also knew that unless the CEO is involved, no company is going to go home and do it."

So Byrne set up a simple rule—no company would be allowed to tour Wiremold unless they brought their CEO. "All the tours stopped—right away," he told Imai.[2]

A few CEOs, however, did approach Byrne, several of whom you will hear from in the pages following. Byrne and Koenigsaecker both went on to inspire many Lean journeys and became key players in a small but growing community supporting the enterprise-wide adoption of Lean.

CHAPTER 4

A NEW WAY OUT
OF FINANCIAL CRISIS

It is not necessary to change. Survival is not mandatory.

—*W. Edwards Deming*

Although Lean makes its biggest impact over decades, not years, it is important to remember that it originated in part as a series of measures to turn a financially troubled Toyota around. Lean's first win was the dramatic improvement in productivity that allowed Toyota to grow its capacity at a time when it was unable to invest in new resources.

Many Lean transformations since that time have experienced early windfalls from quickly identifying and eliminating large amounts of obvious waste. In fact, many Lean CEOs freely attribute their early progress to having been "so bad" in the initial stages. Whatever the cause, such a boost is exactly what a troubled company may need to successfully emerge from a crisis.

Grabbing this golden opportunity, however, requires a significant change in thinking from the chief financial officer (CFO). Companies facing fiscal challenges are typically caught in a death spiral that is all about dollars: creditors lose confidence and cut off the cash supply, the ability to deliver to customers weakens, customers defect, and the cycle continues.

In traditionally managed companies, the primary weapon is triage guided by the company's financial statements. The company divests itself of the facilities, equipment, or employees who are deemed to be creating the least profit in hopes that a leaner, more viable company will emerge from what remains. The information that drives these decisions, of course, comes from accounting.

The weakness of this "cut and hope" approach is borne out by the high failure rate of Chapter 11 restructurings in the United States. By some estimates, over 70 percent of these companies do not emerge, and those that do often limp along until the next crisis.

From a Lean perspective, a key problem here is that the accounting information used to drive these decisions is only indirectly related to the activity that satisfies customer demand and makes money. Consequently, the information can be confusing, irrelevant, or misleading.

MISLEADING NUMBERS, DISASTROUS DECISIONS

One of the first accountants to take practical steps to solve this disconnect was Jean Cunningham, coauthor with Orest Fiume of the book *Real Numbers*[1] and one of the leading voices in Lean accounting. Cunningham was CFO for the Louisville, Kentucky–based Lantech during its Lean transformation that began in 1991.

Cunningham cites several reasons why traditional accounting isn't much help in a crisis. First of all, accounting reports are delivered after the fact and do not provide timely information that can help managers make quick decisions. Three weeks after the end of the quarter, it is too late to address the problems in the quarterly report.

Furthermore, GAAP (generally accepted accounting principles) accounting statements aren't designed with the internal decision maker in mind.

Jean Cunningham: The problem is that we've gone so far toward what the external funders need to know that we have lost the focus on the people who are making decisions about the performance of the company and what they need to know.

Financial information can also be dangerously misleading. When a company is seeing a significant drop in sales, for example, traditional financial statements can understate the seriousness of the situation because of the way unsold inventory is reported.

Jean Cunningham: With standard cost accounting, you initially get rewarded by making more stuff and putting it into inventory regardless of whether you're selling it or not.

So not only have you been lulled into making more inventory to protect your income statement, but you're also lulled into thinking when sales drop that you're not going to be hurt as badly as you really are. So it becomes a sort of death spiral, and when it catches up to you, you've waited longer than you want to wait to take action.

Another dangerous blind spot is that standard cost accounting obscures the line between fixed costs and variable costs, leading to poor decisions about discontinuing product lines.

Jean Cunningham: Traditional accounting systems treat all costs as variable. So when a company loses $100 in revenue, they tend to say, "Okay, if the gross margin is 30 percent, then I lose $30." But in reality, a lot of the costs in manufacturing—your facilities, your management, your benefit programs, your insurance, all these sorts of things—are really fixed, or they're fixed in the shorter term. So with a 30 percent gross margin, your variable contributions to profitability—your variable margins—might be more like 60 percent. So you're really losing $60 of profitability, but half of it is hidden.

In other words, labeling all costs as variable gives the false impression that when sales drop, all those costs will go away proportionally. So managers may think they are helping their business by cutting the loss leaders, but they may be cutting their throats.

The disconnect between what accounting reports are saying and reality was aptly summed up by Cunningham's former boss, Pat Lancaster, cofounder, chairman, and former CEO of Lantech, and inventor of the stretch wrap technology that launched the company in 1972:

The problem is the perception that when you get your monthly report, you now know about the vital issues in the business. And Lean would say and I would say even more strongly from my experience that you don't know the details of the business based upon accounting.

The reasons for this are interesting. First of all, accounting is yesterday and certainly not tomorrow, and it's based on two big sins—standard costing and material resource planning (MRP). The argument is that you can flow your product, raw materials, and product components to the best singular, lowest-cost position using standard costs and this MRP algorithm. I don't want to say it too strongly, but I really think that if you drive your ship or fly your airplane based on the two instruments of standard cost and MRP, you will pretty much drive yourself into a waste condition that is almost unimaginable.

AN ACCOUNTING CYNIC DECLARES WAR ON WASTE

Lancaster hired Cunningham in 1991, when the company was coping with the challenges that ignited its Lean journey.

Lantech, founded in the early 1970s in Nashville, Tennessee, is a classic American success story. The name is a contraction of "Lancaster," the last name of the brothers Pat and Bill who founded it, and "technology." The company's stretch wrapping technology, which could be used instead of the more expensive and cumbersome shrink wrapping, was a major innovation in the packaging industry. Not only does the approach allow the work to be done with less material, but because it skips the heat-treating stage, it makes the process much quicker and adaptable to a wider range of applications. When the energy crisis hit in 1973, the energy efficiency of this approach became another significant advantage.

For 15 years, the company had virtually no competition. However, after it lost a patent suit in 1989, low-priced clones of its technology began to appear on the market. Prices plummeted, and the company was soon in crisis. At that time, Lancaster was relying on standard cost accounting to guide him. Convinced that he needed a new approach, he brought in Jean Cunningham, who subsequently became the CFO.

Lancaster knew he needed to make major changes on the plant floor to become more competitive and also knew that he needed to get a more accurate reading of his company's finances. Lantech had installed a costly MRP system, but Lancaster was finding that the company's financial systems were a hindrance rather than a help. As it turned out, he and Cunningham saw eye to eye on this.

Pat Lancaster: What Jean Cunningham had was a proper nonreverence for the profession of accounting, which enabled her to see through these problems and to really get an organization dedicated to busting through them. She did an absolutely wonderful job of that along with me. By the way, I'm an absolute accounting cynic as well, so we busted a lot of icons together. Then she was able to put together a regimen that was at the very least not a barrier and at the most was supportive of Lean concepts.

Lancaster conducted an extensive search for a vice president of operations who could rebuild his manufacturing. After screening hundreds of applicants, he hired Ron Hicks, a Danaher veteran who had first seen Lean at Jake Brake and had developed his skills working with Japanese senseis at Hennessy Industries in Nashville. Hicks came to implement Lean with no compromises.

With Lancaster's support, Hicks began to make radical changes on the shop floor, reconfiguring the plant to create flow. Seeing Lean unfold in the company was a huge epiphany for Cunningham and the beginning of her journey in Lean accounting:

That was my moment! That was when I knew that this was the greatest thing that we could possibly do to make more money. This was going to make our business work. If we could do this, this would be the best thing that we could do.

Twice the Productivity with Half the Space

Working with the outside consultant Anand Sharma, the company attacked its manufacturing processes through a series of *kaizen* blitzes.

Pat Lancaster: We were very, very small relative to his other clients, but because we were small and anxious to move fast, he gave us a tremendous amount of help and got enormous results with us.

His early-on strategy at the time was called *kaizen*, which now is called one-week *kaizen* or a *kaizen* blitz. The idea is to jump in with both feet with a few principles and a little learning. What happens is that a group of people will reorganize a particular job within the space of a week.

We used this idea very successfully for the first three or four years. If you're pursuing commonsense modifications that help align the organization with customer value, you can make some very positive changes very quickly, and it's incredibly effective. Especially if you're a sloppy organization to begin with.

By 1993 Lantech was profitable again, and the next year the company was once again a top performer. Factory space was down to roughly half, lead times had shrunk, productivity had doubled, and inventories had dropped significantly, all while revenues doubled and market share shot up from 38 percent in 1991 to 50 percent in 1994. The turnaround was documented in *Lean Thinking* by James P. Womack and Daniel T. Jones[2] and became a classic Lean success story.

As the company's shop floor journey evolved, so did the accounting department. Cunningham worked with the management team to develop a series of reports that supported the company's Lean transformation. Unnecessary steps were eliminated, processes were streamlined, and soon the department was supplying managers with current information; furthermore, members of the accounting staff were able to get involved in improvement activities. Labor cards, matching of invoices, and other tasks were eliminated, and the company began to close the books within hours, as opposed to weeks, of the end of the quarter.

Lean, however, is a long journey, and in the late 1990s it was clear that there was more work to be done. The *kaizen* improvements that had been so successful and the energy that had gone into them were starting to diminish.

> *Pat Lancaster:* The problem with the *kaizen* improvement approach is that it doesn't sustain itself. That's the Achilles' heel—stuff that doesn't have a systemic basis doesn't really stick. This is a fact of life, and there isn't any way around it. We tried for six or seven years to find ways to reenergize the returns on the benefits that we got.
>
> For example, we'd do what is called a *kaizen* newspaper, where you document your progress and make your claims, and in most cases the claims are valid. However, 90 days later half of these were gone, and a year later another half was gone. Two years later you could barely can find the tracks in the sand.
>
> So the *kaizen* blitzes were valid and they remain valid today, but you have to be able to sustain as well. When companies talk about how many *kaizens* they have done and that becomes the metric, I'm reasonably convinced that that becomes a diminishing method at some point.

The quest to take Lantech's Lean transformation to the next level was to be picked up by a new CEO: Pat's son Jim, who took over the reins in 1995. What Jim Lancaster discovered was that the key to embedding Lean practices more deeply into the organization was to create a strong management culture. We will pick up that portion of the story in Chapter 7.

RESCUING A FAMILY BUSINESS FROM THE BRINK

Another company whose Lean transformation started from a financial crisis is the Ariens Company, based in Brillion, Wisconsin. When Dan Ariens took over the leadership of his family's company, orders were declining, distributors were defecting, and the company was sitting on a growing mountain of debt.

> *Dan Ariens:* I took over the business in 1998 as the CEO, and at that point we were in need of a turnaround. We had a lot of debt, and banks were in workout for me. I would say we were a year away from closing shop.

The Ariens Company had been founded in 1933 by the inventor Henry Ariens, the grandfather of the current CEO. The company began with rotary tillers and other farm equipment and then moved to the consumer market with a line of lawn mowers and snow blowers.

In the period leading up to the recession of the early 1990s, the company ran into financial difficulty. An outside CEO with a reputation as a turnaround specialist was hired, and in an attempt to improve the situation, the company entered new markets, consolidated operations, and took measures to increase productivity.

However, the company began to accumulate a huge volume of unsold inventory, and soon it became clear that the crisis was more severe than the financial reports were indicating.

> *Dan Ariens:* The prior CEO had designed a bonus plan that rewarded people for absorbing more overhead, but of course, this was creating income that wasn't real. I took over with a ton of inventory on hand, two shifts of labor running, and orders shrinking.

Ariens had studied Lean principles and had used them in his previous role as plant manager since the early 1980s, and he knew about the dangers of high inventories. Although his scope had been

limited to plant operations, he was aware that there was more to
Lean than what happens on the shop floor:

> When I was plant manager here in the early 1980s, I read a
> number of the books about world-class manufacturing, and I
> read the early books about Toyota and Lean when they came
> out. I was pretty impressed with the way people were working
> together toward common goals. There was something very
> holistic about this as well in terms of value streams and how
> everything fit together.
>
> The lightbulb for me, though, was understanding what
> waste is and where it exists in organizations. It's not the waste
> so much in the process of making the components—it's all
> the other things that go around to make them ready to make
> the component. From the design system, to the accounting
> system, to the manufacturing engineering system, and the
> process design, and the processes themselves. There are many
> steps before you even drill the hole.

Ariens's insight that Lean was about more than manufacturing
proved to be pivotal. It revealed the scope of the change that had to
be made to save the company:

> It was a very stressful time, and we needed that holistic
> approach to change the way we did business, not just the
> way we manufactured. So I brought Lean to the whole com-
> pany and really drove it hard from my vantage point and
> never let go.
>
> I was also very impatient with people who didn't get it. I
> used to say we're either going to change the people or change
> the people. That was very hard; it was tough love, but we
> were in a turnaround. I still remember the day. It was April 1,
> 1998, when I terminated the entire executive team except for

two guys. I had to gut the place to get the right kind of leadership in place. We rebuilt from those early days.

We then went out looking for people who had experience in Lean. Our first hire was Bob Bradford, a guy who had worked with Shingijutsu, as our VP of operations. So he built our manufacturing team, and I got marketing and accounting staff that started to understand Lean accounting. We created all that into the mid-2000s.

The first efforts were in manufacturing, but the Lean journey quickly began to spread from the shop floor to the offices.

Dan Ariens: That started with one of our manufacturing events, when we discovered that our supervisors were spending about a day a week on payroll issues. We said, "What's wrong with the payroll system?" We had the equivalent of about three and a half people doing all kinds of wasteful work on managing the payroll system, making sure everyone got paid the right amount. It had to do with when they punched in, how they punched in, the punch clocks, the software system—all those things were redundant.

So we did a *kaizen* event in payroll, and we went from three and a half people—in terms of equivalent hours of work—down to one in that one-week event. At that point, we realized that conventional accounting practices are full of waste that we could eliminate.

And then we did customer service, and we did more back in accounting, and then we went back to the call centers. And the accounting thing—changing the way we did our manufacturing, the labor and overhead absorption stuff, converting that all to a clear expense that someone owned—was a real change. We didn't get to that point, though, until probably 2004.

The transformation was characteristically buoyed by the early successes.

> *Dan Ariens:* We did have those early successes, and we made a lot of noise about it. We celebrated that, and they were fairly visible things, like our Sno-Thro assembly line. We went from a very linear assembly line with the roller conveyor and the person at station 1 all the way down to station 32. People didn't even know each other's first names, because they couldn't even communicate. So we quickly went from 30 to 15 stations and created cells. Those early wins really started to get people to take notice.

When Slower Is Better

Workers, supervisors, and managers had built their careers by making as many pieces as possible. However, creating flow often meant that people had to slow down. The idea of scaling down production to meet demand was counterintuitive to many in the company, including Ariens:

> There is an awful lot in what we call Lean management that sounds like an oxymoron. One of the lines I remember that caused me to stop in my tracks was when we were challenging capital and the big machines we needed to make a lawn mower deck. One of our senseis at the time—we used Simpler Consulting—said to me, "Dan, the question you have to ask about equipment is 'How slow can you make it go?'" You're not trained to think that way. You think, How fast can this press pump out components? And he was absolutely the opposite. Of course, this makes perfect sense, because there are going to be constraints that limit how fast your line can

go, so controlling the speed of the machine is the only practical way to maintain flow.

Today we have a group, and I think it's the most innovative group in this company, that's called the Ariens Right Size Machine Group. Through them, we make a lot of our own manufacturing equipment. We design it to go very slowly and make one piece at a time that fits within the demand pull. We're only pulling components through that work center, and now today we're trying to figure out how to automate that as slow as it can go. People don't think in those terms.

Not every employee, however, was able to embrace the change. As production was scaled down to meet existing demand, it was too much of a change for people who had spent their lives making as much as possible.

Dan Ariens: This wasn't for everybody. One guy in particular who was a foreman of our machine shop said, "Dan, I'm too old for this. I don't get it, I'm not going to get it; I'm going to be a problem to you." He was like 62, and he said, "I'm just going to retire." We had a lot of that. People who just didn't get the enigma. We'd say, "Go slower," and they'd say, "You're crazy."

While the work processes continued to improve the performance of the company, Ariens had to keep the auditors and the bankers happy. Previous financial reports had many of the costs absorbed in inventory. With inventories declining and fewer labor hours, overhead appeared to be increasing.

Dan Ariens: Our biggest challenge here was to get our auditors to understand what we were doing and to get a clean and approved audit so that we could keep banking. I think it's very difficult to bridge that gap. I really think that many public companies may never get there—and that's unfortunate—because the regulatory environment for a public company is much more restricted than for a private company.

The hardest thing internally was being able to allocate a real expense to a real owner, for instance, having a manager who owns the cost of powdered paint so that it's not part of the overhead that flows through.

You could see how there was a real misnomer in how we were managing the business. The more you managed to reduce labor, the bigger the challenge of trying to absorb this overhead number. As the question "Who's going to own that?" got more and more prevalent, we realized that we had to do things differently. So we figured out how to quantify what we call 9000 series stuff—things like lubricants, Locktite, powder coating—into our bills of materials.

Another aspect of the financial management that was holding them back was the piece rate incentive system. This was a tough one to remove, because it had a long history in the company. This change was perhaps the most stressful for Ariens:

There are times when you go home at night and you don't sleep, and you say, "How is this going to come out? How is this going to work?"

One of the biggest things that we figured we had to change pretty quickly—that was back in 2000, and we were really smack in the middle of our turnaround—was that we were a piece rate incentive plant. We were basically paying people to make more components, and they were driven by that. The way I put it to employees was—and here's another oxymoron—you're not going to be more productive.

The piece rate incentive plan was 35 years old at the time. Some people were used to having the so-called gravy jobs, while others had jobs where it was more difficult to make the incentive number. So we had to average all that out.

So I would stay awake wondering, Are they going to be okay? Are they going to come in to work? Are they going to quit?

Trust as a Company Value

Being able to change a 35-year-old incentive process required a lot of trust. Ariens earned that trust early on:

This is a small town. I'm sitting here in Brillion, Wisconsin, population 3,250. I went to high school here, and my family is part of this community. If I was a CEO and you dropped me in Chicago, I certainly would do the same things, but I'm not sure I'd get the same kind of respect.

That's key, because what we were doing, especially at the beginning, called for a great deal of trust. I could tell people to just hang in there with me and eventually it would all make sense.

The other part of this is that I've also made it very clear that I'm the guy taking the hit for all the big decisions. When I terminated most of the leadership team in 1998, I had always felt, and still believe, that most of our good-quality workforce in the plant is not responsible for a lot of the problems or mistakes that happen. These happen from managers. You've got so much talent in your plant. How are you managing that, and how are you managing your customer base?

When the workers saw that I was starting at the top with making changes, I think that said to everyone, "Okay, this is a company that's not just going to fire me because we don't have work." That's the way I've always treated it. People who come in here for a wage job, we want them very engaged, we want them to know that they're part of the family, part of the team, and they're part of the problem solution here.

When I give talks about our Lean journey, I tell people that the biggest thing is that we have built a culture around here where we trust each other. When we have that, we know that we can take some risks on making changes in our plant. People are going to have a little patience and see it through, or they're going to be part of the team that makes it all work out. Trust is such an important component to having a Lean culture.

Trust is perhaps the glue holding the company together, and Ariens insists on mutual respect in all interactions. This is not a slogan on the wall but a basic rule that governs all activity in the company.

Dan Ariens: We really emphasize the family atmosphere here, and I reinforce that through our core values and our mission statement. I give a 20-minute speech to new employees that covers the basic principles we believe in, such as be honest, be fair, keep our commitments, respect the individual, encourage intellectual curiosity. I tell them I'm going to be really impatient if you break any of these core values, because it's a matter of trust. If we can't trust each other, it won't work here.

For his part, Ariens feels that his most critical role is making sure that the company has the right people:

Ideally, you want high performers who are great in your culture, but I always tell people that if we have a real high performer who is weak in terms of culture, we're very impatient there. We'd much rather keep someone I call great in the locker room. If we had a great quarterback and he was just an absolute jerk, I'd get a new quarterback. That's one of the most important roles I've got—to make sure that we have really good chemistry, and that means having people who are a part of a team.

We had a guy called Tim, and he's left us, but his famous quote was, "There's no I in 'team,' but there is an I in 'Tim.'" Wait a minute; that's not going to work here.

The result is a collaborative spirit throughout the company.

Dan Ariens: Everybody really does work together here. I don't really say that—but a new employee will feel that right away. You notice it in a meeting: "I'll just grab that, you grab that, I got this, I got that." We share responsibilities. Part of that is everybody wears every hat that they can, as opposed to "that's not my deal, that's not my department."

Leading Beyond the Balance Sheet

Ariens believes that the CEO is essential in allowing Lean culture to take hold in a company. His primary reason, though, is not that a CEO is needed to tell people what to do. The point is that it takes authority at the top to remove some of the deeply embedded barriers to Lean transformation.

Dan Ariens: Without it, things happen here and there, but they don't become holistic, and the whole business doesn't benefit from it. A Lean CEO should be saying, "Okay, there's more to Lean than what I can manage with a balance sheet, financials, customers, bankers, shareholders, and all of that."

I do think the CEO really is the most important in getting a full Lean journey going. I won't take credit for what we've done, but I certainly say that a CEO driving a very focused, energized effort and relentlessly talking about continuous improvement is one of the most important things that can happen.

REBUILDING AFTER A MARKET COLLAPSE

The experience of going from Lean tools to Lean management in response to a crisis is not unique to Ariens; organizations in many industries have followed this pattern. One CEO who brought Lean to the enterprise in this way was Steve Brenneman, CEO of Aluminum Trailer Company Inc.

Brenneman owned two companies: Nappanee Window, a manufacturer of doors and components for the recreational vehicle (RV) industry, and Aluminum Trailer Company (ATC), a manufacturer of recreational and commercial trailers. He was actively running Nappanee Window at the time and began experimenting there with Lean concepts in 2005. His approach, he said, was superficial:

> At the time, I thought that improvement was all about reducing direct labor, and I saw Lean as a way to do that. We moved the tables more closely together, and that eliminated steps for making doors. I thought that was obviously better for the business and better for everybody. But I didn't really understand how improving our inventory turns was going to help us or any of the big picture concepts of overall waste elimination.

Then came the Great Recession of 2007 and 2008. The company had invested heavily in equipment to make its own aluminum extrusions, and suddenly it was faced with a massive decline in revenue.

Steve Brenneman: Our business gets hit hard in downturns, because then people basically stop buying RVs or boats or anything that they don't really need. They'll put some of those purchases on hold for a couple of years. So in our area, you don't experience a 20 percent drop in sales; you experience a 60 percent drop.

Ultimately, we had to shut down the door business. As I was selling off the assets, I picked up *Lean Thinking* by Jim Womack and Dan Jones.[3] Maybe it was the gravity of the situation I was in or maybe it was because I just saw things from a new perspective, but *Lean Thinking* is just what really did it for me. I read that book page by page, and walking through the plant as I was getting ready for the auction, I could see all of our mistakes. Now I had a framework and a context to put everything in. I saw what we did, and I saw how I as a leader could learn how to become operationally excellent using Lean as a method.

Brenneman turned his attention to the trailer business. Aluminum Trailer Company was also in a crisis situation, and that was where his real Lean journey began. The first task was to stop the bleeding. With the assistance of consultants Ed Miller and Frank Giannattasio, who were veterans of the Wiremold transformation, the company began to conduct a series of *kaizen* events to create flow and remove waste from its processes.

Steve Brenneman: We were in crisis mode as well, because we had gone from $26 million in sales in 2006 down to $10 million in sales in 2009. We were in the midst of that $10 million in sales year, and the guy running the business had a finance background. He was able to make layoffs and stay ahead of the cost curve, so we continued to break even from a cash flow standpoint. Fortunately, we didn't have as many fixed costs as I'd had in my other business.

At the time, we were occupying two buildings with a total of 100,000 square feet, and my first big decision was to move out of the second building, which shrank our floor space down to 50,000 square feet. The rest of the management team was worried that if sales did come back, we wouldn't have the space we needed. But with Lean glasses on, I knew that it's really about the throughput across that square footage. I saw the mess that we had, and I knew that we were going to set to work in cleaning that mess up and becoming better.

So we cleaned up a lot of the mess, established a supermarket, took all the materials off the line, and began to supply the materials back to the line in small quantities. This brought our annual inventory turns from about 5 up to about 10. By doing that, we were able to free up enough cash to get caught up with all of our vendors. That gave us a level of stability that we hadn't experienced before.

Note that it wasn't bank loans that got ATC up to date on its accounts payable; it was cash freed up by improving the business through a series of *kaizen* events.

Once ATC had gained some experience with *kaizens*, the company began to run them without outside assistance, with Brenneman himself as the primary leader and facilitator.

As the Lean journey progressed, Brenneman, like Ariens, soon found that the existing piece rate system was conflicting with Lean improvement:

We were doing some improvements with *kaizen* events, but as we learned, we were still a piece rate shop, and the further we went with it, the more we saw the disconnect between piece rate and what we were trying to do from an improvement standpoint.

My head of operations was really the one who was pushing for that change. We would want the guys to stop and do 5S or stop and fix problems, and they were so focused on the piece rate system that they didn't want to stop putting production out the door to do improvement work.

At the time we had decided to bring a consultant in to walk through our business and talk about value streams. We had already split into three production lines. He told us that we couldn't just separate production lines but that we had to also separate the functions in the office, divide them up, and then align those with the production lines. We decided this at the same time we decided to move off of the piece rate system.

The organization of the company into value streams is not just a bookkeeping exercise; it represents the way all of the work at ATC is organized. Employees, both on the shop floor and in the offices, are divided into three teams, each dedicated to one of the following value streams:

Value Stream 1: For customers who want a standard, high-quality trailer with little or no customization. These trailers are made quickly at a minimal cost using standard parts and standard work processes.

Value Stream 2: For customers who want special features on a trailer, for example, a vehicle carrier. A thousand options are available, which the team tries to standardize as much as possible to lower the cost. These trailers take longer to manufacture and cost more than the trailers in Value Stream 1.

Value Stream 3: For customers with very specific needs who want trailers that require a significant amount of customization. These trailers are designed to order in consultation with the customer. This team builds ATC's largest trailers.

Each value stream has its own salespeople, designers, and fabricators, and so there is very clear communication regarding all aspects of a customer's order, and the people building the trailers have a clear line of communication with the customer. This approach also gives the company a very precise picture of its costs.

"It Was Ankle Deep in Trash"

Working in the context of a value stream often requires workers to question long-held habits and sometimes to go against their instincts.

Steve Brenneman: I think Lean becomes second nature once you've been immersed in it, as I am. But if somebody says Lean is just common sense, then they don't understand Lean. I can tell story after story about our transition where it absolutely went against all common sense.

For example, three years into our journey, our production floor was still typical for a trailer manufacturing plant. It was ankle-deep in trash—metal cutoffs, liner panels, wood cutoffs, caulk tubes, etc. So every time you moved the line, you swept everything into a big pile, and then you moved the line, and you created the next ankle-deep trash heap.

We decided that this didn't make sense anymore. Anyone can clean up at the end of the day, but we do not want trash on the floor during the day.

So we told our workers, "When you tear a liner panel off, don't just throw it on the floor. We'll give you canisters on wheels, and you just take the recycling canister right along with you and tear that off and put it right in the canister. Don't put it on the floor."

People had the hardest time understanding it. They said, "That doesn't sound Lean, because now I'm taking so much more time to tear that liner off. It doesn't make any sense. Now instead of taking two seconds to tear that liner panel off, it takes me a minute to go get the recycling container."

So for the worker on the line who's engrossed in that daily work, this was not common sense. Common sense would say walk by this trailer and take those liners off one by one, as fast as humanly possible.

But looking at the big picture, if everybody follows this, we can move the line in 3 minutes rather than 15 minutes. Now we don't have tires with screws in them at the end of the line. And we won't have that broken ankle that one of our foremen got by stepping out of the trailer onto an empty caulk tube.

That's why CEOs and managers have to understand Lean at a very deep level. You can't really explain it by the tools. You have to see the big picture; you have to understand Lean at its best. You can't just copy things that Toyota did.

Brenneman believes that his experience in having to shut down a business left him with an indelible picture of how waste can destroy a company and how essential it is to pursue the kind of operational excellence that Lean transformations aspire to.

Steve Brenneman: I had gone through a difficult time just before learning Lean, so I became that Lean driver not because I'm smarter than everybody else but because of the pain I had experienced in getting to the point where I really understood Lean. It made me really wake up to how important operational excellence was and how Lean was the tool to get us there.

Brenneman understood, however, that that kind of transition was going to take time; that's part of the territory with a Lean transformation:

I had to learn that becoming Lean is not a race. As long as you are focused on continuous improvement forever, it's not how fast you get there, it's the depths that you go to and the quality that you get from it.

So I don't mind that there are still folks on our production line who after five years still think that this is stupid, and that 5S is a waste of time, and that all this improvement work should just end and we should just go back to building trailers. Just yesterday, I put some numbers together for our companywide meeting, which we hold every month to go over how well we did and talk about profit-sharing plans.

I felt that when it comes to productivity, the numbers make it pretty obvious that we're doing the right things for the right reasons. I hear those detractors sometimes, and I just think, How can you think back to what we were and say that this doesn't work? Seeing the data didn't work for some of them, but you hope that eventually it will.

The numbers were by any standard impressive. Net income had climbed from a small loss in 2009 to a positive 8 percent in 2012, and long-term debt had dropped nearly 50 percent during that period.

Even more impressive, however, is the reduction of inventory and the effect on the operations. Inventory turns have gone from 5 to over 15. When the company reached its previous high of 26 million in sales volume in 2013, its raw material inventory was only 850,000, down from 1.2 million in 2009, a year that had seen only 10 million in sales.

Shortages, in which a fabricator didn't have the materials to complete a job, were down substantially from 35 to 40 incidents a week to 5 to 10, and this was done with nearly triple the sales volume.

"Why Does the Business Exist?"

Once the value streams became established in the company, the improvement activity began to change. There was less emphasis on five-day *kaizen* events and more emphasis on daily improvement.

Brenneman brought in new people to lead the improvement activity and began to focus on long-term strategy:

> My role then started becoming more of a Lean strategist—guiding the leaders in their standard work and helping them develop the standard work of their folks. We still aren't great at that, but we've come a long way.
>
> In the past six months I've started going back and really focusing on our 10-year vision. How does Lean fit together with what we want to become? As we got more Lean—and I assume other people are this way—we started focusing less on the financial things and more on people development: vigorous learning, mindfulness, quality, quality of life, those kinds of things. Now, to tie that all together, I'm leading the movement toward a 10-year vision.

The vision is all about becoming a great company, which is about a lot more than numbers, Brenneman says:

> People will say, "We don't have 20 years to change the culture the way Toyota does." So then you start to go back to things like "Why does the business exist?" Well, if the business exists only to increase shareholder value, then obviously it makes sense to only reprogram the culture just enough to make the tools work. Because if it's about shareholder value, then you can't focus on 20 years or 50 years.
>
> I think there are a lot of leaders today who understand that Lean can't just be about the tools, but are they really willing to seriously consider any purpose other than shareholder value?
>
> So that is why we are really digging into our vision. If we really want to build something great, it has to be way more than shareholder value. Otherwise, employees work just hard

enough to not get fired and we pay them just enough so that they don't quit. It can't be about anything else. You can say all you want about people are our most important asset and all that kind of stuff, but if it's about shareholder value, then it just doesn't light up.

This kind of vision can be driven only from the top. Like Art Byrne, Brenneman insists that when companies come to visit, they bring their CEO:

I think that if the CEO is not willing to come along on the tour, the company can take Lean only so far. If people go back to their business and the CEO doesn't understand and thinks that this is all about reducing direct labor and reducing head count, they won't do anything with it. You'll get some line managers and the continuous improvement guy, and they'll get all excited, but then they'll do absolutely nothing. This sounds harsh, but that's a waste of my time.

I make exceptions, but we're quickly getting to the point where we're not going to make exceptions. Maybe companies will benefit in the long run if people can go to their CEO and say, "The only way they're going to do this tour is if you come along."

FORESTALLING CRISIS IN 2008

While Steve Brenneman was coping with the fallout from the recession, another manufacturer, although not in immediate danger, was embarking on a similar journey. The Steffes Corporation, with plants in Dickenson and Grand Forks, North Dakota, employs approximately 300 people in the manufacture of oil field products, off-peak heating systems, and custom metal fabrication.

CEO Paul Steffes and President Joe Rothschiller have managed the company as a team for the 1ast 26 years. Although they have common goals for the company, their backgrounds and personalities are entirely different.

Steffes is a mechanical engineer and the company innovator. In addition to leading the company's R&D efforts, he has become a noted authority on thermal energy storage, giving talks frequently and advising utilities on demand balancing, renewable energy, and related issues.

Rothschiller is a business manager with a background in accounting who became an avid reader on the practical aspects of management. He discovered Lean in the early 2000s and began to bring Lean methods into the company.

Initially, Rothschiller explains, the company used Lean tools the way most organizations do: to reduce costs in selected areas. There was little or no change in the overall management approach or organizational culture.

Consequently, few in the company understood the thinking behind Lean, and in some cases Lean was causing more harm than good. For example, by reducing materials and parts inventories, the organization was experiencing stock-outs, and Lean was being blamed. The company was growing at 30 percent a year, and so Lean seemed superfluous and was shelved between 2005 and 2008.

Rothschiller's study of Lean, however, had revealed that there was a lot of waste in the company's operations, and in the period leading up to the crisis of 2009 he was convinced that Steffes needed a strategy to become more sustainable. During 2009 the company faced a 30 percent decline in revenue, and that got Steffes and Rothschiller on the same page.

Paul Steffes: Maybe I'm an old-school guy, but when it was explained to me how we must be light and nimble and continuously improving, I certainly agreed 100 percent. Whether you call it Lean or call it continuous improvement, I recognized that the target is always moving and we must continuously improve or we're history. As a designer who is always trying to have a vision of the future, I also have always felt that the company has to reinvent itself every five years.

I think that the decision to really ramp up our Lean efforts had to do with circumstances: 2008 was a wonderful year, but 2009 was a 30 percent reduction year, and we didn't lay off or right-size for nine months, and so it made it a painful year. It did fit in that we were able to get people to dedicate real energy to learning the process.

Lean seemed to have the principles and the structure where we could drive the efficiency and the productivity that we knew we needed if we wanted to survive.

Taking Lean Company-Wide

With Lean established as a key priority, Rothschiller and Steffes began to plan a much more comprehensive implementation of Lean that would include not just manufacturing but all aspects of the company.

Joe Rothschiller: I felt that Steffes had to become a Lean company to survive the next 10 years even though we had just come off the best financial year ever. We were headed into a down year in 2009, and this time my approach to Lean was different with our senior team. The first time around we had approached it from a Lean manufacturing perspective and looked at cutting costs and waste. The second time was the correct strategy—to enable growth even in a down market. It was all about continuous improvement.

As we were looking at the economy going down in 2009 and 2010, it was a time when the management team was on board. They weren't busy with growing 30 to 40 percent a year, and they said, "You know what? It's time to look internal. It's time to become a better company to compete down the road." At that point we hired a consultant to help us provide Lean, and we hired two people to focus 100 percent on continuous improvement in our company.

The company selected Brian Maskell, a respected specialist in Lean accounting, as its Lean consultant. They also took advantage of employees' available time and a state-sponsored training program to bring Lean skills into the company. The bronze-level certification covered the basics, such as 5S, standardized work, total productive maintenance, and flow, and also, as Rothschiller notes, showed employees that Lean was not a far-fetched idea from management but a discipline that was widely accepted by other manufacturers in the state.

The organization then started conducting *kaizen* sessions to eliminate waste, free up space, and set up cells to create flow. Rothschiller led the first *kaizens* and made it very clear that unlike the company's earlier approach to Lean, these sessions were about starting a companywide culture of continuous improvement.

What we did then, and we still do it today, is make every *kaizen* report-out happen across the company. The entire senior team is invited to that report-out to listen to what occurred within that *kaizen*. They're not going there to hear about cost savings—it's about how a team improved something from 200 a day to 700 a day or where now we've taken our on-time delivery on this product line from 70 percent to 97 percent.

All we want to hear about is, "What is the continuous improvement that you came out with? We're not looking for dollars—we're looking for continuous improvement every day, every hour, every minute. What did you guys discover?"

The exercise of creating capacity initially seemed superfluous to some, but the teams made progress, and Lean thinking began to take root in the organization.

Joe Rothschiller: We knew that we can't just live within a 12-month world. We have to look forward and say, "How do we maximize the use of our square footage?" It becomes quite interesting how, after you dive into this over a year's period, it becomes part of your culture where everybody has the same vocabulary in terms of our Lean journey.

Rothschiller saw that the culture was changing when Lean started to creep into casual conversations. For example, an employee returning from a road trip reported that he had watched an airport window washer using a batch approach. The job could have been done faster and more easily, the traveler noted, if the worker had applied Lean principles.

The Reforming of a Minute Merchant

Rothschiller, who frequently speaks at Lean events, cites three prerequisites for successful Lean adoption:

1. Get 100 percent management commitment.
2. Structure the organization by value streams.
3. Implement Lean accounting within the value streams.

The emphasis on value streams reflects the commitment to bring Lean to the entire organization and to forge a closer link between financial management and the operations of the business. Rothschiller's accounting background had made him all too aware of how accounting can get in the way of improving the business:

In the GAAP world, the CFO is a minute merchant. In a Lean world, the CFO is all about flow and cash flow. If you're counting minutes or hours to apply overhead to the cost of a product and then afterward looking at what's the variance report, you are wasting a significant amount of your time.

The CFO has to get over that. Five years ago, I could tell you the labor, material, and overhead on every component of what we made. Today we say, "Who cares?" What does the product cost through the value stream? Quit doing all these transactions in the system and variances and follow-ups for nothing. All that research people are doing on variances is something that happened 45 days ago.

In 2008, Rothschiller oversaw six functional departments, each of which supported all of the company's product lines. As a result, decisions were often isolated from the customer. For example, the purchasing department was focused on getting the best prices even when the result was large piles of unused materials that tied up cash and took up valuable space.

Joe Rothschiller: As a manufacturer, there's the thinking that a truckload is better than a box, because you never know what the customer wants. When you buy a piece of equipment, you don't buy the 6-foot that you need; you buy the 14-foot because you might grow into it. So you're always buying more than you need, and things become monuments in the plant. We had to change our thinking around that.

Value streams, in contrast, allow managers to closely align expenses with demand and customer value. The key, Rothschiller says, is making the value streams as comprehensive as possible:

A lot of Lean companies have their general and administrative functions separate, and the only places they put value streams on is in a manufacturing plant somewhere. So their value streams are more like product families.

We don't do that. We went with 100 percent—everybody in our company is in a value stream. Each of our value stream managers is a division manager as well and has final responsibilities for everybody in the value stream. They have their own sales, their own inventory, their own purchasing, their own accounting.

Rothschiller assembled a cross-functional team of 14 to scope out the requirements for the first value stream. One of the difficulties was that the routines of traditional cost reporting were still ingrained in the company, and so people had to break the habit of thinking of overhead and variances and focus instead on cash flow and scaling expenses to correspond with immediate demand.

Another challenge was understanding the role of the value stream manager. In contrast with a traditional divisional manager role, a value stream manager was expected to keep in close touch with the workplace, which involved a daunting list of daily routines and responsibilities. Rothschiller decided to be the first to take on this new role, and he was surprised at how demanding it was:

I can be very honest with you—when I drew this thing out on paper, I said, "I don't know how I'm going to do this." How do you fit that into your schedule already?

You discipline yourself; that's the biggest key, and it worked very well. I was here, we did the meetings, we did the board, we did the metrics, we put things in place, and I can tell you that about a year later, when I was ready to hand it over to the person who headed up that product area of the company, I was making that person the value stream manager. I handed him my value stream work, and he looked at me and said, "There's no way." I said, "Actually, in 30 days you'll disagree with yourself. Just do it day in, day out, and it becomes natural."

Once the routines in the first value stream were established, the entire organization was restructured around six value streams. Four of them—heating products, oil field, manufacturing, and off-site provider—were created around product categories and generated revenue. Additionally, there were two internal value streams: support services, which consisted of corporate accounting, human resources (HR), and safety, and new product development. As the revenue-producing value streams got large enough, they were given their own administrative personnel, such as an HR person or a financial analyst.

The value stream structure removed the organizational constraints that would otherwise separate business decisions from the work that generated value for customers. The numbers everybody watched were no longer in the computer system but on visual display boards in the plants, where workers updated them on a real-time basis.

Joe Rothschiller: We have lots of billboards and inventory boards that our people certainly trust more than the computer system. We are trying to detransactionalize ourselves every day. All our people know that the inventory board is more accurate than what the system is going to tell you, because the system has to catch up. The board is actual by the minute, by the second. We introduce lots of new product, and our people are to the point of saying, "Unless you give us *kanban* quantities and a billboard out here so we can see what needs to be built and when and give us the red, green, yellow signals, we don't even bring it to the floor."

The common metrics provided a basis for continuous improvement that was shared companywide. By progressively improving flow, the company was able to grow the business 50 percent annually with minimal investment in capacity. In 2013, the company sold three times the product it had sold in 2008, which had been a banner year, with the same square footage. Lean vocabulary is now used throughout the company, and continuous improvement is firmly embedded in the culture.

However, the journey continues, and Rothschiller is ever aware of the dangers of retrenchment:

> The biggest thing for us is disciplining ourselves and saying, "Wait a minute. Are we defaulting into the old ways of thinking, or are we staying with the Lean way of thinking?"

Although Rothschiller is a believer in letting people find their own ways of improving, he occasionally has to be more direct:

> At one point, I had to write a purchasing policy that said you can pay 10 percent more for any product you want if you can get it here on a weekly basis instead of a monthly basis. I wanted our purchasing people to understand that flow is very important and storing product and getting truckloads is not good. It's the whole supply chain. You have to work on the supply side too.

Lean thinking has to be reinforced on the sales side as well.

Joe Rothschiller: Those spikes sales will kill you. Everybody dances on the table when they sell three truckloads of something, and then production sits back and goes, "How are we going to do this?" Then your on-time delivery falls apart.

It's a complete, balanced system. Spike orders are no good; you want level flow. There was an interesting face on the salespeople when we said, "Quit giving discounts for truck-load orders and give them the cheapest price to order one."

Back to the Roots

For Paul Steffes, who continues in his role as innovator and designer, the real story about Lean is that it has given the company the capability to change with the times. It also, he notes, helped bring the company back to its roots:

> I like the way that our employees, right down to the floor, are involved in *kaizens*, have input, and take ownership of manufacturing processes. Lean is a structured process that makes it possible for 300 people to do things the way I believe my father did when this was a one-man shop. So it brings me back to the days when it was just my father and me in the company.

CHAPTER 5

❖

CAPACITY WITHOUT
CAPITAL EXPENDITURE

I n 2009, General Motors sold over 6.5 million vehicles worldwide. The bad news is that it had the capacity to manufacture 8.8 million vehicles.

Manufacturing capacity represents a significant investment in facilities, equipment, support infrastructure, and salaried employees, all of which show up as fixed costs in a company's financials. Capacity utilization consequently becomes a bellwether for a company's financial health. Companies such as GM start losing significant money when sales drop below 80 percent of capacity, and when the decline hits 75 percent, as it did in 2009, a company moves into bailout territory.

To forestall such catastrophes, companies engage in various capacity planning exercises. The idea is to do the math carefully before investing in production-related resources, weighing a variety of options, such as outsourcing, partnerships, licensing, and overtime. Financial analysts use a variety of formulas to quantify the risk factors and determine precisely how much capacity it is prudent to add.

The Achilles' heel in all these calculations is dependence on the dubious art of demand forecasting. When the forecast is way off, as it was in 2009, no magic formula can save the day. It is no surprise, then, that when a company is rendered insolvent by a crisis in the economy, management is likely to blame "factors that nobody could have predicted."

There is, of course, a very different way of approaching this, and the secret sauce in it is one of the basic tenets of Lean: instead of buying capacity, build it over time by using existing resources and investments.

Identifying and eliminating waste is the method of choice for building capacity in a Lean environment. As results confirm again and again, Lean companies, through ongoing continuous improvement, free up significant amounts of plant space, equipment, and employee hours and then grow into that freed-up capacity. The resulting "asset-light" business model leaves them far less weighed down by fixed costs and consequently far more resilient in economic downturns.

"MY DAD HATED INVENTORY"

The Lean alternative for growing capacity started to enter the boardroom conversations at Vermeer Corporation, based in Pella, Iowa, in the mid-1990s. The company, founded in 1948 by inventor Gary Vermeer, employs approximately 3,000 globally in the manufacture of hay bailers, wood chippers, stump grinders, and other outdoor equipment.

At the time the discussions began, the influence of Lean was starting to grow in North America, and there were a number of excellent role models. Two board members advised the CEO, Mary Vermeer Andringa, to consider Lean as an alternative to expending capital in order to grow.

Mary Andringa: In the 1990s, Vermeer had two independent directors who were seeing and hearing early success stories of Lean. One of the directors at that time was the vice president of operations at HON, an office furniture manufacturer. He was quite pointed that we really needed to look into Lean. He challenged us to reconsider our recent history of adding plants, floor space, and people as we grew—all of which added capital expenditures that he claimed weren't likely to be necessary if we implemented Lean.

We did some strategic planning in the mid-1990s and indeed saw that one of our biggest opportunities was to reduce our cost of manufacturing and improve our gross margins. So we took our independent director's advice and started looking at companies that had started their Lean journey.

We had good examples close to home. We looked at our director's company, HON, and also learned from Pella Corporation, a premier window manufacturer headquartered in the same community as Vermeer. Both companies had been on the Lean journey already for several years. Interestingly enough, Pella Corporation pursued Lean in part because the CEO of HON was one of its independent directors who was advocating for Lean as well. It was amazing how this Lean story was spreading.

The Lean message resonated well at Vermeer partly because the founder, Andringa's father, had been asking many of the same questions that people with a Lean perspective were asking.

Mary Andringa: My dad hated inventory. He used to ask questions like "You mean we've got this whole building for central receiving? Why can't we just bring things directly to the plants, where they're going to be used?" We do now. And he also made a big point about how we built these batches of things, and we put them under a roof somewhere, and then we'd find them two years later when they were obsolete, and we'd have to scrap them. He understood how terrible waste was.

Andringa and her management team began to study the Lean practices of HON, Pella, and other companies. Once the decision was made to adopt Lean, Andringa brought in a veteran from the Lean transformation at HON as vice president of manufacturing. One of the key revelations was that Andringa, as CEO, would not only have to sponsor the transformation but actively lead it.

> *Mary Andringa:* Shortly after we made our decision to adopt Lean, I went to a manufacturing conference where I met Art Byrne. He told me, "If you're going to lead this, Mary, you need to be on one event a month in order to understand the strengths and weaknesses of your people and processes and your products."
>
> I took that very seriously, and got very involved, and pretty much demanded that of my direct reports. So that's how that started.

The Go and See Imperative

One of the difficulties for managers in the early stages of a Lean transformation is that much of the waste that Lean targets is not visible in the company's financials, and therefore the financial reports that managers are accustomed to working with aren't much help. Consequently, managers need to learn new skills to understand how processes become wasteful and what can be done about it, and the best learning environment is the shop floor where the value is created. Boot camp here consists of active participation in five-day *kaizens*.

"Go and see," accordingly, became a constant imperative at Vermeer, and participation in *kaizens* was a requirement not just for technical managers but for those in support functions as well. Andringa herself participated in dozens of *kaizens* throughout the Lean journey.

This new role drew managers out of their comfort zones and it took strong leadership to bring a new way of thinking into the company, but attitudes soon changed.

Mary Andringa: When I said to my leadership team that all of them should try to be on at least three events in those beginning years—six if they were involved in operations—I got some pushback, particularly from some of the sales folks, who said, "We travel too much."

Obviously you have to adapt your expectations to some of those things. But my CFO, for instance, continues to be on shop floor events once a year, and he requires his team to be on the shop floor as well. Seeing waste there actually helped them understand the whole financial picture. Being on and learning from the manufacturing floor helps you understand all sorts of processes better.

For example, understanding waste on the shop floor helped our financial people look at their area of responsibility differently. They challenged themselves to look closely at the steps it took to close the books at month end, which was at least a 10-day process. They started to ask questions: How much time were people spending on month end? And how often did they have to wait on information from others? And how often, because there wasn't a disciplined approach, did things get out of whack and cause more waiting?

Well, that team took it down to five days after an event. And then through continuous improvement in the next few years, they took it to three days.

The go and see imperative applies to Vermeer's board members as well.

Mary Andringa: I can be a bit of a pain about Lean sometimes. When we are invited as a board to go to a plant and see what has happened, I have a hard time fathoming it when some of my fellow board numbers don't think they need to go through a plant. We don't make it optional for our boards. They need to go through the plants and hear the stories.

Of course, there was lots of good news in the financial reports, but that took some time and some patience.

Mary Andringa: The hard thing for the CFO is how to justify the expenses, people, and energy going into Lean. You don't do it one event at a time—you have to look at it cumulatively. In our case, we had, after a year or two, turned quite a bit of inventory into cash, but all that hadn't flowed through yet to the bottom line. So it was absolutely critical that my CFO was on the same page.

One challenge was that in spite of the good work, team members weren't seeing any improvement in their piece of the profit sharing. I came up with the idea of giving everyone a free day, which we called an inventory day. It was a thank you for the fact that they were helping us on this Lean journey so that we didn't just have inventory stacking up. That made a huge impression on people, and it really brought inventory into the daily conversation.

Over the company's journey, the teams made dramatic improvements on the shop floor. Product lead times went from 52 days down to 2.5. Hours per unit dropped from 80 to roughly 24. All this led to a significant increase in capacity with existing resources. In 2012 there was 40 percent higher revenue than in 2000, with 10 percent less staff in spite of two economic downturns in that period.

An interesting feature of Vermeer's journey is the degree to which it brought a Lean culture into its sales organization. The results have been phenomenal: salespeople not only learned about the problems that order spikes can create in a production system but also discovered how Lean could be used to help dealers improve their own processes.

Mary Andringa: We've gotten some of our sales folks to really take hold. They go on events at dealerships and on customer job sites, taking this Lean journey far beyond Vermeer facilities. We had one great event where we had a couple of Vermeer team members go to a dealership that had multiple branches. They looked at their accounts payable, their accounts receivable, warranty, and a number of other processes, so it was a big team split up into subteams. They made huge progress in developing standard work so that all the different locations were doing things the same way. The point is, the process works.

And it's good for our team—they are connecting with their stakeholders and adding value to their organizations but also continuously learning about the process along the way.

Vermeer has also used Lean to help dealers generate the capacity to sell more products. By designing their products with common, standardized parts, they allow dealers to reduce their spare parts inventory and support a larger range of products. Also, a program of replenishing dealer stock as soon as a unit is sold means that dealers do not have to maintain inventory and can sell a wider range of products.

In addition to improving the supply chain, the work here has provided a common framework through which all stakeholders can work together toward common goals.

Mary Andringa: All of our industrial dealerships in North America have been involved with one or more *kaizens*. Many of them have someone on the team who has become their Lean guru. But the interesting thing is that we have learned how to work through issues using the same principles and the same language. We map out the process and get from the present state to where we want our future state to be. And it actually takes out some of the tension in what could otherwise be a conflict situation.

Sustaining the Gains and the Passion

One of the biggest challenges for a CEO is that production environments change, and there will always be new situations for people to adjust to.

> *Mary Andringa:* The problem is, as you grow, you bring in new people on the line or new managers or group leaders, and you start to see abnormalities. All those variables make it difficult. And when we make multiple products on a line, we add variation. It's hard, because nothing stays exactly the same. Spurts in your sales, which are great, can also add complexity and pressure, and then you sometimes start to lose ground on your Lean journey.
>
> So you can't put Lean on automatic pilot. Taiichi Ohno talks about this—he would say that after Toyota had been at it for 40 years, he thought they were just starting to get it. And that's the truth. We have been on the journey now for 16 or 17 years, and we keep learning that we're still not doing it as well as we want to do it.

Looking back, Andringa sees Lean as something that was absolutely necessary for Vermeer:

> If we hadn't gone on this journey, we would have retracted. This is really the only way to stay competitive. We have had price increases, but not nearly as many as we would have had if we weren't on this journey. And those price increases would have meant losing market share. Instead, we've actually gained market share.

In keeping with the tradition of sharing Lean expertise, Andringa continues to be a tireless Lean advocate. Her many roles include serving as chair of the National Association of Manufacturers, a member of President Obama's Export Council, and an active participant in Lean initiatives for the state of Iowa. Vermeer is also visited by people from every sector who are interested in cutting waste and improving their operations.

> *Mary Andringa:* At Vermeer, we love to have people come, get on the line, hear *kaizen* presentations, and then ask, "How does this apply to me?"
>
> In terms of different disciplines, we have had more medical professionals visit Vermeer than any other discipline to get on the line, see the process, and then ask, "How does this apply to medicine?" They come in thinking about their administrative role, their healthcare provider role, or their insurance role, but only when they're out there do they see it. We've had lots of other industries, like construction, visit, and it's amazing what they are able to learn about waste on their job sites. We have people from government come in as well, asking for help. Some of them get it, and some of them, not so much.

PUTTING A LEGEND ON A SUSTAINABLE PATH

Andringa's influence as a Lean advocate extends to her role as a board member of Herman Miller, Inc., a Zeeland, Michigan–based designer and manufacturer of furniture for offices, institutions, and homes. Founded in 1923, the company became associated with the work of legendary designers such as George Nelson and Charles and Ray Eames. Today the company is one of the largest furniture manufacturers in the world, employing over 6,000 in eight manufacturing facilities, with revenues approaching $2 billion.

Capacity in the commercial furniture sector in which Herman Miller operates is particularly challenging because shipments are made to order and are subject to considerable fluctuation. Companies therefore are under pressure to add more capacity than is economically viable for fear of delaying orders and losing market share.

When Mary Andringa joined Herman Miller's board in 1999, she began to bring Lean into the conversations about capacity, raising concerns very similar to the ones that had been voiced by Vermeer's board:

> On the Herman Miller board, there had been discussions early on about needing to find more floor space, factory space, bring in more capital expenditures. I would ask, "Are we sure we're going to need this? Lean will let us do that with the capital equipment we have and the people we have."

Herman Miller had already made significant progress with Lean through work that had begun in the late 1980s. As Matt Long, Herman Miller's vice president of continuous improvement, explained, the company already had a strong participatory culture that had been developed since the 1950s. Like Vermeer, Herman Miller studied nearby Lean companies and got significant help from one of its suppliers. In 1996, the company signed an agreement with the Toyota Supplier Support Center to work with it on its Lean transformation.

Matt Long: Before we signed with Toyota, we had gotten some help and guidance from one of our suppliers, Grand Haven Stamped Products, which invited us to participate in its *kaizen* teams for six months. This gave us the great learning experience of converting a cell from traditional manufacturing to TPS, and that's when the lightbulbs first went on for us. They also helped us connect with Toyota, which led to the agreement.

After about three years, we became a showcase company for Toyota. They saw us as a living, breathing example of TPS outside of Toyota—something that they were able to use to show other companies what the system looks like outside of automotive. So they started using our shop floor as part of their local Midwest training for TPS. Every quarter, they would hold a workshop in Grand Rapids or in Spring Lake and open it up to the public to teach about TPS. They would use our shop floor to tour them through to show what it looks like. That got started in the late 1999, and it's still going.

The company's early success with Lean, however, was limited primarily to its integrated metal technologies facility in Spring Lake, Michigan, and senior management did not take an active role in supporting it. The leader who was to change that was Brian Walker.

Walker had come to Herman Miller as the CFO and subsequently held the role of president and COO before becoming the CEO in 2004. He recalled his major epiphany about Lean and the role he would have to play:

> My big learning with Lean came when I was still COO. Our practice of Lean at the time was pretty much limited to one entity within the company, and our attempts to take Lean companywide were really getting nowhere. One day, about four longstanding employees whom I had grown up with in the company told me they wanted to meet me at a local pub. These guys were essentially the drivers behind the adoption of Lean.
>
> They sat me down and told me that if I really wanted Lean to happen, I would have to get actively involved. This meant going to meetings, being present on the shop floor, and making some decisions to show that I was really committed. I suppose this would apply in almost any situation in business—leaders can talk about change, but if they aren't willing to try it themselves, it never really gets done.

As it turned out, I was tested soon after that conversation. We were trying to make improvements at one of our plants in western Michigan, and I was participating in a *kaizen* event. The plant had adopted a lot of the ideas that IBM was promoting at the time around automation in manufacturing. They had put in a lot of robotics, automated carts moving things around, inventory systems.

By the end of the night, our *kaizen* team came to the conclusion that this inventory system was just a massive system for managing waste. Furthermore, it was taking up 10,000 square feet of badly needed space. We agreed that the best thing to do was to get rid of the waste and get rid of the system.

This was about 11 at night, and one of the guys who worked in the area handed me an acetylene torch. So I started cutting, and we spent the next couple of hours tearing this thing down. When we were done, the team decided that I would be the one to tell Mike, the owner of the system, what we had done.

So I walked into Mike's office the next day, and he asked how the *kaizen* event had gone. And I said, "You know your little inventory management system?"

He said, "Uh huh."

I said, "We cut it up and threw it in little pieces out in the parking lot."

He looked at me and said, "Are you sure it's right?"

And I said, "No, but the logic made sense, and we decided it was a monument that we had to get out of the way to show people we were serious about supporting their efforts and trying something different."

That was actually a kind of tipping point where people realized that we were really committed to Lean and to working with them to make major changes.

There were many more stakeholders to convince, and conversations with board members were particularly difficult. As it turned out, the most powerful argument was to let board members see freed-up capacity with their own eyes.

> *Brian Walker:* The hardest thing was describing the benefits to our board when we first started with Lean. We'd have conversations like this:
>
> "When are you going to be done?"
>
> "Never. We're never going to be done."
>
> "When are we going to capture benefits?"
>
> "We don't know."
>
> "Do you think Lean is really positive?"
>
> "Yes, we do. But it's hard to describe what it will look like after you've done it."
>
> Being able to show them rather then tell them was a lot more convincing. We had built a new facility and filled it with equipment, but through Lean improvements, we were able to move everything to other facilities.
>
> So we took the board there and said, "This is the advantage of Lean." And they said, "An empty building?" And we explained that we had used Lean to empty the space ourselves and now had the capacity to grow without capital expenditure. I would say that was the best picture we ever gave them.

According to Walker, circumstances forced the issue, and the company moved aggressively to bring Lean to the enterprise:

> In the downturn of 2000–2001, our business dropped 40 percent, and there was literally a question of how we were going to survive. We had been progressing on our Lean journey, but we were kind of doing it at a nominal inch-by-inch pace, and all of a sudden we were faced with this crisis. We

saw we were going to have to make some big moves out of necessity—big jumps in terms of reducing square footage, putting things closer together. Those were the things that really leaped us forward in our Lean journey.

Those are the times when you have to ask, "Am I making these moves that are going to be okay just for today, or am I really making moves that will have lasting benefit?" Sometimes when you're in the middle of a crisis, you can often get folks to reset things in ways you never could with a normal method where the pain is too great.

We did this work over a three-year period, and we made almost transformational moves that still pay great dividends today.

One of the most dramatic changes was triggered by an unexpected event. During that difficult time, Walker and his executive team were visiting customers to help support the sales effort. When Walker was explaining how the company had reduced lead times, a customer shot back, "If you're doing such great work, how come it takes six weeks to get my Aeron chair?" Although the chairs were manufactured in minutes, it turned out that there were significant delays in procuring components and in distribution. Walker immediately challenged the Lean team to broaden their scope to the entire "order to cash" value stream. This was, according to Long, a strategic leap that brought the Lean journey to a new level and continues to drive progress today.

Over the several years following the downturn, the company was able to grow revenues by 50 percent while keeping head count constant. Lead times overall have been reduced from eight weeks to four weeks, and floor space requirements have been cut nearly in half in many parts of the operation.

Ironically, the freed-up capacity allowed the company to move out of the Spring Lake facility that had hosted the company's first Lean successes.

Looking in the Mirror

Leading a mature Lean company is difficult given that the environment is fragile, results are often difficult to perceive, and the journey has no end point.

> *Brian Walker:* We haven't had a problem sustaining the things that are easily measurable—where we can apply metrics. It gets tougher when you have slow, gradual change that isn't as tangible.
>
> The question is, how do you make sure that the whole deployment from the leadership all the way down to the people on the shop floor has this kind of constant reinvention? If I'm reinventing all the time and never assuming it's done, it's like I don't have to worry about maintaining, because I'm not really maintaining anything. I'm actually always trying to make it better. So if you can stay in the focus of "I'm always trying to make it better," maintenance isn't a problem.

Even in a mature Lean environment such as Herman Miller, what worked yesterday will not necessarily work tomorrow. This, says Walker, is his biggest challenge:

> In terms of leading a Lean company, I think the hardest thing for a leader is to be willing to observe your own team, particularly things that you helped create, and be critical of that. That is a really hard skill to learn—I think it's the one thing we don't spend any time really learning in school. Nobody really sits down and considers how you take a problem that you've largely created yourself and get real enough with yourself to realize that what you created was wrong. That's a really hard skill to have.
>
> It takes time as well. In your first two or three years as CEO, you're mostly looking at problems that somebody else

created. Then all of a sudden, after 10 years, there is not a problem that is not your problem. You created every one of them, maybe unwittingly, but you created them all.

That's probably where leading Lean gets really tough for folks, because you may have developed a methodology for doing business that was fantastic for a period of time, and now it needs its own reinvention.

One of the issues Walker confronted was maintaining balance between improving and maintaining standard work and making sure that workers remained emotionally connected with the product.

Brian Walker: I think it's hard to love a process. But if I know that the process creates something at the end that I can fall in love with and that I hope others will fall in love with, it completely changes the emotion behind the work.

So one of the things we've really had to work hard at in the last 12 months in our new operation is reteaching our folks on the shop floor that what they're actually making is furniture. It's going into people's homes, and it's going into their offices, and you have to make something palatable and something that people are going to keep in their eye for 20 or 30 years.

So it's interesting. I think you go through these phases where you constantly have to ask, "Well, we got really good at that aspect, but we've probably caused something else to be not where we want it to be. So how do we bring the dial back up on that?"

It's like changing your lifestyle to lose weight but finding that because you're not going to restaurants, you don't see any of your friends. So that's a different outcome: What do I do about that? How do I rebalance around that?

This is not just a question of being able to identify issues and make improvements. Sometimes the challenge is seeing what went right and getting that message out.

Brian Walker: When you look at the day-to-day issues, Lean is like dropping water on a pebble. You don't notice the pebble changing, but if you come back 10 years later, the pebble has changed to something completely different. That's sort of how Lean works.

We have an operation down in Georgia that produces a very high-end product line. Their margins have historically bounced all over the place. When they were really busy, they had good margins, but when they weren't busy, their margins were really bad. So they went in and out of profitability constantly.

However, that team has really jumped on Lean in the past year, and all of a sudden, while their margins haven't wildly jumped up, they're consistently at the high level now.

Now, to be frank, if you asked me what was the one thing they did, I'd say it wasn't one but a series of things over four years. You can kind of see it, but then you realize, "Wait a minute; these guys are turning their inventory faster," or "Look, their quality has gotten better." It's one thing at a time.

If you watched Lean in time-lapse photography—looking at each step along the way—you might go, "Yeah, okay, that's kind of cool," but it wouldn't seem like a big deal. But if you saw the whole picture from beginning to end, you'd say, "Wow, this is amazing."

That's really what you have to do with Lean—give people that picture. We have some plants, like our chair plant, where it's super-easy to see, because things are moving extremely fast, and you can really see the dance of Lean authority. People walk in, and they instantly go, "Holy mackerel! You literally can make these chairs in 17 seconds! And you turn the inventory every day!"

Perhaps the toughest part of Walker's job is dealing with the dual reality of never being finished and always questioning, but at the same time providing a persuasive vision of the future.

Brian Walker: One of the toughest things is balancing where you want to be five years from now and having enough investment going there versus getting some semblance of short-term results so you have the credibility to continue to invest for the future. That's the constant balancing act where everybody would prefer to be one or the other. But I don't know that you ever get that luxury.

What my job boils down to is being the great allocator of resources. You're never going to make everybody happy when you're in that role. When somebody brings me an idea, it might be a great idea, and I can say it is really great, but there may be five others that I think are more important and are greater right now.

So you have that constant need to try to get people to think about new ideas but also realize you will have to say to some folks, "We're not going to work on that right now." So prioritization and thinking through that is a tough one.

I would say the other journey that I've personally been on is how you paint a big enough picture that people are emotionally engaged with what they're doing versus doing it because they have to or because the company is trying to meet some particular objective.

The company's financial position has made the boardroom conversations a lot easier.

Brian Walker: We have a very light asset business compared to most people. We generate lots and lots of cash, we turn our assets over very quickly, and I think that speaks for itself when people compare it with other companies in our space or in manufacturing generally.

So it's actually relatively easy today to tell the story about why we're doing what we're doing. To be frank, the word on the street is that if you hear somebody else in our industry talk about starting their Lean journey, we've become one of the benchmarks for that.

Teaching others is an important aspect of Herman Miller's ongoing Lean journey.

Brian Walker: We do help other companies, and a lot of them come in to visit our plants. Toyota didn't charge us, with the understanding that we would help other people in the same way.

Our customers come in to learn about what we do, and we've taught lots of people on their Lean journey. For obvious reasons we don't help people in our own industry, so when we help other companies, our people learn about other industries, and this often triggers thought for us about something we could do differently.

According to Long, however, some of the biggest learnings from the visits are what the workers learn about their own processes:

Matt Long: I often apologize to our people for the time these visits take from their normal jobs. The answer I get back from them so often is, "Don't apologize. By me having to explain it to other people, I really have to think about my own system. And there's a level of accountability that I have to have that I might not have otherwise. So it helps me to stay on the journey."

CHAPTER 6

❖

A REALISTIC APPROACH
TO WORKER MOTIVATION

One of the most common marching orders for new leaders is to address a situation that is being presented as a workforce motivation problem. Often a new hire walks into an us-versus-them environment in which managers and employees are pitted against one another in a zero-sum game. The symptoms may include poor morale, low productivity, quality issues, lack of teamwork, or even outright hostility toward the company's management.

Conventional wisdom in the early 1900s was that the manager-worker relationship was inherently adversarial and that the key weapons for ensuring a productive workforce were pay and threats. Frederick Taylor, whose views were widely followed, believed that by linking pay to output one would not only ensure compliance but motivate workers to put out their best effort.

Psychological research since that time has shown that human motivation is far more complex than that. In his famous 1968 *Harvard Business Review* article titled "One More Time: How Do You Motivate Employees?" the psychologist Frederick

Herzberg cited numerous studies in outlining a much more comprehensive view:

> The findings of these studies, along with corroboration from many other investigations using different procedures, suggest that the factors involved in producing job satisfaction (and motivation) are separate and distinct from the factors that lead to job dissatisfaction. Since separate factors need to be considered, depending on whether job satisfaction or job dissatisfaction is being examined, it follows that these two feelings are not opposites of each other.[1]

In his two-factor theory Herzberg separated motivating factors from demotivating factors, which he called hygiene. True motivation, he argued, comes from conditions that cause an employee to feel challenged, trusted, recognized, valued, and able to learn and grow. Conversely, workplace aspects such as company policies, supervision, relationships with the boss, and basic work conditions are table stakes: they can demotivate if they are not satisfactory but do not create a genuine desire to do the work. Interestingly, Herzberg also included pay in this category.

The key here is that the motivators Herzberg cited are intrinsic to the work itself. Conversely, common HR motivators such as perks, shorter work hours, human relations training, and employee counseling are extrinsic and consequently do not create true motivation.

By these definitions, Lean creates the ideal environment for motivating workers. Recognition, variety, autonomy, and the opportunity to learn are all intrinsic to the employee's role in a culture of continuous improvement. Furthermore, these aspects are not the result of an artificial intervention cooked up by an HR department or consultant but are based on the real needs of the customer.

There are, however, two important caveats. Lean is hard work, and for the magic of motivation to kick in, there has to be the authenticity that can be achieved only when senior management truly believes and is directly involved. Also, motivation is not a cure-all for every production problem; management must be committed to listening to workers and providing the tools they need to do their jobs.

A BUS COMPANY TURNS AROUND

When Jorge Pinto took on the role of CEO at Caetano Bus in 2005, he knew that he would personally have to play a major role in instilling a new way of thinking in the company.

Caetano Bus, founded in 1946, is the largest bus body manufacturer in Portugal. Situated near the city of Porto, the company fabricates a varied line of municipal and tour buses, including the well-known Cobus brand of airport buses. The majority of Caetano's products are exported, frequently through joint ventures with other automotive providers.

In the early 2000s, the company began to experience production problems: poor quality, rising costs, and erratic delivery performance. Much of this was attributed to a poorly motivated workforce. When a major customer started complaining, the situation became urgent.

Jorge Pinto: We manufacture the Tourino line of buses for Mercedes, and we were under fire from our friends in Germany because of our high production costs, which were related to manpower. It was taking 1,200 production hours to make a bus, and I needed to reduce this to 800 to make this profitable. There were also some quality issues.

The workplace culture problem at Caetano had a long history.

Jorge Pinto: Changing the behavior of our people, if you will, was one of our biggest challenges. We have very low turnover, and our average age is quite high, so we have a lot of people who have been here for 15 or 20 years. So a lot of people would say, "Why do we have to change what we have always done?"

Pinto, who like many Europeans refers to Lean as *kaizen*, learned the approach at Bosch, whose production system is modeled after Toyota's.

Jorge Pinto: I think most of the automotive world now is somehow *kaizen*-oriented and that this is the normal management way. However, it is clear that this really has to come from the top. Our projects at Bosch were always successful because top management was saying, "We want this to happen."

The approach taken was to teach workers about Lean tools and then enlist their help in solving the productivity problems the company was facing. The efforts began as a pilot project focused on the troubled Tourino line. As a first step, the Kaizen Institute was engaged to provide basic training on shop floor methods such as 5S, visual management, standard work, and supermarkets. Then teams were formed to take on the quality and delivery problems.

Jorge Pinto: We put together some *kaizen* teams, which we called agents of change, to lead the improvements. There were some difficulties at first, and we had to change some team leaders, but when we finished the project, we started to see results.

A big part of this was that we changed how workers thought about productivity. Normally, productivity was understood as "I have to work more; I have to make more of an effort." I told them that productivity is nothing like that, and I used the example of Formula One cars to explain. If we don't have the right tools to change a tire, it takes a lot of effort and we get covered with grease. In Formula One, they can do a tire in seven seconds with absolutely no effort. So for our workers, productivity was not about more effort and being more tired at the end of the day. It was about working together to create the conditions to be more productive.

The improvements involved relocating one of the assembly lines to the opposite end of the facility to allow for wider aisles, which in turn made it easier to supply the workstations with larger preassembled components such as roofs, pipes, and dashboards. A cart system allowed a comprehensive range of components to be delivered on an as-needed basis to the assembly stations, freeing workers on the line from the tasks of unpacking, sorting, and transporting.

To increase flow, some categories of work were removed, and workers took on a wider range of functions to minimize transport of the workpiece.

Jorge Pinto: The work we did involved reconfiguring work flow patterns in order to balance the workload, providing better tools, and even making some design changes that helped make assembly more efficient. This meant that some workers had to take on multiple functions, and that, again, took a lot of persuading.

Labor laws in Portugal made this aspect of the change particularly challenging.

Jorge Pinto: In Portugal, if you are classified as a welder, you have a job description that specifies the scope of your activity. So if you want a person who is classified as a mechanic to do welding, that person can refuse legally. So a lot of this had to be negotiated on an individual basis, and we had to fight with some, let's say, very hard-minded people.

However, as the Tourino line became more orderly and efficient, workers found that their environment had improved and that they felt much more connected to the work. Soon other team leaders were asking about *kaizen*.

> *Jorge Pinto:* When the project was finished, I had some team leaders of the other assembly lines come to me and say, "We want the same solution that we have in the Tourino line, because now they have better conditions, it's cleaner, and people have a much better understanding of the work flow." This was a very interesting effect and I would say our biggest indicator of success.

Shifting the Transformation into High Gear

The effort was then expanded to the Cobus line beginning in 2007, and in addition to replicating the success of the Tourino line, the company added several innovations. By preassembling large portions of the body rather than building them up on a chassis, the teams were able to reduce assembly steps and decrease the amount of floor space needed. The approach also resulted in a better fit between components and consequently better quality and less rework.

The results were also improved by closer collaboration with suppliers, such as instructing them to refill empty containers on demand.

Overall productivity gains on the Cobus line were significant: production increased from 400 to 700 vehicles per year without adding personnel.

After the downturn of 2008 and 2009, the plant had plenty of spare capacity and a solid reputation in the Caetano group. When the group management team began discussing where to locate the new aeronautics plant, Pinto convinced them that Caetano Bus was up to the challenge:

> What I fought very hard for was to locate the aeronautics plant in our existing facilities here in Porto, because I felt this would help us compensate for the loss of volume we faced after the downturn of 2008. We have three buildings here, and what we did was free up 8,000 square meters so that we could dedicate one of the buildings to the aeronautics business. This meant changing our system for supplying parts to all the bus lines and cleaning out everything that was not absolutely necessary in the other two buildings so that we could compress the existing lines.
>
> This was a huge reduction of space, and we completely remade our production supply chain. We made the big physical moves as we were approaching the summer shutdown and then continued for several more months to fine-tune the solutions.

Although the productivity numbers are impressive, the big change was in the workforce. A factory that less than a decade earlier had been stagnant because of a retrograde culture was serving as an example for the rest of the group. Pinto had a déjà vu moment recently when he visited a plant that resembled Caetano Bus of not too many years ago:

> I won't mention any names, but I was visiting a supplier that makes a very complex product with around 1,000 parts. As we walked through the plant, we saw that there were metal containers full of parts everywhere in production. This was more a warehouse than a factory, and I looked at some papers that were there, and I saw that some of these parts were three or four months old.

I was with one of my managers, and I remember telling him, "We should bring some of our people to see this plant, and they will see why *kaizen* is so important." What's amazing is that this was the president showing us the plant, and he was so proud of it and convinced that he was doing the right thing.

Leading this kind of change, Pinto said, has been an experience that has affected him as well:

It's changed me a lot, because it's something that you internalize yourself. I'll give you a very small example. I'm a person who sometimes forgets where I put my keys. *Kaizen* taught me that if I always have to think of places to put my keys at home, and in my car, and in my office, I will never forget them. I guess that's what we call mistake proofing.

I've also become very conscious of waste. When I'm in an airplane and watching them serve our meals, I find myself looking at the work flow and asking, "Why couldn't they do that with one person instead of two?" People aren't used to thinking this way.

Kaizen has also changed not so much my management style but my perception of the importance of people. When I was a young manager, I used to say that people were the most important asset I had, but I never felt that very deeply. But as CEO here at Caetano facing all these projects and challenges, when I say people are my best asset, I really feel it deeply. That means that if I don't have the right people in the right places, I cannot go too far.

In 2011, Pinto saw his responsibilities expand to include Germany and China, and he hired a chief operating officer (COO) to take over the day-to-day *kaizen* activity in the Porto plant. When the group decided to build a plant in China, the team from Portugal was actively involved in the design, and one of them went to China to help set up production.

Like other Lean CEOs, Pinto acknowledges that many challenges remain, and that the journey is never complete:

> I think *kaizen* helps everybody improve and makes us more competitive, but applying *kaizen* in indirect work situations can be very difficult. In engineering, for example, you also have to deal with new tools, new information, new methods of analysis, and the speed of technology. So the challenge there is, How can *kaizen* and continuous improvement cope with such a fast-changing world? How can I make my project people much more productive than they are today? What am I to do? There is never enough *kaizen*.

BALANCING CREATIVITY WITH DISCIPLINE

Changing an organization's work culture can involve taking aim at some aspects while carefully preserving others. This was the situation when Pierluigi Tosato, a leader with considerable Lean experience, was hired as the new CEO of Acqua Minerale San Benedetto, a global bottler of water and nonalcoholic drinks.

Situated near Venice, Italy, the company runs one of the largest bottling operations in Europe. Brands include San Benedetto, Primavera, Batik and Tropico fruit drinks, and Energade sports drinks. The company also has partnerships with major brands such as Schweppes and Pepsi-Cola.

San Benedetto promotes a value proposition that reflects health and environmental awareness and is constantly innovating to make lighter bottles that use less plastic. The company's innovative edge is supported by a strong creative culture in which employees fervently believe in the product.

At the same time, there was a lack of focus on company objectives, and spending had gotten out of line.

Pierluigi Tosato: I came to San Benedetto as a *kaizen* guy. I've been working as a CEO for 20 years, and for half of that time I've been using *kaizen*. The reason I introduced it to San Benedetto was that the company needed to have not so much a turnaround but a reshape. There was a lot of inefficiency, and the company had lost focus toward its goals and its objectives.

Although Tosato uses many tools from the Toyota Production System, he dislikes the term *Lean* because he feels that it implies a top-down approach. *Kaizen*, in contrast, implies the bottom-up approach that defines Lean culture:

If you adopt a bottom-up approach and you listen to people, they will give you the solutions for the issues, and the end results are more sustainable. This also keeps people motivated, and you can keep improving much more than with Lean.

What Tosato wanted to preserve was the participation in the innovation processes that had given the company its leading edge.

Pierluigi Tosato: San Benedetto is special in that we are the only beverage company in the world that has its own engineering company. We design the bottle lines, we design the products, and we design the packaging. We have the lightest bottles in the world. We are a technical company, and everybody wants to have a say in the innovation process. Even though the company had problems when I took over, that participation was very strong.

So I wanted to have a more efficient company but not lose all this participation, know-how, and culture of innovation. *Kaizen* may not be ideal in general terms for every company, but it is ideal for San Benedetto, because it forces the people to have a say and to participate in the process of improvement.

Part of the efficiency problem was a lack of discipline in spending. Consequently, Tosato felt that before improving the culture, he would have to change the rules.

Pierluigi Tosato: For the first 18 months, we began with some cost cutting, which was unpopular. We did not dismiss any personnel, but we took away a lot of privileges that were not sustainable for the market situation. Of course, if you take away privileges, people who are used to them are not happy.

So we saved a lot of money in a very short amount of time, but I felt that because these efficiencies were done top-down, they were not sustainable. Also, we had lot of quality issues in our products, and a lot of them were the side effects of this cost cutting. There was a lot of demotivation, and also the general environment in the company was not the best.

I still believe that when you're hired to turn things around, as I was, you need to do cost cutting; you have to do it in the first 12 months and then forget about it. Because then you have to move toward development, new products, new market, and so on. At the beginning, if you find a situation where costs are not under control, you have to do it in a very short time without thinking about it.

But of course you might have side effects that are not positive. So we quickly moved on to phase 2, which was *kaizen.*

The *kaizen* efforts began with the most urgent area: a bottling line that was serving a major North American brand.

Pierluigi Tosato: Our approach was to start with a pilot as opposed to trying to bring *kaizen* to the entire company at once. I should mention first that we were bottling for big multinational American companies, and we had some very serious quality issues. So we started the first pilot project with *kaizen* to address the quality of one line.

We started working with Carlo [Ratto at the Kaizen Institute Italy] to teach the *kaizen* principles, first of all to the top management, then to the middle management. Then we did some value stream mapping to identify what was going wrong and what solution we could identify to solve the quality issues.

The quick win was that we fixed all the quality issues for these big American companies. But for me it was just a quick win and just the beginning, because I was already succeeding in changing the culture of the company. The culture in the past was "Let's produce millions, billions of bottles, no matter what. We don't care what's coming out of the company; what's important is to produce the number of bottles that the market is demanding."

We started changing the culture, and the people started to look at the quality of the bottles and also the efficiency of the processes and the scraps. They also began to think in a *kaizen* way that the cost that matters is not the cost of one department but the total cost of the company. It doesn't make sense to be efficient in the plastic department making empty bottles, which are scrap, and then lose a lot of efficiency in the filling lines.

People had been working in silos. With *kaizen* we started looking at the full process, and we started working as a team. We were moving from a functional organization to a process organization, because this business is about processes.

Making these changes throughout our organization, of course, is a huge task. Our biggest plant has 27 bottling lines and is one of the biggest factories in Europe. Getting over 1,000 people to work as a team is not easy, and we are still in that phase.

One of the big milestones has been to stop treating quality as a separate function and make it integral to production.

> *Pierluigi Tosato:* We now use common KPIs [key performance indicators], not single KPIs. These are the KPIs of the company. For example, we used to have a separate group responsible for controlling the quality of the products, while the products were made by production workers. Today, basically, I don't have the quality control people—the production workers are looking after quality and controlling what they are doing, the way they do at Toyota. This was a big step.

The next big step will be to move the new way of thinking beyond the walls of San Benedetto and into the supply chain.

> *Pierluigi Tosato:* Our next phase will be to involve the suppliers. Of course, we also have constant dialogue with our customers about *kaizen*, and that has worked really well. Sometimes we bring them to the *kaizen* steering committees, because we want to be also very transparent with the customers. I think this has been a great success.

Everything Can Be Improved

One of the keys to success at San Benedetto has been financial performance. Although the organization has done well on that front, Tosato is clear that this approach requires a long-term view:

> If you do *kaizen* well, your indicators all look good—quality is improving, you have less scrap, you have customers satisfaction, and you improve the efficiency. However, this may take some time at the beginning. If you were a typical American company looking on a quarter-by-quarter basis, then you

might not get what you were looking for. What *kaizen* will give you is sustainable results for the next five years.

Perhaps the moment of truth for the cultural change came when the chairman of the board visited the plant. He had no previous knowledge of Lean or *kaizen*, and as the event unfolded, it turned out that no introduction was necessary.

Pierluigi Tosato: I invited the chairman of the board to visit. He was nearly 70 years old and had never heard about *kaizen*. I also invited a few production workers to speak up in front of him. At the beginning they were very shy, as you can imagine, but he was very pleased to see these people talking about quality and improvement. He felt the passion of the people, and I didn't have to communicate anything—he understood. He felt the motivation and the passion of the people talking to him.

Kaizen, however, is not an aspect of management. It is comprehensive and becomes a way of life.

Pierluigi Tosato: Kaizen is something you use everywhere, not just where you're producing things. You can *kaizen* the work of the people in the offices and the R&D. You can *kaizen* even your CEO job, your private life, and the way you train. For me it's not a method; it's a philosophy. Either you have this philosophy or you don't.

At the end of the story, we rely on people. *Kaizen* changed the culture of this company, changed the mindset of the people, and makes everybody work better in the company.

CHAPTER 7

❖

BUILDING COLLABORATIVE
MANAGEMENT TEAMS

Despite its crucial importance, its high visibility, and its spectacular
rise, management is the least known and the least understood of our
basic institutions. Even the people in a business often do not know
what their management does and what it is supposed to be doing,
how it acts and why, whether it does a good job or not.

—Peter F. Drucker

In traditionally run businesses, managers often are expected to
generate tangible results by means that are anything but tangible.
The skills that are deemed essential—decision making, negotiation,
problem solving, motivation of others—are loosely defined, yet
a manager who fails to make the numbers is quickly judged as a
failure.

Leaving a person to sink or swim violates what may be the most
important pillar of Lean: respect for people. In mature Lean organizations, it is a given that managers are workers like their peers on

the shop floor and need clear guidelines for their activities and the right tools and processes to be successful. Furthermore, managers in Lean organizations count on their superiors to help them improve and remove any barriers that stand in their way.

This calls for a paradigm shift in the way an organization is run. First of all, it requires a significant culture change, particularly with managers who built their careers by practicing top-down autocratic management.

It also requires the removal of systemic barriers that prevent employees at all levels from succeeding. Standard cost accounting and silos, for example, prevent cross-functional teamwork and often incentivize behavior that is contrary to the interests of creating customer value. Firefighting duties and wasteful activities such as paperwork can prevent managers from spending time with and supporting their people. Lack of knowledge can be the biggest barrier of all.

These deficiencies are far less obvious than, say, the lack of a screwdriver on an assembly line, yet they are equally debilitating. Consequently, creating an environment where managers can succeed in a predictable way is one of the most challenging tasks for a Lean CEO. This challenge often persists even in organizations that have had considerable success in improving their shop floor processes.

"I WAS HEARING THE SAME STORY . . ."

In Chapter 4, we saw how Lantech turned its business around by cutting waste and creating flow in its plants and regained a leadership position its sector.

However, Jim Lancaster, who had assumed the CEO responsibilities in 1995, began to have concerns that Lantech's Lean journey was losing momentum:

We were running *kaizen* workshops a couple of times a month—lots of resources, lots of people, using the same folks who helped us with the conversion. I started noticing that at the report-outs, I was hearing the same story I had seen three years before.

The reality was, you could walk into an area and you might see some small things that came out of the workshop, but the whole thing wasn't having any impact. We'd taken *kaizens* throughout the company, including the office, accounting, purchasing, customer service, but you could see this problem everywhere.

Initially, Lancaster thought that the Lean transformation had reached a point of diminishing returns and that it was time to broaden the scope of the business in order to grow. He embarked on a strategy to become a leader in secondary packaging—packaging that companies use within their facilities—and expand into other technologies beyond stretch wrapping.

Jim Lancaster: I decided that the strategy should be to maintain the Lean culture that we had and to grow the company by finding adjacent markets. I thought that it would be great if I found an adjacent sort of product that happened to be overseas and I could use their distribution channel to take my stuff from here so that we could grow.

So we, top management, pursued that for a couple of years, and we made a couple of acquisitions, and as you would guess, we focused on them, and the core business started to deteriorate a little bit. And what I mean by that is profit margins deteriorated a little bit and our rate of innovation slowed down. We were still the leader and we weren't in financial trouble or anything, but we just weren't rocking the way we were before.

Lancaster, getting more concerned, began to consult with his colleagues in the Young Presidents' Association, an executive association in which he is active. A suggestion that seemed logical was that he was too nice and wasn't holding his people accountable for results. Lancaster turned to some outside talent for help:

> I hired a couple of veteran managers who were very good at that sort of accountability culture that you see in larger companies—a "let's set the number for the month, and then let's talk about it, and if you don't hit it, then there had better be a darned good reason why" sort of an approach. So they came and started to do that, and business got worse.

Lancaster realized that this was a much larger problem than he had anticipated and that he would have to get much closer to the operation if he was to solve it. After some reflection, he decided to go back to basics. This time he brought in Bob Morgan, a Lean veteran from Delphi who had been trained by the Lean senseis at Toyota; Morgan agreed with the stipulation that his advice would be followed.

> *Jim Lancaster:* He basically took me all the way to the beginning by running me through standardized work workshops on the shop floor. And I spent, believe it or not, a year on the shop floor with my steel-toe shoes virtually every day. I handed the daily operations over to an ops manager and did this for virtually a year, basically relearning the business from the ground up.

What Lancaster learned in his year on the shop floor was how to see the work; essentially, it got him much closer to the operation than he had ever been and in a much better position to create a management environment that would reinforce the fragile Lean gains the company had achieved. As Lancaster explained, this was different from the earlier journey:

> When we had originally started our Lean transformation, we were a medium-size business that was winning because

of our innovation. In terms of our processes, we were probably particularly ugly. So we got a particularly large lift from Lean initially. We went from really bad to pretty good but not great, would be my summary of it.

This time around, it was all about really understanding how to see work. What does work look like? How do you design the work? And then after a period of time, how do you manage to maintain the work so that what you put in place sticks?

So since about 2007, what we've really been focused on from a Lean perspective is how to maintain and improve work. This is different from the initial conversion. We had flow going, we had production lines, we were no longer batching, everything was being made to order already.

But we've gotten at least as big a lift out of this second level as we did from the first lift. And I've got all kinds of different stats on things like quality improvement, quality levels, all kinds of stuff. And basically it's the management system that's made the difference.

So the management system is where I spend my time. I have a very standardized, specific way that we manage. And we've got it in place in our plant in Europe and here, and it is incredibly powerful. This is very unlike 2001 and 2002, when I was doing my traditional CEO stuff of looking out in front, figuring out what is going on, looking for a direction to go in, and then turning the wheel so that the organization would go in that direction.

I was good at all that, but the problem was that when I turned the wheel, it wasn't attached to the tires of the car. So it took a long time to get any movement. So I depended on my gregarious capability to go through three or four layers of management to get a turn made.

That's not the case anymore. I can literally turn this organization in a day. We're far more agile and far more connected to what's actually going on all over the organization. My guess is that I'm far more tactical in running the organization than I ever was 5 or 10 years ago. And I think I'm far more tactical than most CEOs are. But I think that allows me to be more strategic, because I know what we can actually do.

Teaching Managers to See

The key to Lantech's success with having the steering wheel attached to the wheels, as Lancaster put it, is that managers are in tune with what's happening in the workplace. However, as people quickly find out in Lean situations, seeing on the shop floor is not that easy.

> *Jim Lancaster:* When you start to get really involved with what's going on on the shop floor, you begin to see how hard the job is that we're giving these people. You see the problems very directly. But when you're on the third or fourth floor, and you're in a meeting room, and somebody's telling you about it, it looks very different. They look far more trapped in labor practices and politics and culture and strategy and some big system, which makes them seem much more complicated.
>
> When you're down on the floor, you say dang, the guy needs a screwdriver that's not broken, and it would be nice if he had the material, and it's pretty stupid if the stuff shows up scratched or broken.
>
> The problem is the people who won't engage with the detail level enough to understand it. They'd rather try to follow some high theory of everything that you read about in *Harvard Business Review.*

What managers need is real experience, not knowledge of techniques.

Jim Lancaster: My experience is that very few of these principles work as a direct teaching. I can tell you how pull works, or I can explain to you how standardized work works. But people have to have experiences. I had a call this morning with my GM in Europe, and he ran a workshop last week with some very important new managers we have over there, and we spent the whole hour talking about each student, where they were, and what they could articulate versus what they believed, what experiments we were going to set up for them so we could find out where they are, and what kinds of workshop assignments would help them move forward.

I got to this point only after I understood the power of getting a manager to understand these principles. The power they then have is so huge that you're then willing to invest big in getting them there. But you can't get there by sending them to a class. They've got to actually do things, and they actually have to work, and they have to get reinforcement for it and then start to have fun with it. People have to be able to say, "Dang, I did this."

Simply being taught a technique and then using it, Lancaster said, is not enough to create that experience. For it to really sink in, the manager has to use it to solve a problem and succeed. What Lancaster tries to do, therefore, is set up situations in which the technique will help them out of a jam:

I'll set the problem up and stay enough in the background to make sure that the save actually happens. And then he gets that experience, and he'll know it when he has the next project.

Unless people have seen something work, it's just an academic exercise. It's fun to talk about and you sound smart and all that, but that won't stick in a culture.

Accountability Without the Shame and Blame

The glue that holds all this together is the management system itself. The system isn't that complex; it's applying it that takes time.

Jim Lancaster: We literally got the management system going in about 10 days some five years ago. And then we built on it—we bolted stuff onto it.

But learning how to drive the management system and support it has been difficult. What do you do when an area performed less well today than the prior day and so they have reds on their measurements? You want people to see the urgency of solving whatever problems are cropping up, but you don't want to shame them. The subtleties of how you deal with that are what we've learned, and we on the management team coach each other on that. It takes six months to a year for the trust to build up to the point where people will share their problems with their manager.

The thing is, if you don't get the problems visible, then you can't fix them. And with most companies I see, the object is to hide all the problems. That's what's so beautiful—once you have all the problems visible, the whole strategizing thing gets easy. All we've got to do to beat everybody else is not screw up as much. And we've got plenty of screwups to work on, so it's not that hard.

We also try to have a sense of humor about this. If somebody goes for three or four weeks and has virtually no problems—no reds—I say, "It's time for a cookie," and I actually bring in one of those oversized chocolate chip cookies and present it to him. So I'll say, "Congratulations, this is great, now it's time to reaverage all those numbers for the last 90 days and redraw the line."

If it's a quality measure, we'll say. "Okay, you've been running at 0.7 defects for 90 days, and there's been only one day where you've gone over the top, so let's reaverage down to 0.5." And guess what. I'll get reds again. Which is great, because then I've got something to work on.

The challenge is, if you're dealing with problems all the time, to keep people feeling good about what they're doing. Because otherwise it feels like you're screwing up every day.

Another aspect of this is what happens when people make mistakes. Lancaster never blames the worker:

You have to believe in the system and why we have it. When I investigate when somebody made a mistake, there's almost always a reason. Generally people don't make a mistake because they're just plain lazy or they felt like making a mistake or whatever. I think that 99 percent of people want to go home feeling like they made a contribution that day and did a good job. And I don't care whether you're stuffing envelopes, answering the phone, building a machine, you're a salesman, whatever.

So 99 percent of the time, the reason that mistake was made is that the process is difficult, they didn't have a material that worked, they were either not trained or the training was out of date, or the process didn't facilitate the work well enough so that they could do it reliably.

Just an example. We get bad picks. Material handlers are picking parts for a machine, and the material has to show up on the production line in sequence, like an automobile line. So we get these bad picks. And it's easy just to say, Well, the material handler is not reading the bill of material; they're just trying to pick from memory, and that's the problem.

If you go down that road, you can't solve any problems. You go talk to the material handler, tell him he needs to read the bill of materials, and then when he gets promoted, you just start over again.

So we go watch him pick the part that was picked wrong, and 75 to 80 percent of the time you're going to find that there's a part that looks exactly like it sitting on the shelf right next to it, or a part number where if he just transposed the last two digits it looks exactly the same, or something of that nature. Or we don't have enough space on the shelf, so somebody stacked a little extra inventory in there and it scooted over into the other side.

Our employees are generally being our heroes every day in realizing something and saving us. Sometimes they don't realize it and don't save us, and then that's when the mistake happens.

The same thing applies to managers, but the context is different. For managers, the key material is information.

Jim Lancaster: When a manager makes a mistake, a decision mistake, it's because he didn't have the criteria to make a decision. I'll never forget, we were doing these management workarounds some years ago, and Bob Morgan was here with me. We were at the inside engineering stop, and we had lead times posted, and they had gotten really short—we were down to a little over a week.

And I said, "Guys, what are you going to do when you run out of work?" And they looked at me with this blank stare. And then they said, "Well, we'll figure out some improvement projects here."

So I said, "Great, once you run out of work, you're going to figure out what the improvement projects are, then you've got to scope it, then you've got to get it approved. So your guys are going to be sitting around for days while you get all that stuff figured out? How about if we get the job jar all ready so that when they run out of work, they'll have a bunch of things to do?"

And they said "Okay," and I'm walking away, kind of shaking my head, saying, "Why didn't they think of that? These guys have been around here forever."

And Bob looked at me and said, "How did you know that a week out is when you ought to have that planned?"

And I said, "Well, it's always that way. If it gets past four weeks, we need to look for other resources to come in and do the engineering or we're going to get too late and our customers are going to get mad at us. But if it goes under a week, we're going to start having holes in the schedule and our engineers are going to open up."

So Bob asked me, "Have you ever told them that rule of thumb?" I said, "Uh . . . nope."

So the next day, we posted a bracket on the lead times—when it goes below this, you've got to make sure you've got a job jar that's well articulated with scopes and objectives for improvement projects. If it goes over this one, etc.

So I don't have to save them on that anymore. And there is a series of hundreds of those things that have happened over time where you can inject that leadership or management know-how back into the standards. And you don't have to save the world every single time.

All this reflects a new way to look at accountability.

Jim Lancaster: Accountability is very important. But it's not what I thought it was. It's not about setting goals and then shaming people who don't hit the goals. That's not what accountability is. Accountability is about making sure that everybody understands where we're trying to go. Asking them about the piece they can pick up and move and then staying close enough so that they do the things to try to get there.

But if they don't get to the goal, that doesn't mean they necessarily did something wrong. It might mean that they weren't set up for success by something I did or whatever. So it's about supporting them so that they can be successful. And accountability means coming back with an action, or something they did next, and a plan for what they're going to do next. "I did this, this, and this, and this is what I learned, this is where I am, and this is what I want to do next. What do you guys think?" If they're doing that, I'm happy.

BREAKING DOWN THE SILOS

Silos or fiefdoms that support individual or group interests at the expense of the entire organization are one of the most destructive forces in business. When divisions, departments, sections, or individuals won't share or collaborate or, even worse, try to impede one another's progress, the organization ceases to operate as a cohesive unit.

Breaking down such disconnects is one of the most important challenges for a Lean CEO. Building customer value and eliminating waste throughout a value stream is impossible without cross-functional cooperation. Conversely, setting up value streams is often the moment of truth when silos are forced into the open.

The effectiveness of Lean in creating rapid and visible improvements often serves as a catalyst to bring a collaborative spirit to an organization. This aspect was the primary reason Lean was initially brought into PLZ Aeroscience.

The company designs and manufactures specialty aerosol products in five manufacturing locations in North America. Rivalries between two divisions in the company were impeding progress, and in 2009, the company appointed a new CEO, Ed Byczynski, to take on the problem. Byczynski had had previous experience with Lean.

Ed Byczynski: I was brought in to resolve a cultural issue with the management teams. When I first joined the company, there were two primary business units—one was a contract packaging house, one was a branded private-label house. They had two very different ideas when it came to manufacturing processes as well as sales and marketing of their products. The two groups had gotten to a point where they really didn't talk to each other.

Byczynski felt that Lean was the best way to bring the kind of cooperation that could solve the rift between the two factions.

Ed Byczynski: It was really a question of how do I go about pulling these folks together and getting them to understand that we're trying to move in one direction. It just seemed logical to me that Lean would be the best way to do that. The way I put it to the team was, "Look, I'm going to bring a person into the organization who's going to look at our business processes in a different way. We are too entrenched, and we want to create a new environment in which to operate."

So initially, I was using the Lean process not so much to eliminate waste and do value stream mapping and all the other things that you want to engage in as to get teams to talk to one another and understand that there may be a different way to look at someone else's process or system.

At the same time we were able to get those groups to get that conversation flow going, which then led to our current state and future state activities. It really bonded the team.

To provide consulting support, the organization brought in Jean Cunningham, who helped not only with the shop floor aspects but in setting the right expectations for how Lean would affect financial reporting.

> *Ed Byczynski:* I think you have to build expectations initially around what you're trying to accomplish on a longer-term basis as it relates to Lean, and you have to understand up front what the short-term issues are that are going to arise as a result of that. I will say again that if you have the right person helping you through that process, you'll understand what initial issues you're going to face, including the inventory draw.

The conversation took place through a series of *kaizen* events aimed at improving processes in the plants. Cross-functional teams included operators, maintenance staff, a representative from finance, a Lean facilitator, and often individuals who were not directly involved. Byczynski has actively participated in many events as a "regular" team member, gathering data, finding root causes, and helping formulate solutions:

> When you're involved in those Lean activities and you're on a cross-functional team, you're no longer the boss; you're really part of that team in terms of trying to solve the problem that you're working on or you're trying to find the waste in the business process. There's no place for really a boss at that point.

One of the key areas initially was finding problems that were slowing down the operation and not allowing the machinery to run at the recommended speeds. Because the company ran identical equipment in 12 facilities, improvements could be leveraged significantly, and participants began to see the power that Lean has to transform companies.

Ed Byczynski: In many cases, we found that the problem did not require a significant amount of capital expenditures. It really just required a cross-functional team of people focusing on recurring problem areas within those processes.

To me, that was really about us understanding the power of Lean from a manufacturing perspective and what *kaizen* events can do toward addressing those repeated concerns that we had.

Buy-in, as in any organization, was not instantaneous. The toughest part about bringing Lean into the organization, Byczynski said, is getting people to change their thinking:

What happens in most cases is that people feel like they know everything there is to know about that piece of equipment they're working on. People on the floor have a high level of skepticism about the power of Lean when they're accustomed to a non-Lean way of thinking.

When you originally start to talk to them about how you can increase, let's say, run speeds to the manufacturer's suggested rates or whatever it might be or you're trying to identify a way to solve a problem on the shop floor, I think that they are reluctant at first to see the merits of problem solving or looking at current and future states.

But once they begin to see what can happen as a result of that exercise, they immediately begin to get excited about the power of Lean. Once that happens, the culture and the plant will start to change.

We've actually had people who didn't even want to wait for the Lean activity to come into their area. They started on their own because they had some experience working on a cross-functional team and would bring that over to their area. They can become very engaged in the process because they see the power of what can be done through it.

Getting people to see Lean and what it can do is the key, Byzcynski said. However, visiting an area is not enough:

> I would say you have to be an active participant on a team to really understand what Lean is all about. I think it's hard to read a book and really apply it, but if you're on a couple of teams where you're engaged in a *kaizen* event, and you do the value stream mapping and the current and future states, and you start to look and see where the opportunities exist with the elimination of waste, then I think you can easily figure out how it's done.

Building an Impressive Track Record

During the first five years of PLZ's Lean journey, revenues nearly tripled to $425 million, and the company had become successful at acquisitions. Byczynski attributes this to better collaboration on the senior management team that resulted from the Lean transformation.

Byczynski brings Lean into every company PLZ acquires, driving improvement according to a set of standard work metrics:

> We have a standard set of metrics, and we implement those immediately. When we see that the metrics aren't aligned with what we feel are the targets that we want to achieve, we engage in *kaizen* events with the new team to get them focused on how we get our metrics to where we want them to be.
>
> Whenever we're engaged in acquiring a company, I go in with the senior team and work with the new teams. It's been very beneficial to us, because we can actually begin to push this into the new organization. We've probably made now five acquisitions, and there's never been a time when those operators were engaged in any type of Lean practices prior to us acquiring them.

For Byczynski, Lean is business as usual:

Lean is one of those things that never go away. Once it becomes a part of your culture, it's kind of the way that we continue to operate our continuous improvement process going forward. We continue to build the organization, the cultures are now a good fit, and our senior management team is pulling in the same direction, so we can begin to focus on continuing to look for opportunities in the area of waste elimination, reduce our labor costs, our operating expenses, and things of that nature.

CHAPTER 8

---◆---

PUTTING PEOPLE FIRST

Let people realize clearly that every time they threaten someone or humiliate or unnecessarily hurt or dominate or reject another human being, they become forces for the creation of psychopathology, even if these be small forces.

—Abraham Maslow

One of the business casualties that we don't hear about in the news is that millions of workers go home every day feeling that they are not valued by their employers. Behind this treatment of employees is a widely held view among managers that workers are dispensable, and the more dispensable, the better. The subsequent humiliation leaves many employees, even those who are well paid and not threatened by layoffs, leading lives of quiet desperation.

Of course, companies don't admit publicly that they treat their employees like commodities. Reception areas are full of vision statements and mantras about companies' people-centric views, and the phrase "our employees are our most valuable asset" has become such a cliché that it is the subject of ridicule, not to mention derision in Dilbert cartoons.

Few have been as vocal about the treatment of people in the workplace as Bob Chapman, chairman and CEO of the St. Louis–based industrial machinery manufacturer Barry-Wehmiller. The company is a highly successful multidivisional corporation that employees nearly 7,000 worldwide. Chapman is a man on mission. In his frequent speeches, he decries the business practices that he blames for much of the malaise in the United States.

> *Bob Chapman:* We're destroying lives. We are sending people home feeling unappreciated. Eighty-eight percent of the people in this country feel they work for an organization that does not care about them.

Strong words from a CEO who started his career by following all the traditional rules and built a $2 billion organization.

> *Bob Chapman:* I had a very traditional business background—undergraduate in accounting, graduate MBA at Michigan, public accountant. I eventually entered the business my dad ran in 1969. As a young businessman, I played the traditional game, applying everything I had learned about making money and creating value.
>
> At the same time, I was raising a family of six kids and was serious about being a good parent. I didn't connect the two at the time—one was my personal job, the other was business, which is where most people are.

After weathering a series of challenges in the 1980s that he "barely survived," Chapman developed a knack for acquiring undervalued companies and maximizing their value, and Barry-Wehmiller grew rapidly. In 1987, a group of acquired companies was spun off on the London Stock Exchange. The issue was oversubscribed 35 times, making it the subject of a Harvard business study.

Now highly respected and in a strong cash position, Chapman created a formalized vision for the business that he called Growth, Value, and Liquidity. Using this as a road map, he concentrated on the historical core business of the company. By 2000, Barry-Wehmiller had grown tenfold to $200 million in revenue.

But Chapman never forgot his kids and the fact that his life at work and his life at home were separate. Clearly, there was something missing from his vision, but he wasn't sure what.

Then, in 1997, he had an epiphany that was to transform not only his management style but the lives of thousands of employees:

We had just bought a company that had a significant after-market business as part of its total revenue, so I flew down on my first day of owning this company to meet with the leaders. I decided to meet with the customer service team first, a group of 8 or 10 people who took orders over the phone for parts and service. I walked in early Monday morning and was having a cup of coffee, and it was March Madness, and they had some kind of pool going. I'm not a fanatic about sports, so I wasn't interested in what people were betting on, but I'm interested in people's behavior.

So I watched people just laughing and talking, their body language, comments about how this team won, etc. The closer we got to eight o'clock, when the office opened, the more you could see their body language convert from fun to "Now I have to do my job." I don't remember thinking consciously about it at the time, but in hindsight it's crystal clear what was happening.

Chapman then tried something that surprised him as much as it surprised the rest of the people in the room:

I walked down the hall to have my first meeting with the customer service team, and I walked in and introduced myself as the owner of the company. And then I did something I'd never done before—I don't even know where this came from. I said, "We're going to play a game. Whoever sells the most spare parts wins, and if the team makes the team goal, then the team wins."

Immediately there were objections—people had 10 different reasons why this couldn't work in this company. But they began playing this game, and we saw dramatic improvement in performance and behavior—it was like the March Madness spirit I had seen in the cafeteria. People really wanted to win, and they were having fun doing it.

I went back 13 weeks later, and their sales were up dramatically. So I asked, "What happened? I don't understand." And they said, "Mr. Chapman, you've got to understand what it's like in customer service. When the phone rings, it's often about a problem, so you hope somebody else picks it up. Now, because of the game, we're down there asking the switchboard operator, 'How do you decide who gets what call?' because we want to answer the phone."

I had no idea that this would affect results—I just wanted people to have fun. But I started hearing more and more stories like this. Normally companies would say, "We have a problem in customer service. We need to bring in a training specialist to teach people how to do a better job." But I didn't need to tell them anything, I let them have fun, and their creative abilities, their natural abilities came forth. It was amazing.

Chapman tried this in a few more situations and got similar results. The exercise was deceptively simple—introduce a game to change the mood—and it proved to be very powerful:

Around 2000, I realized we were on to something. I didn't understand it, but it was certainly much bigger than simply the game and customer service. So I got a group of thoughtful people together—not senior executives but people in a variety of functions—and we gathered together and we reflected. I gave some articles to our leadership just to stimulate thinking. Then I went through the experiences we had had and asked people, "What do you think is going on here?"

Then we started writing things down on a sheet of paper. Keep in mind that this was the Enron era, when business executives were rated lower than politicians and lawyers. Our company was growing fast, and we were doing well, but what did this mean? Was Enron successful when they created massive value that disappeared overnight? What is success? The answer to me was clear—we would measure success by the way we touched the lives of people.

The phrase "we measure success by the way we touch the lives of people" became the headline for the document that emerged from those conversations, which they named the Guiding Principles of Leadership (GPL). The one-page document lays out the company's core values, emphasizing trust, respect for individuals, teamwork, and the importance of each and every employee having a meaningful role in the company.

However, one big question remained:

We knew that companies like Enron had all kinds of great visions and value statements hanging on their walls, but they were broken companies. How could we be different and bring our vision to life in the hearts and minds of our people?

A Delivery Mechanism Based on People

One of the companies Barry-Wehmiller had recently acquired, now called Marquip Ward United, had brought on Jerry Solomon as its VP of finance, charged with the task of launching the company's Lean transformation. Solomon, a Lean veteran who has published several books, knew from experience that most Lean transformations fail because they are unable to create a companywide Lean culture. He immediately saw a natural fit between the Guiding Principles of Leadership and Lean.

Chapman initially saw Lean as "another quality fad" but very quickly saw the connection between Lean and people.

Jerry Solomon: Bob was working with a group of people on the Guiding Principles of Leadership at the time. When he told me about the principles, I said, "Lean is exactly that, Bob—it is about respect for people and all of those kinds of things that are inherent in the foundation for the Guiding Principles of Leadership."

We had a number of conversations about this and finally came to the conclusion that we're both trying to do the same thing in a different way. It was like a jigsaw puzzle in the sense that you had Lean that was a bunch of tool-driven concepts, and you had the Guiding Principles of Leadership, which was all about the people side. They really fit together like a jigsaw puzzle.

So Bob came to the realization that the Guiding Principles of Leadership are absolutely of paramount importance, but there really is no, for lack of better word, delivery mechanism or no distribution system with which to deliver them throughout the company. And Lean was a wonderful delivery mechanism if done right.

If Lean is done wrong, and there is entirely a tools focus, and we're beating up people, and we need results, and it's all about the numbers, it's not going to sustain itself, which many companies have proved. But if done right and with the core principles of the Guiding Principles of Leadership, by integrating the two we could have a sustainable model that really brings the respect for people element that is sorely missing in a lot of Lean transformations.

Chapman, however, was not initially impressed with the Lean activity he saw. When he attended a presentation by a consultant the company had hired to make improvements in its Green Bay plant, he found that the presentation wasn't about people at all but about targets and numbers. Chapman was so upset that he had to get up and leave the room.

Then came another important "aha" moment.

Bob Chapman: I was invited to a report-out the next morning on one of our early Lean successes in the Green Bay plant. I suggested that the people involved give a report to our executive team. So, at 7 a.m. this group of unprepared people, mostly assembly workers, were asked to come in and present to all the presidents. So they came in, and much like the consultant the day before, they talked about how their project had reduced inventory, shortened lead times, reduced costs, and improved quality.

I listened to all of this for about 10 minutes. I'd never met these gentlemen before, and again, I have no idea where this came from, but I asked the presenter, "Steve, how did this change your life?"

I had no idea what Steve was going to tell me. There was a long silence, and then Steve said, "My wife is talking to me more."

Here we were with all this Lean data, and I was stunned. "I don't understand, Steve. Help me."

Then Steve proceeded to tell me one of the most profound stories I had ever heard. "Do know what it's like to go to work for a place where you're just another number?" he said. "You punch your time card, you go to your workstation, and you're told what to do. You're not given the tools you need to do it. You get 10 things right that day, and nobody says a word, but you get one thing wrong and you get your ass chewed out. Your manager complains about your salary and your benefits, and by the time you go home at night, do you know what? You don't feel very good about yourself. When I went home and encountered my family, I realized I wore that feeling. It affected my relationship with my wife."

Steve went on: "Now I've got a chance to contribute my skills with my team members, see those ideas translated into improved results. When we ask questions, we get answers. In this environment, I feel better about myself when I leave this place. I feel I've been heard and I've contributed. When I go home, I feel better about myself and I'm nicer to my wife. When I'm nicer to her, she talks to me."

I turned to Jerry Solomon and said, "Jerry, we may have a new metric in Lean—the reduction of the divorce rate in America."

Another individual who saw the connection between the Guiding Principles of Leadership and Lean was Dick Ryan, a Lean consultant who had cut his teeth working for Art Byrne at Wiremold. The two men and their wives had been paired in a foursome at a golf course in Oregon and were having an impromptu dinner when Chapman started discussing the principles. Like Solomon, Ryan was intrigued.

Dick Ryan: I said, "Bob, I don't know if you practice this or if this is something you and your leadership team hang on a wall. But if this is a live document, and you practice this type of leadership with your associates and treat people this way, and you add the Lean tool kit to that, then you will be able to write a new book on Lean."

The two kept in touch, and in March 2006 Ryan signed on as the leader of the Lean journey at Barry-Wehmiller, charged with establishing Lean practices throughout the enterprise.

Aligning Methods with Beliefs

The decision to bring Lean to the whole organization required a strategy. This led to another major vision document for Barry-Wehmiller. In keeping with the company's new direction, the document was subtitled "The Merger of the Guiding Principles of Leadership and Lean Enterprise."

Bob Chapman: We decided that we were going to approach Lean very differently. In fact, we decided that the word *Lean* gave the wrong message. Instead, we called it L3, an acronym for Living Legacy of Leadership. This reflects our principles, so we built our own process around Lean based on that idea.

The document reinforces the Living Legacy of Leadership, with emphasis on pillars of Lean culture such as respect for workers, continuous improvement, cross-functional cooperation, and daily communication.

As Chapman points out, the vision bets strongly on the sincere desire of people to make a positive contribution in the workplace. In other words, if a company removes the barriers that prevent employees from realizing their potential, the employees will do the rest. Furthermore, Chapman is adamant that providing fulfilling work for employees must be the number one objective that trumps all others: treating people well cannot be a means to some other end.

> *Bob Chapman:* We need to do this for the reason that we want to take our people to a better place and that Lean is a way of fully engaging people in the process of continuous improvement and allows them to feel appreciated and validated for the gifts that they share with us.

In other words, the Guiding Principles of Leadership provide the vision, and L3 provides the Lean strategy for fulfilling this vision.

The Snowball Gains Momentum

The L3 office at Barry-Wehmiller provides training and support resources for any division that wants to go Lean. The strategy is not to force but to encourage: each division must decide whether to undertake the journey.

Those who do find themselves joining a community. Classes at Barry-Wehmiller University are in person and encourage representation from different divisions. Instructors bring their practical Lean experience to the classroom, and learners also participate in benchmarking trips to other companies. The university is also being used by Barry-Wehmiller customers and companies that are part of the community, including the U.S. Navy.

All the companies Barry-Wehmiller acquires are introduced to GPL and Lean, and the positive reception is building momentum in the entire company.

> *Jerry Solomon:* When we acquire a new company, people see that we've been solving the same problems that they have, so they are very anxious to learn. The other thing is that these new companies send people to these classes, and they build

that bond which is the culture side of it—getting to know the people and seeing the culture that Barry-Wehmiller brings to the table. All this is up front and center when Bob looks at an acquisition candidate.

The snowball is going downhill, and it's gaining a lot of momentum and getting very big. This will be the Barry-Wehmiller way. And it's just getting more roots being implanted each and every day.

As a Lean CEO, Chapman sees his primary role as making sure that the principles of leadership are followed, which he believes is the prerequisite to Lean success. For him, employee engagement is the ultimate dashboard.

Dick Ryan: Bob's focus is on people. He's never been on a *kaizen* event, and it is unlikely that he ever will. His main interest is making sure people are inspired and engaged. The leap of faith here is that when our team members use their gifts and talents to improve processes and eliminate waste, they ultimately help the company achieve continued financial success. It is maintaining this balance between people-centric leadership and business performance that makes Barry-Wehmiller special.

The leap of faith is more than a bet on future returns. For Chapman, it goes much deeper than that, as Bob said:

Recently at a conference, somebody from a major corporation asked me, "What return on investment are you seeing in this, Bob?"

"So why would I try to calculate the return on investment of being a good steward of the lives entrusted to me?" I replied.

And he said, "Well, our accountants would go nuts if you didn't do that."

I said, "I never even asked my accountants about something like this. This is a fundamental belief."

"What Would a Caring Family Do?"

When the economic downturn hit in 2009, Chapman faced a familiar question from the board. With orders down 40 percent, was he planning any layoffs?

> *Bob Chapman:* When the impact of the loss of orders began to hit, I was alone on a business trip in Europe. I immediately spent some time reflecting on how best to respond to this crisis within our vision. New thinking emerged. I asked myself, What would a caring family do when faced with a crisis? The answer came to me easily: the family members would all take a little pain so that no member of the family would have to experience dramatic loss.

Rather than lay off employees, the company agreed on a series of measures by which everybody would share the burden. Executive bonuses and the 401(k) match were suspended, and every team member took four weeks of unpaid time off. Improvement efforts were ramped up too: people attended classes, launched major improvement events, and participated in a variety of team activities.

The exercise was a huge morale booster, and the company emerged quickly to post record earnings the next year. The 401(k) not only was reinstated but was increased to show thanks for the sacrifice the workers had made. Then there was an unexpected bonus.

> *Bob Chapman:* Although we had been on a leadership journey centered on our guiding Principles for more than seven years,

many team members still weren't convinced of our sincerity. Walking the talk during this tough period did more to confirm our beliefs and strengthen our culture than anything we could ever verbalize or proclaim through a framed mission statement on a wall.

Engaging the Greater Community

Like many Lean CEOs, Chapman has spread his message widely, giving speeches and actively engaging with the Association for Manufacturing Excellence (AME) to change the focus to one that more closely reflects people-centric management. Today, thanks to Chapman's influence, AME is talking about a renaissance.

Chapman's message to the outside world is blunt: there is something fundamentally wrong with the way organizations do business today, and it goes back to the dawn of mass production.

Bob Chapman: Henry Ford's message to his workers was, "You've got 15 seconds to put a hubcap on every model, and just do it all day long. I'll pay you well, but I took away the dignity of your job." When we created organizations capable of mass production, we never saw it as an opportunity to profoundly impact people's lives and to be good stewards of their lives. So we never learned, and we never developed good leadership.

What did we study in our business schools? We studied successful companies. How did we define successful? Financial success. So we wrote case studies about financially successful companies because they had to be good. We created management classes, we created management degrees, we created jobs in management. And what is management? It is telling people what to do. That is management. It's not about the human dimension of life; it's about process and numbers. So we never learned to be good stewards as one of the principles of organizational dynamics.

Chapman is as tough on many Lean companies as he is on traditionally managed ones:

I think that the way Lean is practiced, it emphasizes putting people in an environment where they contribute, but there's not any attention paid to engaging people. Lean does ask for people's ideas on making things better. But it doesn't do it for the right reasons. It does it because we realize that these people know more than we do, but we don't give them credit for that because it is all about process improvement, not releasing the human potential.

My proposition is that you have to start from "We actually care." And then from that environment we give them the tools to care, which means allowing them to release the human potential, not the process potential. The process is just the way we tap into the human potential, and we celebrate the individual, not the numbers. The numbers are a by-product.

Chapman expanded on this:

When somebody comes into our organization and agrees to join us, when we invite them into our organization, we become stewards of that life, just as we are when a child comes into our life. A different level of intensity but the same concept. And the way we treat that person who joins our organization will profoundly affect that person's marriage and the way that person raises his children and interacts with our community.

REEXAMINING "DISABILITY"

As the Barry-Wehmiller experience demonstrates, Lean is a powerful delivery system for building an environment of respect where people can share their gifts and have fulfilling jobs.

But what if the people have capabilities very different from what we consider normal? What if a worker on the line has severe autism or cerebral palsy? What if the worker can't communicate verbally? Is it possible to create a work environment where these people can contribute side by side with "normal" people?

Tom Everill, the CEO of Puget Sound–based Northwest Center, was intrigued by these questions. An idealist of 1960s vintage who became a corporate executive, Everill figured there must be a way to merge these contrasting sensibilities:

> What I noticed in the corporate world is that nothing is impossible. There's capital, there's energy, and there are just astonishing examples of human ingenuity that go into making Toyota, and Boeing, and coffee equipment, and insanely complex financial instruments. So why not apply all this in the name of social justice?

Another early influence on Everill was the work of W. Edwards Deming, who believed that management could do a much better job of creating environments where workers could be productive and happy. Could better management make it possible, he wondered, for companies to have a social purpose?

Everill began to think more deeply about this possibility when he took early retirement in 2006 and enrolled in a master's of science program in management and leadership at the Antioch University Center for Creative Change. He also joined the board of the Northwest Center, which was at that time essentially a social agency funded by a group of businesses.

Tom Everill: Five years ago, Northwest's assembly and packaging business especially was a sheltered workshop, which was basically a daycare center for adults with serious developmental disabilities. Hence the name Northwest Center. It was like a place to house these people. The little custom buses would go out, round up all the people who don't fit into society, and bring them to the center.

The center's business included an industrial laundry, an electronics assembly plant, and a packaging business, and it also helped find jobs for people with disabilities. The center had a good reputation, and its work was a far cry from the days when people with disabilities were, as Everill puts it, "put into institutions, locked up, and never thought about again." However, employment of people with diverse abilities was limited, and when Everill took over as CEO in 2008, he was determined to change that.

Tom Everill: Our journey to Lean started when we said, "This isn't good enough." We were arguing with our local employers, Boeing and Starbucks and Nordstrom, that they've got to hire these folks, but we weren't employing people with developmental disabilities in a lot of our businesses because we didn't think they could do the work. If you wanted to make money, you hired normal folks, and those businesses made money to help fund our programs for people with disabilities; people with disabilities were really relegated. They became the objects of our benevolence.

Our assembly and packaging business, for example, was allowed to lose money, because it was thought of as a program that kept people busy. So we started having a lot of dialogue and debate about this. Around the time I took over as CEO, people were saying, "You have to decide. Is this a program or a business? Because if this is a business, then we'll move people with disabilities out and hire regular people."

As the new CEO, Everill decided to take a different tack on this question that was to change the course of the Northwest Center:

Rather than solving the question "Is this a program or a business?" we began to evolve from either/or to both/and. This forced us to think a lot harder. What kind of solution embraces both? If you can figure out what embraces both, all of a sudden you've got something that's way bigger than one or the other.

Although he had no expertise in manufacturing, Everill believed that the answer to this question would not be found by social workers but by people with deep industrial experience. Therefore, Everill made a gutsy move: he hired Mike Quinn, a steel industry veteran with considerable Lean experience, to take on the new role of vice president of manufacturing. Quinn's marching orders were explicit: turn around the money losers while maintaining the existing workforce.

Tom Everill: We gave the assembly and packaging business to Mike with the charge to think both/and. Mike had 30 years of experience in the steel industry, and he had done a lot of work with Lean. He and his team were brought in to apply what they'd learned from industry. Production leads, production foremen, were hired because of their experience in manufacturing. They did pass a kind of compassion test in that they had to have high emotional intelligence and have the capacity to work with a really diverse workforce. Now there's not a social worker in sight.

Quinn's Lean experience had taught him that when people were provided with the right work environment, their innate desire to make a positive contribution would kick in.

When he first visited the plants, Quinn immediately saw that people were not the problem; it was the processes that needed fixing.

Mike Quinn: When I first walked into our assembly packaging business, I couldn't figure out what was going on. Everything was so chaotic—there were supplies all over the place, finished goods not labeled, and people making things they had no orders for because "we like to make it ahead of time so we have it when the customer wants it."

The excuse was that we had to work this way because of our people. So we started tearing it apart based on the thinking that there was nothing wrong with the people—it was management that was the issue.

Many people might have been daunted by the prospect of creating a profitable business with a severely disabled workforce. Instead, Quinn saw opportunity:

When you first get into things with Lean, there's lots of low-hanging fruit. From a process standpoint, we had no flow at all in a couple of the companies. So we were able to make a lot of headway by just setting up work cells, and identifying materials that they were actually working with, and creating a one-piece process flow. This really eliminated the delays and gave us a huge reduction in inventory and the associated carrying costs.

Quinn had no secret sauce for dealing with this diverse workforce. All he did was apply Lean principles in exactly the same way he had in his previous work with "normal" workers.

Mike Quinn: One of my favorite lines is "just like everybody else." Some of the people we're dealing with don't communicate the same way we do. Some of them can't communicate at all. But it doesn't mean that they aren't capable of doing the jobs. And it doesn't mean that they aren't capable of being really productive. You just need to see how they see the world and start to present it to them in a way that they understand. So you really get down to how you're setting up a work cell. What does the work cell look like? It looks like everybody else's.

What did have to change was the thinking. Everywhere, there were people second-guessing the workers because of their disabilities. In one case, a job coach was checking 100 percent of the brushes made by a worker named Bob because of his disabilities. When Quinn asked the coach to take a closer look, it turned out that approximately six per day were defective, all for the same reason: the screws holding the brushes were not screwed in all the way. On asking why that was, they found that the batteries in the electric screwdriver were running out, and so Bob would throw the incomplete brush in the bin and wait, as he had been taught, for a job coach to come change the battery.

Quinn taught Bob how to change the batteries in a matter of minutes, and his quality went up to 100 percent. In fact, because of his speed, they put three people next to his workstation to package the brushes he assembled, and today the orders are completed strictly according to customer demand.

Mike Quinn: People would point to Bob and say, "He can't do this." And I'd say, "Why not? He gets dressed every day, he gets on a bus, and he comes here. He's certainly capable of changing the battery in his drill."

People were also used to the idea that disabled people needed to be protected from their environment. Nonsense, said the industry veterans who were now running the show.

Tom Everill: The social worker would say, "Well, you can't operate forklifts while the clients"—the euphemistic term for people with developmental disabilities—"are on the floor because someone might get hurt." And the manufacturing people were saying, "You're kidding me. We trained them. They don't get hit by a bus when they're coming to work; you just teach them." The manufacturing people expected that people who experience the world in a wide variety of ways would be able to do it, and they can.

From a manufacturing perspective, we're not doing anything unique. If a person has autism or Down syndrome or cerebral palsy, that might have implications for how they learn, but it doesn't mean that they can't do the work. Our job is to align the needs of the customer with the capabilities of our workers and the way they experience the work, and Lean does that very well. It's respect for people and involving people in figuring out how to satisfy the customer. So far it's worked incredibly well.

The successful transformation of Northwest's businesses emboldened the management team to raise the bar. If their workforce could perform as well as the workforce in a normal business, could they perform even better?

Tom Everill: Our successful transition from either/or thinking to both/and thinking revealed that the total here was greater than the sum of its parts. In 2013, we really started to explore an even higher order of thinking, which you might describe as "because." Our business is already successful not in spite of our diverse workforce but because of it. Mike and his team have really started exploring how to leverage the unique way in which our employees experience the world to the advantage of the work and the customer.

For example, in each of our work pods in our electronics factory, we intentionally have at least one person with autism.

We hire people who have a really highly obsessive capacity for repetitive work, for perfection, for concentration, which are characteristics frequently cited as disabilities in people with autism. Well, those qualities aren't disabilities when you're making intricately complex magnetic components or surgical equipment and aerospace or solar power insulation.

When we integrated our shop floor by bringing in people with diverse abilities and really started making good use of the talents of every employee in each work pod, our productivity went up, our quality went up, customer satisfaction went up, and so did our profits. All of these trendlines are just woven together, and they all go in the same direction.

One of the results from this diverse workforce is a stunning quality record that companies with normal workforces simply cannot compete with.

Tom Everill: One of my favorite stories is about the secondary packaging work we do for Starbucks. We're not dealing with their social corporate responsibility people or their diversity people; we're dealing with the production people, because they've never seen quality like what we can produce. We have an employee who frequently does our quality control work for us. We did 390,000 holiday gift packs in 2012 for Starbucks, and this guy did a nine-step quality check at the end of the assembly line, and among 390,000 we didn't get one back.

Starbucks called Mike and asked, "How did you do that? We've never seen perfect before; we've never worked with a vendor that was perfect." The secret is our workforce. We have people who can do stuff that you and I can't. Now we do all of Starbucks' secondary packaging. We did 1.1 million holiday gift packs this year, and we have projects all through the year.

People with diverse abilities are not just star performers on the line. They have also helped Quinn and his team find work processes that are simply better. For example, in a kit assembly job, the standard practice was to arrange the six items in a kit side-by-side on benches so that workers could access them from left to right. But there were a couple of workers who did not look left to right—they looked straight ahead—and so those workers constantly had to reorient themselves.

Quinn found that when the task was divided so that two people did three items each, the job went much faster than it did when each of them assembled the entire kit. Then came the surprise: when Quinn tested it, he found that the new process would be faster for people like himself as well. Any assembler, regardless of ability, could now do the job faster without twisting and turning and reaching all day.

In the electronics assembly business, a woman's disability led her to suggest a new way to attach a wiring harness to a transformer that is now the standard method for the process. These stories are common. The point is that as Lean pioneers said a half a century ago, the workers understand better than anybody else what the problems are.

There is no longer a perception by the management or the customers that Northwest Center is looking for "busywork."

Tom Everill: This is challenging work by any standard. In our assembly and packaging business, we're not making one product or a suite of products; we're constantly changing. So our people are building processes on the fly and disassembling them over and over again, which is a real challenge for our workforce, just as it is for other companies.

As Northwest Center's reputation for quality and on-time delivery grows, so does the business. From 2011 to 2014, revenues grew 500 percent.

"You Could Do This Too"

Everill, however, believes his mission has just begun. Citing statistics from the United States Centers for Disease Control and Prevention, he notes that one in six Americans has some level of a developmental condition, ranging from learning delays to attention deficit disorder to autism spectrum disorder. Many of these people are under the care of social agencies and are often placed in menial jobs that, he says, are wasting their talents.

Everill is out to prove that this is a huge opportunity for businesses:

> We bring businesspeople through here and tell them, "Look, you could do this too." Northwest Center shouldn't have to exist, and that would be our goal—to affect the consciousness in the community so much that Boeing and Starbucks and Nordstrom and Costco are falling all over themselves to build a diverse workforce and harvest the benefits of it.

Whether or not Everill is able to change the world, he has proved with the help of Lean that business and social justice are not mutually exclusive.

Tom Everill: When the exigencies of running a fairly complex midsize conglomerate get to me, I go down and stroll on the production floor and get reminded why we are here. Our employees are really amazing people, and it's really neat to go down on the floor and see people who probably wouldn't pass the job interview anywhere else doing world-class work for global brands. Growing the business 500 percent over three years with perfect quality scores makes it worth getting up in the morning.

BRINGING NEW LIFE TO THRIFT STORES

Can a thrift store run on a shoestring budget compete head-to-head with a multinational clothing chain with a powerful brand? With the help of Lean, Jim Martin, the CEO of Goodwill in southern Oregon, proved that it can, and his model of Lean retail stores is spreading to Goodwill outlets across the United States.

> *Jim Martin:* We don't look at the Salvation Army or St. Vincent de Paul as our competitors. We're competing with Kohl's, TJ Maxx, Old Navy. When you come into our stores, they are cleaner, more efficient, and more organized. We size, we colorize, and we rotate our merchandise, and we're vigilant. An Old Navy shopper might go there once or twice a month, but a high percentage of our shoppers are in our stores every day, because we're putting new product out every day.

The secret sauce in this transformation is people. Like Northwest Center, Goodwill Industries hires people with cognitive disabilities, and like Everill, Martin found many of the same prejudices: tasks critical to running a profitable business are handled by normal people, and the disabled are tucked away in back rooms where mistakes don't really matter.

Martin wanted to change that. He knew that many in the ranks of the disabled are cheerful, energetic, and highly motivated, exactly the kinds of people you want in a retail environment. Furthermore, Goodwill is in an increasingly competitive business that is very sensitive to the atmosphere that people are able to create in the stores.

By studying several large retail chains that were using Lean to improve their stores, Martin, who prefers to use the term *kaizen*, saw an opportunity. The idea of eliminating waste and providing value made a lot of sense to him, especially when he considered the amount of waste that was present in most Goodwill facilities.

Jim Martin: I had been visiting the more successful Goodwills, and one of the things that I noticed very quickly was that the production areas in the less successful stores were very messy, whereas in the more successful stores they looked like Marine Corps barracks. So we all put our heads together to figure out the best way to improve these rooms, and *kaizen* was clearly the preferred method.

With no budget, and using teaching materials donated by the Kaizen Institute, Martin began to apply 5S to clean up the stores in his region:

There was almost an immediate bump in sales as we *"kaizened"* each production area because we were able to get more products on the floor at a faster rate. We cut down on the time that it took to get merchandise from the donation door to the sales floor.

As it turned out, there was much more to Lean than cleaning up a few warehouses. As Martin's team members explored the possibilities, they found there was a much greater benefit: the ability to employ individuals with disabilities in the stores. The first area was stock rotation. With the use of a system of color-coded tags, employees could work the shop floor, doing jobs that had been previously done by "normal" employees. One at a time, the team experimented with labeling, creating picture guides for workers who could not read, and training employees to use price guns.

Jim Martin: What *kaizen* does is, it breaks down every process. And as a result, you have the opportunity to find jobs where you can insert that into the workforce. It's not busywork; it's real work. It may take an extra step, but it doesn't deviate from the stream and actually it makes it quicker.

The improvements at Goodwill in Eugene bear many of the hallmarks of a successful Lean transformation. Capacity, measured in sales per square foot, doubled between 2003 and 2013, and profitability increased as well, making this one of the top-performing regions in the United States.

The surprise was that as the transformation progressed, Martin, like Everill, found that he had a superior workforce compared with many companies that employ only "normal" people. The worker dedication is unusually high—Martin says that in a snowstorm, every single worker will show up—and there's an atmosphere of friendliness in the stores that would be difficult to train into a group of normal people. Furthermore, there are tasks whereby the disabled can beat a nondisabled person, such as scanning books into the e-commerce system:

> *Jim Martin:* Repetitive scanning of books for some, including myself, would be very difficult to consistently do for eight hours. But there are a number of individuals whom we work with who work well in that environment and outproduce by a significant margin folks without developmental disabilities.

Goodwill Eugene, operating today from nine stores and 11 donation centers, is now respected not as a charity but as a business. Martin says that realtors who would not return his calls years ago now call him on a regular basis to let him know when store properties come on the market. Martin now assists other regions and is opening new territory for Goodwill across the state of Alaska.

The biggest reward for Martin, however, is seeing the changes that this has made in people's lives:

> This job has taught me to never underestimate the value of an employee. It's amazing what giving the right work structure

and the right work environment to individuals with really substantial barriers can accomplish.

As well, I've grown to respect the incredible value that earning a paycheck has for individuals. There are a lot of folks we work with where we're their first job. They've been told all their life that they couldn't get a job and could not be successful. But here we are—we have one break room, we have one Christmas party, we're an integrated organization, and everybody works together. It's really something that it's great to be a part of.

W. Edwards Deming would be proud.

CHAPTER 9

BUILDING THE LEARNING ORGANIZATION

There was no manual and we could find out what would happen only by trying. Tension increased daily as we tried and corrected, and then tried and corrected again.

—*Taiichi Ohno,* describing the
development of the *kanban* system at Toyota

One of the casualties of North America's industrial decline during the 1970s was the reliable business forecast. Demand was no longer behaving as planners expected, and during the ensuing years, globalization, rapidly evolving technology, and environmental constraints accelerated this trend of uncertainty, turning formerly stable markets into moving targets. Phrases such as "adapt or perish" soon became the watchwords of modern business.

From this situation came the revelation, shocking to some, that applying what worked in past no longer guaranteed future performance. In 1990, the concept of the learning organization—one that could beat the competition by quickly acquiring the knowledge needed to adapt to changing conditions—became common currency with the help of Peter M. Senge's seminal book *The Fifth Discipline*.

Like Deming, whom he greatly admired, Senge envisioned a new era in which learning would be recognized as a key determinant of competitive advantage:

> The old days when a Henry Ford, Alfred Sloan, or Tom Watson learned for the organization are gone. In an increasingly dynamic, interdependent, and unpredictable world, it is simply no longer possible for anyone to "figure it all out at the top." The old model, "the top thinks and the local acts," must now give way to integrating thinking and acting at all levels.[1]

Learning in this context, however, isn't about acquiring factual knowledge or processing reams of market data. It's about a high level of engagement that accelerates the art of observation and the sharing of ideas in the interest of commonly held goals. Deming called for a fundamental revisiting of the way people work and learn together:

> We must restore the individual, and do so in the complexities of interaction with the rest of the world. The transformation will release the power of human resource contained in intrinsic motivation. In place of competition for high rating, high grades, to be Number One, there will be cooperation on problems of common interest between people, divisions, companies, competitors, governments, countries. The result will in time be greater innovation, applied science, technology, expansion of market, greater service, greater material reward for everyone. There will be joy in work, joy in learning. Anyone that enjoys his work is a pleasure to work with. Everyone will win; no losers.[2]

By 1980, the learning organization had a long history at Toyota and other Lean companies in Japan, a fact that Senge and Deming clearly acknowledged. When Kiichiro Toyoda exhorted his team in 1945 to catch up with American companies, he was counting on the brainpower of Toyota's employees; it certainly was not going to happen with big machines.

The evolution of Lean that followed strongly reflected this. Developing people is, of course, one of the pillars, and the specific practices—*kaizens*, PDCA, the Five Whys, the Ohno circle, the manager as coach, the emphasis on training—all support the concept of the learning organization. In fact, Lean arguably promotes the learning organization above all else.

EMPOWERING PEOPLE TO LEARN FOR THEMSELVES

Transforming the organization to one that truly learns and adapts is a demanding proposition for the management team. To succeed, the CEO must provide clear direction for employees and at the same time accept an atmosphere of considerable uncertainty. Piloting a ship decisively is tough when you do not know the route.

One thought leader who has studied this role very carefully is Kevin Meyer, who possesses a unique set of talents. Trained as an engineer, he became a Lean consultant with a special interest in the relationship between Lean and Zen Buddhism. Meyer honed many of his ideas about leadership during his eight-year tenure as president of Specialty Silicone Fabricators (SSF), a midsize medical device fabricator that currently operates two plants in California and one in Michigan.

Meyer, who was consulting for SSF in 2004, was offered the job unexpectedly and accepted under the condition that he would have latitude to experiment. Other than make money for the company, there would be no specific objectives. In other words, he would be free to learn.

Kevin Meyer: It wasn't "here are your goals for this quarter and next quarter." If it had been that, I wouldn't have been nearly as interested—there I'd be managing more than leading.

So having fewer boundaries really appealed to me. But I can see where an executive coming out of a much larger corporation would really want to know what they were expected to do and what the boundaries were.

SSF was an ideal candidate for the journey of discovery that Meyer envisioned. The company was a custom shop that had a variety of manufacturing capabilities: extrusion, molding, sheeting, dip casting and coating, and assembly. Its products were in a continual state of reinvention.

Kevin Meyer: SSF is a contract manufacturer, and we had very little knowledge of true demand. Because we were making custom one-offs, we didn't care about things like overall equipment capacity utilization. There were machines sitting idle all over the place. But that was value, because we could take on something very quickly and get it done.

Although his engineering training and prior experience with medical devices gave him a good understand of the company's processes, Meyer knew that the knowledge the employees had accumulated was critical to any strategy:

The people had much more experience with the company and the product than I did. They could come up with solutions that were better than what I could just edict based on other backgrounds, and I still think about that quite a bit.

Lean thinking was new to the employees, however, and Meyer needed to have them on board to move forward. Telling them about Lean, however, was not going to be enough.

Kevin Meyer: I don't think it's possible for an organization that hasn't been exposed to a Lean operation to really see it. They can hear, "Yeah, we can reduce cycle time and waste," and all those kinds of things, but Lean is one of those things you've got to experience to truly understand the power.

And if I look back at SSF, we started with some of the simple stuff like 5S, but when it really grabbed hold was when we started sending people to things like the AME Southern California Lean tour, where they put people on a bus for three days and you go to seven wildly different companies—a hospital, a glassblowing shop—and they always come back and say, "Oh, my gosh."

So I really grabbed hold of that, and those guys became the dual proponents of implementing the things I was talking about. I think you have to experience it. You can't just learn about it.

Meyer began by rolling out Lean tools in a logical sequence, but eventually decided that the order should be determined not by a plan but by the problems employees were grappling with in their day-to-day work:

There was a time early on when we were trying to learn two major tools a year without understanding why, and we got a little ahead of ourselves and decided to step back. I can remember when my QA manager asked me, "Why are we doing any of this?" So we decided to stop working on implementing any tools unless there was a defined problem.

So we'd identify a problem, identify the root cause, and then ask, "What might be some options?" Then we'd come up with several possibilities that I would either give people or they would find on their own. Some would work and some wouldn't.

We applied this to adopting tools in general. Should we try total productive maintenance? We'd go a little way down that path, and then maybe we'd say, "This shouldn't be a high priority for us in terms of resource consumption; let's focus on this other tool instead."

There are also some interesting stories about how some Lean tools in the wrong application actually create costs. I think that it was good for us to see that. We needed to figure out why we were using tools in the first place.

At the end of the day, this was creating a culture of experimentation. The conscious part was about what the problems were and digging into the root cause. And it was allowing people to try solutions to it.

This trial-and-error approach to implementation meant that many efforts were started and then dropped. This troubled Meyer initially, but he soon realized that it was also part of the learning experience:

If anything, I felt bad about the number of things we were abandoning. And in hindsight, maybe that's not a bad thing. The more you try, the more you can abandon as long as you understand the underlying reasons in each case for why something didn't work. It's about that learning in itself.

What the process yielded was an approach to Lean that was unique to SSF. This meant that Meyer was forced to rethink some of his ideas about Lean:

The underlying situation that determines customer value is different in every company. Lean has to be built on optimizing value for the customer from the customer's perspective, and there also has to be respect for the people side in the decision making, so I think it has to be different in each situation.

For example, there can be cases where there is more customer value when you're having a little bit more inventory.

I also think there are too many people who are focused on building up their Lean toolbox. I think the best Lean companies get really good at understanding the value and treat the tool set as just ideas that you use to create your own tools. There are a lot of things we did at Specialty Silicone that I couldn't really put into 5S or TPM or any of those buckets. But they optimized customer value.

So we did shoot from the gut on some stuff, because it felt right from a customer value standpoint, and we tried to refine that down to some level of standard work. We never got into the classic weeklong *kaizen* event—we could just never do that. But we did a lot of TWI work that then turned into *kaizen* when we broke down the process.

Humility with an Air of Confidence

Leading people to find their own solutions involves a delicate balance. There has to be assertiveness and empowerment at the same time.

Kevin Meyer: There has to be humility, but you have to project this air of confidence that things are okay. When you're not humble, I don't think you can project that in a trustworthy kind of fashion. When you're humble, you're out on the floor more, and you're talking to people on their level, they trust you, and they feel that you've got their best interests at heart. If you spend all your time in the executive suite and come out for a speech here and there, you create an environment of fear or concern. And that in itself hinders performance in people.

Meyer's managers, however, found it difficult to give up their traditional reactive roles and shift their focus to coaching and supporting their people.

Kevin Meyer: The manager-as-mentor role is something my staff struggled with. I wanted them to be on the floor, in their operations, even if they weren't manufacturing, and I wanted them to be teaching.

But first I had to teach them. They were some of the first people I sent out on Lean tours. But it was still a struggle—to break them away from the firefighting that you have in pretty much every department. Even when they improved things and had reduced the firefighting, it's almost as if they felt more comfortable dealing with the paperwork and the phone calls—fixing problems rather than envisioning the future and guiding their groups toward that. Of course, some were better at it than others.

Meyer also found that managers didn't know how to work with one another. An unexpected team-building exercise helped improve that:

When we built our new building, we had a lot of discussion about where the managers should sit. Should they be with me in a group on the second floor, or should they be dispersed out on the shop floor in their operations? In the old facility, they were for the most part with their operations. But the big downside there was that they were spread all over, so they didn't know how to work together.

So when we started construction on a new building— we actually had to demolish a building—I moved my entire staff and me into a triple-wide. The walls were so thin that everyone could hear what everyone else was doing. So they could hear the problems other people were experiencing and intervene and support, and it became a very cohesive group.

Another tough issue for the CEO is confronting managers who put up strong opposition to Lean. Meyer believes that much can be learned from them as well:

Jim Collins, the author of *Good to Great,* talks about getting the wrong people off the bus as fast as you can, and there are a lot of Lean people saying that as well. I've had a couple of manager-level employees who have really made me question that. The questions they asked annoyed me at the time because I just wanted to forge forward, but they were very good questions. I wish I had listened to them more.

So it bothers me when I hear Lean people say you have to get rid of the barriers as fast as you can. Are they a barrier, or are they providing another kind of input?

California Edges Out Michigan

Although Meyer's approach might sound somewhat tentative to traditional managers, the results were anything but. In his eight-year tenure at SSF, the company made the following improvements:

- Cycle time: five weeks to five days
- First pass yield: 65 percent to 99 percent
- On-time delivery: 70 percent to 99 percent
- Opened new U.S. plants and initiated sales to China and India
- Developed significant new manufacturing capabilities

Meyer's biggest source of pride, though, is that the knowledge of his employees became so valuable that when it came time to build a new plant, staying in California won out over Michigan, even though the move would have included the incentive of a free building. Clearly, the learning organization had become a reality.

Meyer reflected back on his strategy:

I think it was the right thing, with a couple of caveats. Change took a lot longer. I sometimes wonder what would have happened if I had gone in there and said, "Thou shalt do 5S and you will do value stream mapping and have a solution planned by week 2," and that kind of thing. Would the transformation have been faster, and therefore more cash created? Maybe, but on the other hand, it's more sustainable now, since the employees have discovered it themselves. I think that's a good model.

Most of the time, I guided people and they learned. And I think the Lean transformation may have taken longer because of that, but I think it became more rooted in the culture then.

SHARING IDEAS AS A STRATEGY

Ideas and knowledge are essential to Appvion, formerly Appleton Papers, one of the largest employee-owned companies in the United States. In an industry dominated by players with massive production capacity, Appvion has a century-long history of differentiation through its expertise in formulating and applying coatings. The company was a pioneer of carbonless paper, an improvement on the older and messier carbon paper technology, and later was a leader in the development of thermal paper for fax machines.

In 2005 Appvion was facing both a challenge and an opportunity. The market for its largest product category, carbonless paper, was in decline, and that was hitting revenues hard. At the same time, the company had a strong track record in innovation and an impressive staff of qualified engineers and scientists.

That year the company appointed Mark Richards to succeed the retiring CEO, Doug Buth. Richards had achieved notable success during his six-year tenure as a group president at Valmont Industries, and Lean had been very much a part of that picture.

Richards's appreciation for Lean stemmed from an interest in organizational culture that he had developed at an early age. It all began when his father, a longtime General Motors employee, got him a summer job working on the line at Oldsmobile. Richards worked hard at GM, sometimes doing "doubles"—16-hour shifts—but what he remembers most was that people did not share information.

> *Mark Richards:* I was very into team sports and pretty collaborative and was surprised to see that there wasn't much team spirit at GM. When there was some kind of breakdown, a bunch of people would show up, basically swarming the event and trying to fix it. The operator wasn't part of this process, and that seemed odd to me.
>
> I remember talking to a gentleman who ran a very complicated machine that was basically gauging the cadence of the line, and the machine would constantly go out. I asked him why, and he said, "Probably this, this, or that." I said, "Why don't you go tell them?" and his response was, "Because they didn't ask me." I never forgot that.

Richards's formal introduction to Lean came when his newly hired VP of operations, Keith Hoffman, suggested that it would be a good strategy for Valmont. What interested Richards was that this was about empowering the workforce, something he had not seen at GM. His superiors did not understand Lean but nonetheless gave him the latitude he needed.

> *Mark Richards:* The position of my superiors was, "Well, it's your business to run, but you've got to hit the numbers." So over the next six years, we really drove Lean, and for the first time ever, we beat our return on invested capital thresholds in Europe. We also turned China into the black, and we grew it. The infrastructure business at Valmont became its largest division during that period.

When Richards was offered the top job at Appvion, it seemed the perfect opportunity to instill a Lean culture of empowerment. Lean experimentation was already taking place, and the employees were enthusiastic and willing to learn.

Mark Richards: What I found appealing at Appvion was that it is an employee-owned company—actually, one of the largest. They had some real challenges, too, and I wanted a challenge. Their largest business at the time when I came, accounting for 80 to 90 percent of their sales and earnings, was based on a product line that was decaying 8 or 9 percent a year. It was in the late stage of maturity. But they had other capabilities and needed a leader to come in and begin to do something.

There were pockets of Lean when I got there but no senior management support for it. But after walking around and asking lots of questions, I could see there was a passionate group out there that was very interested in Lean. There had also been a lot of work done on self-directed work teams where supervisors were being removed and workers were being put in place to run their day-to-day operations.

We also had leadership that believed in this style of management even though they weren't Lean guys. They had the approach where you respect and value people, are humble and open to learning new things, and respect the diversity of thought and ideas in the company.

So I saw that we had a good foundation to do Lean here.

Upon arrival, Richards embarked on a long-term strategy to broaden the emphasis on the company's technologies and decrease dependence on volume products in mature industries. A key asset was the company's microencapsulation technology, which is now sold and delivered through the company's Encapsys division. Clients include Procter & Gamble, which employs the technology to reduce the amount of fragrance chemicals used in its laundry soap products.

This departure from the traditional paper business led to the 2012 name change from Appleton Papers to Appvion. The company also entered a strategic alliance to acquire uncoated paper from industry giant Domtar and discontinued papermaking operations at its West Carrollton, Ohio, plant. All this has brought the company closer to its innovative roots, Richards said:

> This business has differentiated itself for over 100 years by making paper special through our ability to formulate and apply coatings, as opposed to being a papermaker. So overall, we are pursuing an asset-light model and leveraging strategic alliances with larger papermakers like Domtar. We've proved that with the Encapsys business, and we're doing some other things that demonstrate that core capability of coating formulation and application.

If Appvion was to hold its own among much larger players, the company would need an engaged and knowledgeable workforce. For Richards, the journey was all about creating a culture that encouraged workers to share their knowledge and develop new ideas:

> It was about laying out, if you will, a future state for the business and then reaching out to the people. This harkens back to what I observed on the line at Oldsmobile—everybody's important. People closest to the work know what's going on, and if you're able to articulate a clear vision of what success looks like in great detail, you'll be so surprised at how people will work to deliver on that and come up with their own ideas.
>
> The key is to create an environment where people feel enough trust that they can put their ideas out there. Often, you have processes that don't work and people are being rewarded for what I call heroic workarounds. When you sit

back and ask if there's a more efficient way, people say, "Well, we've always done it this way, and I never thought we could change it."

So what I'm trying to do is turn the lightbulb back on so that everybody is in a mode of self-audit: What can I do differently? What can I do better? We need an environment where people say, "It's okay to change," and then change by running a set of controlled experiments with defined steps to make what I would call incremental but consistent improvement in the process.

Richards drove the journey personally, appointing direct reports to the role of continuous improvement director and then reappointing them within the operation to evangelize Lean across the organization.

This created an explosion of continuous improvement activity in the company. Between 2006 and 2013, over 120 *kaizen* projects were conducted each year. The results included the following:

- Annual reductions in waste ranging from $12 million to $30 million (2 to 5 percent of cost of goods sold)
- $1 million saved annually on changeovers
- Inventory reduction of 25 percent across the company
- A 25 percent reduction in breakdowns after implementing total productive maintenance
- Reduction in one plant of broken service promises by 90 percent over seven years

Taking the Transformation Corporatewide

In 2009 the company was organized into three value streams, and in 2011 Lean accounting was adopted. Active participation of the company's CFO was key to this transition.

Mark Richards: When I recruited Tom Ferree, our CFO, I was looking for a business partner who was curious and willing to try new ideas. That's often hard to find in an accountant. Tom really breaks the mold—he's got the personality and the vision for this, and he can see around corners.

The first hurdle with Lean accounting, or any kind of accounting, is that the CFO and CEO have a fiduciary responsibility to shareholders or plan participants, and they have to make sure that the control, the oversight, and the compliance are not compromised. The CFO must be able to articulate that very clearly.

To help Tom get comfortable with the connection between that and Lean, we brought in Jean Cunningham, who had been down that path. The trick is to create Lean operating statements that facilitate the speed of decision making while not compromising control. Taking out discussions around applications and standards doesn't prevent a CFO from being able to close the books and capitalize costs. You can have management reports that are direct-based accounting, and you can still preserve your accrual-based accounting.

The second step on the accounting side was about changing managerial reports so that we were managing with direct costs. We felt that getting rid of standards would facilitate the business decision making. I think that was pretty quickly demonstrated to be of great benefit to the business unit managers and to the operating people. Jean helped facilitate that as far as painting a picture of what that looked like and how we needed to get there.

The third step was to move the accounting people from standard accrual accounting, reports, variances, and standards to a direct accounting methodology. This was a transition process of getting people trained up so that they understood.

So we are now into direct costing. There are some additional system things we're changing this year, but we're making very good progress. People are getting their reports and using them, and it's working very well.

In 2013, Richards felt that the Lean journey was reaching a plateau and that it was time to find a vice president who could help raise it to the next level. The candidate selected was a 30-year Lean veteran, Jason Schulist. Schulist was attracted to the idea of working for a CEO who really understood Lean.

Jason Schulist: Trying to convince the top leader is a struggle, and it's not something I wanted to do again. I really wanted the opportunity to take it to the next level. So I was interested in what vision Mark brought to the company. I was interviewing them as much as they were interviewing me.

Rather than implement a predetermined Lean agenda, Schulist felt that what was needed most was alignment, which would open the door for building continuous improvement capabilities:

I stressed in my hiring interview that there were three questions that we needed to concentrate on, and that became my mandate.

1. Are we culturally aligned with our vision, such as the Appvion Way?
2. Does everybody in the company understand how he or she fits into the purpose of this company and the objectives?
3. How do we build the capabilities for daily continuous improvement?

We utilize a five-day course to help build our daily continuous improvement activities. All the members of our leadership team teach content in the course, including Mark, our CFO, our head of HR, and value stream vice presidents. This shows people how important daily continuous improvement is, and it also forces the leaders to really learn the material. This is the only way we do it.

The learning, however, is not a means to an end but in some respects the end itself. The company will have to learn every day to adjust to new circumstances, continuously innovating to discover and fulfill Appvion's true purpose.

Jason Schulist: I didn't create the Appvion Way. I didn't create the values. However, by joining the company, I have signed up for the mission, the vision, and the values. So given the system, the goal is to help us become consistent with it.

A Bold Plan for the Future

Today the company is far different from the way it looked in 2005. Carbonless paper, which once accounted for 90 percent of the profits, now accounts for less than 50 percent. Encapsys is growing at 10 percent a year, and overall, 15 to 20 percent of revenues are coming from products less than three years old.

Mark Richards: This puts the spotlight on R&D, and that's now our prime area for Lean and continuous improvement. I want to build a new state-of-the-art innovation center. This will be a collaborative center with no walls—a very open learning space. We want to apply the Lean continuous improvement model in our R&D and product development in order to recalibrate the R&D group and begin to integrate it into cross-functional teams with operations, marketing, and customers to drive new products faster and more efficiently.

We want new products coming out in less than 70 days. We also want to improve our vitality index, meaning the percentage of revenue coming from products less than three years old. We want to get away from supply-driven invention, where we think up something in the lab and say, "Here, go figure out how to sell it." That doesn't work, and that's not Lean either.

Richards runs the businesses through a series of short- and long-term Lean objectives, which are displayed in an X-matrix format on a "glass wall" in his office. According to Schulist, he is unusual in his ability to question himself:

Jason Schulist: Mark is pretty unique in that he accepts and responds to feedback. How many CEOs can do that? As Mark is introduced to daily continuous improvement, I am able to say to him, "What's your next step?" and then challenge him on that. He knows he's getting unadulterated feedback from me, and that creates good alignment.

Richards reflected on the capabilities required for Lean leadership. If you want to create an organization that is open to learning and new ideas, you have to be that way yourself.

Mark Richards: You also have to truly believe in diversity of thought and ideas and that new ideas can come from the shop floor just as well as from an executive office. I need to be able to learn from people just as they can learn from me. If your style is very much "This is from the top—do it or else" and that has worked for you, then it's going to be very hard to switch to a style that goes 180 degrees counter to that. You can't wave a magic wand and say, "Make me Lean." That won't work because this is cultural, and the CEO and senior leaders have to be the ones who create that culture within an organization.

Generally, managers in this Lean environment have to display a lot of courage and self-confidence. You're getting involved in a journey, and you have to be comfortable with your own self and true to the dynamic you're trying to create in an organization, which is a speak-up, listen-up kind of environment.

THE LEAN START-UP: LEARN FAST OR PERISH

The Lean start-up, a concept originated by the entrepreneur Eric Ries in 2008 and popularized in his 2011 bestseller with the same title, represents a whole new take on the learning organization. Start-ups face the unknown at every turn: customers, products, production capabilities, and ability to execute are all up in the air. Unlike mature companies that engage in long-term journeys to build learning cultures, a start-up faces an immediate and urgent need to learn very quickly from day 1.

In *The Lean Startup*, Ries describes the central role of learning in a start-up:

> In the Lean Startup model, we are rehabilitating learning with a concept I call validated learning. Validated learning is not after-the-fact rationalization or a good story designed to hide failure. It is a rigorous method for demonstrating progress when one is embedded in the soil of extreme uncertainty in which startups grow.[3]

Ries came to Lean thinking through his work as a software entrepreneur. The traditional approach to software development is the waterfall method, which involves a sequence of steps starting with conception and going on to design, testing, and eventually delivery to a test group of customers. Wanting to put their best foot forward, companies try to perfect the outcome of each stage to ensure that the final prototype is as complete and bug-free as possible.

The problem here is that during the months it takes for the product to go through the development cycle, there is no interaction with the customer. If customers are not buying, the company gets the bad news at the very end of the cycle, leading to months of rework, assuming the company has the resources to continue. In the early chapters of *The Lean Startup*, Ries describes how he learned this the hard way.

In response to this problem, a group of software developers got together in 2001 and formed a community around a concept called agile software development. This represents a radical departure from the waterfall method. Instead of attempting to develop a finished product in the hypothetical environment of a development shop, the idea here is to get a "quick and dirty" version of the product [Ries calls this a minimum viable product (MVP)] in front of the customer as quickly as possible and then use customer feedback to validate and improve the product.

Eric Ries: I was using a bunch of practices in the software world that have a connection to Lean, but I didn't know that at the time. The first Lean-related technique I used was what is called continuous deployment in the software world. This is the flow applied to the deployment of a software product into a production environment. So you're putting it in front of customers as it is being developed.

I could see that these methods worked, but I was having trouble convincing other people that they should give them a try. So I needed to get a better understanding of the why behind this. I read every book I could find about management around process and software—I just wanted to understand what was going on.

Ries started with Taiichi Ohno's book *The Toyota Production System.*[4] Expecting to see a set of techniques, he was surprised and initially disappointed to find that Ohno's approach was a philosophical one.

Eric Ries: I thought I was going to get a book of handy tips. Instead, I'm getting this overarching philosophy of work. I thought I was going to learn about all this Toyota stuff, like I'd read about in the newspaper.

But a few things in that book struck me as so powerful that it inspired me to want to learn more. One was the explanation of the Five Whys. Another was his very philosophical discussion around flow and inventory. As I understand it, he was trying to give people the motivation and the philosophical tools necessary to go out and learn the whole system and maybe reinvent it themselves. Because there's a belief here that you could learn the whole system yourself if you just thought carefully and applied the scientific method.

Those revelations led Ries to *Lean Thinking* by Jim Womack and Dan Jones,[5] and soon he found that Lean gave him a conceptual umbrella for the tools that fit under the banner of agile software development.

He also found that Lean added some new ideas that helped broaden his vision. The idea of reducing batch size—in this case a large investment in developer time that accumulated before the product reached a customer—was particularly powerful.

Eric Ries: The thing that caught my eye at the time was the discussion of batch size and the relationship between speed and quality. I had a lot of batch size–related problems, so this was the first Lean concept that made my life dramatically better. And when people asked why I was doing things this way, I was able to say, "To reduce batch size," and then explain what that meant. Womack really gave me the intellectual foundation to explain what's going on, so that was the first stage of my Lean understanding.

There was, however, an important difference. Lean talks about building production capacity with the assumption that there are willing customers out there. In start-ups, this is not a given.

Eric Ries: What I understand now that I didn't understand at the time was that when Lean was developed, we were coming out of an 80-year period of great stability in which most companies didn't have to worry about what to do with their extra capacity. The demand was there—you just made more.

So the Lean books are pretty silent on this point. Sure, there is maybe one sentence about how Toyota had to figure out the transition from light trucks to consumer products. But for me as a start-up person, that's the whole story. Just that one topic.

So I would say that the second big insight that helped me develop my career and my understanding of Lean was that everything we want do in Lean—pull, responsiveness to demand, production leveling—all applies in a start-up context if you make one adjustment. And this is that you're not pulling from a customer order, because we are operating in a predemand or uncertain demand environment. In other words, we are working with our hypothesis about the customer.

So we're building a learning factory, not just a production factory. And Lean is really good at that, because Lean is already a learning system—even on the production side it is very learning-oriented. So we're taking the same ethos but now applying it to a very different problem in a slightly different way. And that unlocked a lot of good stuff for me, and I made a conscious decision to name what I do Lean start-up—to make the connection between these two communities explicitly.

Learning Culture in the Fast Lane

The key to building a learning factory, of course, is assuring a culture that encourages people to share their knowledge and be open to the ideas of others. Like Meyer and Richards, Ries puts the onus on senior management to create the right environment.

Eric Ries: My feeling is that the culture that you have reflects primarily the philosophy of management in the organization, specifically the accountability systems and processes that we employ. Some people view this as me saying that culture is not important, but that's not right. Culture's incredibly important, but it's driven by the past process decisions that we've made. That's why there's such a tight connection between process and culture.

The cultural differences in start-ups, Ries believes, are similar to the classic silos that can be found in larger organizations:

The classic dysfunction that I see is where people in creative functions—artists, engineers, designers—don't get along with operations people who function very differently. They hate each other. They blame each other for problems.

I often see people who are trying to fix this through HR policies and other cultural interventions. I used to think that the way you solve those problems is the way you solve a political disagreement. You take them all out to dinner together and take them on trust-building exercises and have them get to know each other—have a beer bash. For this kind of problem, however, I've seen that that almost never works.

What does work amazingly effectively is changing the process in which people work. Usually, when you see the wrong behavior, you're seeing a siloed organization with two groups throwing work over the wall in large batches to each other, where the feedback cycle to the end customer is quite long and distant and people can be promoted for doing their function well even if it screws the people downstream from them, etc.

So if you fix the processes, you change the culture, because now you have a framework where people can work in a cross-functional way. A start-up is essentially a dedicated cross-functional team that has a shared mission. When they get into the trenches and do work together and solve a common problem and engage in a conversation, those divisions go away fast.

However, you can't do it in a crude way, such as offering them a bonus to work together. You have to embed it deeply in the organization.

The Lean Start-Up Movement

The big story here is that the Lean start-up concept has sparked the emergence of a global best practice movement. The Lean Startup Circle, an online support community founded in 2009, has over 80,000 members, and hundreds of Lean start-up events are held across North America. Of special note is that many of these events bring investors and entrepreneurs together.

Lean concepts adapt well to the intense learning environment of a start-up, and the Lean start-up concept creates a powerful connection between Lean concepts, entrepreneurship, and innovation.

Start-ups, however, are organizations that have yet to face many of the challenges of a company that is in full-scale production. In that later stage, execution, as opposed to innovation, becomes the primary function of the company and the organization grows to support a much wider range of functions.

Jim Womack, whose writing inspired Ries to embrace Lean concepts, observes the difference between the Lean start-up and the "Lean grow-up":

> Starting up and growing up are two phases necessary for every organization. Lean thinking has traditionally been very strong on the second phase and the Lean startup community is adding important concepts to strengthen the first phase. If managers get these two phases right they will never need a third phase, the organizational rework of starting over.[6]

FROM START-UP TO PRODUCTION

One company currently transitioning from start-up to full-scale production is E-Leather, a manufacturer of leather products made from recycled natural fiber. Founded in 2006 in Peterborough, United Kingdom, the company uses an innovative patented process developed by the late inventor Chris Bevan.

The company's primary markets are seat covers for airplanes, buses, and rail cars. E-Leather's product is lighter and stronger than conventional leather, and the process for fabricating it is more efficient from an environmental standpoint than conventional leather processing. The raw material is small pieces of animal hide that would otherwise be considered scrap and put into landfill.

E-Leather's unique product has been enthusiastically received in the marketplace, and customers, notably three of the world's top five airlines, are eager to increase their volume of orders. Consequently, sales are expected to increase from $24 million in 2013 to $136 million by 2017. This gives the company the dual challenge of managing a steep growth curve and simultaneously developing new products and processes and learning how to expand with the most efficient possible use of resources.

Chris McBean, an executive experienced in large corporate environments such as Unilever, became the company's CEO in 2008. McBean had begun to take an interest in Lean when he realized that the discipline of strategic finance, his business school major, did not address some of the issues he faced as a leader.

> *Chris McBean:* Strategic finance is a fairly well-established framework, I think, to find out what the key value drivers are within the business and the market. From my experience in larger organizations, there's quite a strong skill set around that.
>
> But to me, the missing element in many corporates is, How do you take the best people you've got, put them into a business area, and really ask them to drive performance as aggressively and as ambitiously as they possibly can?

The CEO role at E-Leather presented the ultimate challenge. There was the need to tailor the product for the market and to develop a successful go-to-market strategy. Talent and money had to be used very wisely. McBean felt that Lean thinking would be a key component to rapidly scaling the business:

> The heart of Lean is the whole area of getting the best return on your resources that you can, whether that's time, cash, or whatever. Obviously, when you're a start-up, all those things

are severely limited. Equally, the cash you've got only lasts a certain amount of time. So you need to be clear on what you're not going to do so that you can ensure that what you are going to do gets done in the shortest possible time.

McBean began working with the Kaizen Institute in 2013 to bring a Lean improvement culture into the organization. As Dan Alexander, director of the Kaizen Institute UK, explained, the time pressures would have made a traditional development process too slow:

> They needed to move very rapidly. Traditionally, the technical people, if they project manage in a normal way, will never achieve the timelines that they need to achieve for the growth of the business. The expectation from the customer is that they're going to grow at that rate as well. The demand is there from the airlines—they keep pushing to increase the size of their orders.

The first action was to engage the leadership team in a value stream mapping process. However, as Alexander explained, the start-up nature of the business called for an innovative approach. Instead of using the mapping as a basis for continuous improvement of lead times or incremental growth, the current state was compared with three future states that were based on the expected volume in 2014, 2015, and 2016. In each case, the objective was to deliver the added volume without capital expenditure. This forced the team to take a highly disciplined approach to understanding its assets and planning out its process development.

> *Dan Alexander:* It's not about improving by 15 or 20 percent. It's about improving this year by 40 percent. And the target for next year will be 40 percent.

To address the gaps identified between the current and future states, the teams engaged in a series of *kaizen* workshops and daily *kaizens* to attack the bottlenecks in the processes. The emphasis was on their top priority—increasing output—and the process brought an immediate focus on rapid improvements.

Chris McBean: The use of value stream maps within projects is an excellent approach to bring the team to the same understanding of the process. It's a good motivational tool when people see the importance of their work.

It's very easy to work out how to improve a process by 10 percent, but the real question is, Is it value added in the first place, and can you just find a better way of doing something?

Now in some ways it's easier to introduce Lean in a start-up because you haven't got the years of ingrained customer practice. However, it is often harder to ask the question "Is that really the best we can do?" when it is only 12 months since the previous project was successfully completed. So you've got to still challenge yourself.

As McBean explained, unknowns are part of the landscape in a start-up environment, and working with them is part of the skill set and the culture:

In a start-up situation, you have to balance the uncertainties and be prepared to accept them. If you wait for certainty, you're often going to be too late.

So you really have to work out what information is value added. For instance, if you're looking at a production process and there are five variables, you might look at that and say, "Well, actually these are the three physical criteria, and based on those, we've got to make a go–no go decision in six weeks' time. We accept that there will be risks, but if we're 90 percent sure, we can sort the rest out later."

Engaging Employees

E-Leather has a dedicated group of employees who are passionate about the product, including the engineers who helped develop the prototype process with the inventor. Consequently, there is a culture of true believers who are looking to management to support the company's mission.

> *Chris McBean:* Lots of companies set objectives related to cost, production, capacity, or internal objectives or a mission statement. People sit there wondering if management is really committed to the goals and is willing or able to make things different. In a rapidly growing business people can actually see that there is a real need for change. Improvement goals have to be met to meet customer demand and to anticipate the future. So the good thing is that Lean becomes very real for the team.

In addition to showing commitment, the ubiquity of the *kaizen* process in E-Leather has improved communications and helped flatten the organization.

> *Chris McBean:* As we get our Lean approach up and running, it's clearly improving the morale. Also, it makes the communication far more effective.
>
> Even in businesses this size you end up with one or two layers of management. If you communicate through that, things always get diluted. But if you've got people working on *kaizen* projects, they always get a better view of what's

actually important, and they take that understanding away and apply it to other areas of the business as well.

Improving product performance at E-Leather has special significance because it aligns with the company's mission of providing a sustainable alternative.

Chris McBean: I think sustainable businesses have to be able to outperform the high-impact products that they are replacing, so sustainability has to be built into the business model and how it operates.

Employees consequently have been enthusiastic about taking part in *kaizens* to reduce waste.

Chris McBean: We measure every single batch every single day, so we can tell you what the waste was on every single run, and we can tell you what the reason for that is. The guys look at that on a daily basis to prioritize actions and follow up improvements.

As E-Leather progresses from a start-up to a mature organization, the establishment of a learning culture will remain as long as McBean is in charge.

Chris McBean: I think one of the leadership tasks is to be unprepared to say that's done and always challenge it and ask how we can make things better. Lean helps an organization do that in a constructive style.

CHAPTER 10

❖

INTEGRATING A DIVERSIFIED CORPORATION

For investors seeking to hedge their bets in uncertain times, the diversified corporation—one composed of multiple businesses—is a plausible option. Although there is no safe harbor in a crisis such as the Great Recession of 2009, corporations such as GE, Hitachi, and Siemens have utilized multisector exposure to give their shareholders a reasonable degree of long-term stability.

The best diversifieds, however, are more than portfolios of businesses; they combine the benefits of diversity with economies of scale in areas such as procurement, infrastructure, the supply chain, human resources, and market influence.

These synergies cannot be taken for granted. What is required is the leadership and discipline to apply common standards, alignment, and culture to what would otherwise be a group of separate businesses.

Achieving this kind of cohesion is at the top of the agenda for Mike Lamach, CEO of Ingersoll Rand, a $12 billion diversified industrial. In 2009, the company began a 10-year-plus journey to integrate all of its businesses through a common culture of continuous improvement.

Ingersoll Rand was founded by Simon Ingersoll in 1871 as the Ingersoll Rock Drilling Company. The company grew over time through innovation and acquisitions, developing a range of products and services that included drills, pumps, compressors, industrial tools, door locks, road construction, and domestic and industrial climate control equipment.

In the early 2000s, the company was composed of 10 divisions that ran more or less autonomously. Although the businesses had high-performing brands such as Thermo King climate control systems for trucks and ARO industrial equipment, the company as a whole suffered from low margins and inconsistency and was considered average at best among its peers.

In 2007, the corporation undertook a series of major transactions to strengthen its focus on climate control products, industrial equipment, and security. Nonrelated businesses, including road development and heavy machinery, were sold off, and in 2008 Ingersoll Rand acquired the heating, air-conditioning, and controls manufacturer Trane, effectively doubling the size of the company.

Lamach, who had joined Ingersoll Rand in 2004, became Trane's new president, migrating from his previous role as president of Ingersoll Rand's security and safety sector, a division that was spun off as a separate company in 2013.

Lamach came to Ingersoll Rand as a strong Lean advocate. He had discovered Lean as a young engineer in the late 1980s when his employer, Johnson Controls Inc. (JCI), entered into a supplier agreement with Toyota's Georgetown, Kentucky, plant. Through that relationship, JCI worked with Toyota's Lean senseis to develop its capabilities for delivering Just-in-Time.

Lamach considers continuous improvement essential for any company and regards Lean as the most straightforward way to develop it.

> *Mike Lamach:* I can't imagine anybody not having a continuous improvement culture or process inside his or her company. Lean's not the only way to do this, but I think it's the

simplest. It's the simplest way to look directly at a line of sight to the customer and to rally people around that customer experience.

In 2009, seven months after his appointment at Trane, Lamach became Ingersoll Rand's chief operating officer and the designated successor of the soon-to-retire CEO, Herbert L. Henkel. He then set out to integrate Trane with the larger Ingersoll Rand organization and lay out a strategy to transform Ingersoll Rand into an integrated, premier-performing company.

Then came the recession of 2009. With his appointment as CEO pending, Lamach now had two priorities: weather the crisis and set a long-term strategic agenda.

Mike Lamach: It was quite a stressful time. You can imagine the timing of the Trane acquisition at $10 billion and the financing to do that, which was a bridge loan that actually came due in April 2009.

So first we needed to get through the 2009 crisis, and we did, of course—obviously it was very successful. Then there was a long-term view, which meant building a strategy that I would have a decade to implement across the business. The view was that it would take that long to make it something that was truly sustainable.

As Lamach started to look beyond Trane to the larger organization, he saw both challenges and opportunities:

My job initially was to integrate Trane into Ingersoll Rand. What I realized was that there wasn't a lot in Ingersoll Rand that you could bolt into. There wasn't an operating system or a common way in which we did things across the company or common best ways of doing things.

So there was a lot of waste and a lot of opportunity that we could go after, both functionally and from a corporate support standpoint. For example, sourcing across the company was in tiny pockets, and so there was no economy of scale there. Of course, one of the big opportunities in a large, diversified international company, particularly where there are businesses that have a lot in common, is that you would harness that scale.

Lamach believed the company needed a common operating system that would bind the organization through shared policies and procedures:

It was about creating standard work across the company. That would include everything from the way we do organizational design to specifics about decision rights and how individual decisions are made across the company. And then all the way down through how a production system would actually operate and how we would look at continuous improvement in each one of our plants.

Although we expected that the details and the tactics would be different in each division, the standard operating system would ensure that we were integrating the company together and using the best-known way to make things happen across the company. Having everybody, at a minimum, working from that standard would provide a common denominator that we could continuously improve on over time.

The executive team set a vision of what a premier-performing Ingersoll Rand might look like 10 years down the road. The determination of common goals and objectives was key to the integration strategy.

Mike Lamach: We had identified the benefits early on— what we referred to as premier performance in the eyes of our customers, our shareholders, and our employees. In other words, what did winning look like, and what would a top-quartile company look like over long periods of time with each of those three constituents?

The management team selected 16 corporations in the diversified industrial sector and then established a set of metrics that could be used for comparisons with companies in that peer group. The metrics fell into three categories:

- *Shareholder metrics*, such as earnings per share growth and long-term shareholder return
- *Customer metrics*, such as market share and margins
- *Employee metrics*, such as employee engagement and retention

The engine for driving performance against these metrics was called Operational Excellence, which was based on Lean methodology.

Mike Lamach: We set up a strategy in early 2009 to achieve top-quartile performance in all areas for the long haul. As a backdrop to that, Operational Excellence was one of the core areas that we had decided were critical to the company. Behind that, the creation of an operating system with Lean as its foundation was what we chose as the continuous improvement methodology that we would use across the company.

When Lamach assumed the CEO role in 2010, he reorganized the company to allow better collaboration between the different businesses. This included the creation of key centralized positions, including senior vice president for global operations and integrated supply chain, for which he brought in Todd Wyman, a veteran from GE.

The company also began recruiting talent to build a cohesive management team.

> *Mike Lamach:* We had to set expectations, and we also had to make sure we had the right talent in the company. There was quite an effort to get the right people in place who were coaches and leaders who were comfortable working in an operating system and with what we were trying to achieve culturally across the whole company.

A new hire tasked with leading the Operational Excellence strategy was Lean veteran Dan McDonnell, who, like Wyman, came from GE. As McDonnell notes, this was not a typical Lean assignment:

> One of the exciting things about coming here and helping the company is that Mike was insistent that this was going to be a total enterprise transformation, not just the manufacturing parts of our company. While we ended up deciding that our primary approach was to begin the restructuring of the company into true, horizontal end-to-end value stream flow, we also were mindful that we were going to Lean out all of the functional support activities that weren't necessary directly in the horizontals but are there for support. So the long-term intent was to apply Lean to every process in the organization.

Beginning the Journey

Introducing a continuous improvement culture in a company with 50,000 employees was a daunting proposition. By contrast, Toyota was roughly one-tenth that size when it began its Lean journey.

> *Dan McDonnell:* While there were pockets of Lean—this company, just like every other company over the last 25 years, had engaged in a lot of improvement activities—we

were pretty well starting from scratch, and I think we all have acknowledged that. So the real question we faced early on was, How would you even start beginning to think about Leaning out what was at the time a $14 billion global company prior to spinning off the security part of the business?

Because the company had little Lean expertise beyond its executive leadership team, it contracted with Simpler, a Lean consulting firm experienced in working with large corporations, to assist in the planning and training processes as the company hired and developed its own internal talent.

The first step was to develop a goal deployment process. The team chose the traditional *hoshin kanri* format used by Toyota and embarked on a six-month strategy-planning process. In the tradition of Byrne and Koenigsaecker, Lamach insisted on aggressive targets.

Dan McDonnell: Mike had a goal to get to 15 points of operating income, which is a massive improvement for a big company like ours. It was almost doubling our operating income. So that became part of the vision, and it became part of our targets. We certainly weren't planning to do that in the year but over a three- to five-year period.

As a result, many of our initiatives have been linked to our main mission to continuously drive an improvement every year in our operating income percentage and to try to drive our margins up to top-quartile levels. I think if you look at our progress on operating income percentage, it's been nothing but remarkable for four straight years.

Building Momentum for Value Stream Adoption

The journey was divided into two major components. There was the technical side, which included activities such as setting standard work and building to *takt* time, and the social or people side, which involved the development of people and the transition to a Lean culture. Of the two, according to McDonnell, the social side was what the leadership team considered more important and consequently where it focused most of its attention.

Under the new structure, value streams became the framework for deploying improvement activity that would drive business unit performance toward the goals established in the *hoshin kanri* process.

> *Mike Lamach:* We had a disciplined approach to doing value stream mapping and for how we conducted a transformation plan within a value stream. We followed the idea of doubling the good and halving the bad every time we attacked the value stream, something George Koenigsaecker talks about.
>
> We used a combination of rapid improvement events, JDIs, or "just do its" as we called them, and projects that we'd schedule out over the course of a year to go attack the value stream where we saw the most opportunity, which usually meant the most waste.
>
> So typically, a value stream, if it was a product value stream, might be looking to reduce cycle time in half. So we would put together a series of projects, events, and just do its that would be targeted and measurable toward reducing the cycle time to 50 percent of the starting point. In the second year, we would cut it in half again.

To ensure consistent results, the team adopted an approach called inch wide—mile deep. Instead of taking on an entire value stream, the teams would focus on a slice of it where they could have the highest chance of success and then, on the basis of their success, expand the activity into a larger section of the value stream.

Dan McDonnell: What Mike wanted us to do was focus on a smaller chunk of scope and go really, really deep, and get it right, and create goodness, and earn the right to expand. What we've done with every value stream is first scope it with the executive team that operates it by deciding where the starting point of the transformation is going to be and where the ending point is.

The company also set standards for the resources each value stream would have to invest to be part of the transformation program.

Mike Lamach: While we were building our human capability to coach and implement Lean, we had to go a little slower. Initially, we started with 4 value streams, and it went from 16 on to 19, and finally it became apparent that this wasn't really about the number of value streams; it was the percentage of the business in transformation, based on cost of goods sold.

So through last year we got to 40 percent, and this year we'll reach 60 percent. What that means is that for a designated value stream, there is standard work being applied and a scope of improvement activity specific to a particular product line or service.

In each value stream, we would have a value stream leader and a value stream coach, and we would designate between 1 percent initially and 2 percent ultimately of the employees covered in a value stream to be full-time dedicated to the value stream efforts. So if a value stream had 1,000 people, they had to be willing to commit 10 people full-time and within a short period go to 20 people. We used that as a requirement to get started.

The big surprise was that once the early adopters began to post their results, other business units were eager to get on board with the transformation. The Lean support team soon found it had a waiting list.

> *Mike Lamach:* The results were so differentiated compared to non-value-stream work that we had a phenomenon that I've never seen happen before in my 30 years of corporate experience, which was that we had all these businesses and leaders calling on us to move faster so that they could become a value stream quicker.
>
> We were in the enviable position of holding people off until we were sure the value streams we started were taking root and we were continuing to get that differentiated result. So we kept demand very high, making sure the quality of the results was so differentiated from what was happening elsewhere that it was almost like the operating system came with a warranty.
>
> Today, we can tell our leaders that if they commit the people, the resources, the talent, and the energy to this and if they follow the operating methodology around the transformation plan, the results they get will be substantially better than the results they're getting today in the business.
>
> At the same time, we've been resisting the urge to go too fast and to somehow dilute the results or to make this somehow less effective. We want to avoid doing that.

Building Engagement Around Customer Value

The customer-centric structure of value streams has brought a strong focus on the customer experience that all employees in the value stream share. As a result, employee engagement is improving dramatically in the designated value streams.

Mike Lamach: Our work with Lean in the value streams is absolutely focused on the customer and the customer's experience across every element of delivery. So it becomes a very customer-centric model. What I've found is that employees really do get charged up about customer satisfaction and around serving customers. There's something special inside the culture, at least in our company, where customer alignment and empathy for customers have always been strong.

So when you're communicating about improving the customer experience, you're talking to a very receptive organization. That's the first thing that I think binds the whole company.

A crucial part of the transformation is the change in the relationship between workers and managers. The real job of managers in a value stream is to help the workers who are creating value serve their common boss, the customer.

Mike Lamach: We try to invert the hierarchy of the company, and that becomes the job of leaders. I personally spent a large part of the early years out in the organization, participating in rapid improvement events, seeing what was happening where the work was being done, and asking our people what we could do to help them perform better.

So it's more of a servant-leadership model where leaders really become servants to the organization, helping people become more effective in their work. As a result of going and seeing, asking, and listening, organizational leaders at all levels are put into a problem-solving mode.

So their work is about removing roadblocks and barriers for employees in the organization. This can range from a short-term countermeasure to get production back up and running all the way back through a long-term countermeasure to prevent a problem from recurring. The more momentum you can get around problem solving, both temporary and permanent, the more excitement you get from the employees about being a part of that.

What workers are seeing is leaders who listen to the people who know best how to improve the process and are then accountable for making those changes happen. That accountability goes all the way to me.

So we've inverted the hierarchy, and I think that's why employee engagement has gone up so high.

Competencies to Support the Inverted Hierarchy

The servant-leader model frequently puts managers on the line to solve problems on the spot. This calls for exceptional problem-solving skills, an area where a major gap was identified. An extensive problem-solving course was the first major training program that Ingersoll Rand developed internally.

Dan McDonnell: We felt we were not strong on problem-solving capabilities, and we knew that in order to get to premier performance we had to build a real culture of capable problem solvers everywhere in the company. Rather than try to invent something, we adopted Toyota's eight-step process.

The one exception there was that there was no activity of reflection built into it. The reason, we were told by some ex-Toyota people we had hired, is that reflection is so ingrained in the thinking of a person in Toyota that they didn't have it as a stand-alone step. But we felt that in our early maturity we needed people to really reflect at the end of a problem solving or the end of a *kaizen* on what went well, what didn't go well, what was learned, or what could be done differently next time. So we added a ninth reflection step to Toyota's eight steps, and we call it the nine-step process.

The wider and more difficult challenge, however, is showing respect for people. Lack of respect, a legacy of the top-down approach to management, is difficult to eradicate and a matter of ongoing concern for the senior leadership team.

Dan McDonnell: In our new leadership competency model, one of the ways we are trying to develop leaders is to create more of what we call servant leadership versus autocratic, dictatorial leadership. A key is always showing respect for people, which we know is one of the pillars of the Toyota Production System principles. Mike thinks a lot about respect for people, and he expects us, from his senior vice presidents to his team leaders, to treat people with respect every time we interact with them.

This is not easy. People treat each other reasonably well here, but still, there are times where leaders behave inappropriately. We need to help them change.

McDonnell recalls a particular incident. He and Lamach were observing a *gemba* walk and watched while a group leader reported some production results to a supervisor. When asked about outstanding safety and quality issues, the leader expressed concern that both could be in jeopardy because she was short staffed and was relying on insufficiently trained workers. The supervisor ignored her answers and moved on to the next question. That had a profound effect on Lamach.

Dan McDonnell: This was probably the most upset I've seen Mike since I've been here. He just could not believe the sheer and utter disrespect that supervisor showed for that hourly team leader. And this was going on in one of our model value streams!

On the plane ride back, we had many conversations about showing people respect and how we as leaders need to stand up to this kind of negative behavior and how we need to coach people to behave differently.

This is something that's very, very important to our future. We know this stuff goes on every minute of the day around the world. Just because we're not there to see it doesn't mean it's not happening, and we need to change that. This is on our mind as we proceed on our journey—how leaders behave and treat the people who work for them.

The company is constantly exploring ways to improve in this area. One of the more recent additions to the training curriculum, which is currently being piloted, is an 11-week team leader development program that includes 20 percent classroom work, 70 percent on-the-job coaching, and 10 percent reflection. At the graduation ceremony, McDonnell recalls, some audience members had tears in their eyes as graduates reported how the course had changed not only their work but their personal lives.

Dan McDonnell: Forget the processes and stuff like that. What we're really trying to do here is change our people and help them lead better lives for themselves both inside and outside of work. We believe if we can do that, they are going to help our company become great. They are the ones who are going to improve our processes.

The Road to Premier Performance

As the journey progresses, the senior management team tracks progress against the 11 metrics established at the beginning of the journey.

Mike Lamach: We do a quarterly benchmark call with the top 1,000 leaders in the company, and we take 16 other integrated companies, many of which are competitors, and benchmark our performance versus theirs. We've done this now for 21 quarters in a row.

As with many Lean transformations, the company has improved its free cash flow and working capital positions, achieving top-quartile performance. The added efficiency is helping the company progress toward the longer-term goals of margin expansion and market share, which have been moving steadily upward.

What's particularly exciting for the leadership team is that the improvements are being driven by the value streams currently under transformation.

Mike Lamach: When we look at the 40 percent going to 60 percent under transformation, the lion's share of that is seeing margin expansion, market share growth, and employee engagement that are greater than the average across the company. That all contributes to moving the needle from a shareholder perspective where, over any multiycar period in the last five years, we've seen total shareholder return and earnings per share growth in top-quartile performance over that five-year period.

This frees managers who have signed on to the transformation to focus their attention on improvement as opposed to second-guessing how their performance might be perceived.

Mike Lamach: One of our larger businesses was making a tremendous amount of product investment, yet employees in the organization didn't feel that we were winning with customers and that we were going to grow. What's nice about this is that we were able to say from experience and with confidence,

"Stick to the journey on Lean. Let's get our cycle times to be faster than the competition. As a result, quality will get better. We'll take waste out, which may result in being able to reduce cost and potentially reduce price while still growing margins."

So there have been a number of businesses where we've been at it long enough now, for three years in the case I'm thinking about, where you can see the progression of working capital improvement and then operating margins improvement and, simultaneously along with that, employee engagement improvement.

We don't have to look past the results, because we're seeing top-quartile performance against our peer group in the public report information and data that we're targeting. That creates, I think, a sense of accomplishment but also a sense of sustainment that this is working. Leaders in the company can count on that to continue to differentiate ourselves against the competition. And if you do that over a long, long period of time at the same level, that's how you create a Danaher or a Toyota.

The positive financial results are beneficial to employees as well.

Mike Lamach: When you're growing share and growing margins, it creates more investment, more development hours to be spent on people, more opportunity to promote people. We promote hourly employees into 1 percent operational excellence change agents, and we've even promoted some value stream coaches to plant management. There's a bit of a virtuous cycle that we've created, a way of getting exposed to the best talent in the company and creating paths for hourly employees to progress and grow within the company as well.

And regarding job security, when you're growing share and margins and shortening supply chain cycles, you're making competition and foreign competition less relevant. So again, when the value streams have been successful, the productivity has not come from the reduction of jobs; it's come from growth and from margin expansion, where employment has actually increased or worst case fell flat at a time when we might've been going the other way. So it's been a bit of a job security proof to our people as well.

Leading by Example

Unlike many CEOs in conventionally run companies, Lamach doesn't have to rely on briefs and reports to find out what's happening in the workplace. As the value streams continue to drive superior results, he continues to spend much of his time out in the plants and in other transactional parts of the value streams (engineering, product management, sales, service, and support) where value is being created, participating in *gemba* walks, asking questions, and checking in on improvement activities.

Seeing their CEO on the shop floor and in the value-creating areas of the offices, actually participating in the work, Lamach believes, sends a strong message about where the company is headed:

> You have to match your own behavior with what you're trying to do. For me, one of the most critical things when we began to implement Lean and value stream mapping across the company was to make sure that whatever I was doing, I had blocked out the time to be able to travel, go and see, and participate in weeklong events with the hourly workforce: right there, tearing apart the product and putting it back together, looking at the tooling, doing the work, and seeing them and listening to them with regard to their ideas to improve the process.
>
> It doesn't take very long when you're the CEO doing that to see other people understand that that's what they should be

doing too. Then they realize they're having a lot of fun doing it. This is really important, because Lean doesn't work if it's not authentic—if people aren't really enjoying it and seeing how powerful it is.

From my perspective, there's nothing better than walking into a plant two or three years after a rapid improvement event, knowing the hourly team members by name, asking them how they're doing, and mentioning something that's important to them or their families. And then following up on where we stand with regard to the improvements that were put in place and discussing what ideas they have to take it to the next level.

Although the transformation is off to a good start, Lamach acknowledges that it will take many years of consistent progress to make Ingersoll Rand a great company. In 2019, however, he hopes to have reached a critical milestone: the point where the journey the company embarked on has become sustainable and irreversible.

Mike Lamach: I really want to be able to look back over a 10-year period and have those top-quartile employee, customer, and shareholder results. My feeling at the beginning was that if you could do it over a decade, you'd be putting something in place that wouldn't get thrown away in the next turn of leadership. It's something that after 10 years becomes the fabric of the company.

We have a goal deployment system, we have an operating system, we have a transformation methodology, we have a way of reporting on progress, and we have a way to do problem solving across the company. It feels like after 10 years it's going to be a sustainable culture inside the company.

CHAPTER 11

❖

REDUCING DEPENDENCE ON THE CEO

The owner-operator CEO is the classic business hero who on any given day may be found solving production problems, negotiating with suppliers, dealing with government, sorting out personnel issues, getting the roof fixed, or, of course, personally handling customer complaints.

In many companies led by wearers of multiple hats, the CEO *is* the management system. The dilemma here is that much of the company's success may depend on the leader's unique knowledge, talents, and relationships. When the job gets too big even for a larger-than-life CEO, the danger, to cite a phrase popularized in Michael Gerber's book *The E-Myth Revisited*,[1] is that management by delegation can become management by abdication.

Lean offers some interesting perspectives here. First of all, Lean provides a disciplined structure that allows an organization to focus resources on measurable customer-oriented goals, essentially codifying what has made the company successful. Because Lean creates a continuous improvement environment where all employees are asked for input on decisions, the Lean journey allows the CEO to naturally evolve from reactive day-to-day decision maker to proactive teacher, coach, and strategist.

There is a major caveat, though. For Lean to fit in this kind of organization, the CEO has to believe in the same values that Lean thinking promotes. This turned out to be very much the case for Karl Wadensten, the CEO of Vibco Vibrators Inc.

Vibco manufactures vibration equipment for construction and industrial applications in its 50,000-square-foot facility in Wyoming, Rhode Island. The company was founded in 1962 by Wadensten's father, Theodore, an immigrant from Sweden who invented and patented a vibration product suitable for the U.S. market.

Karl Wadensten, who took over Vibco in 1994, had run the company in a manner that was, by his description, somewhat chaotic but fairly typical of small to medium-size North American manufacturers. However, as the business grew and faced tougher competition from overseas, he knew that the status quo was not sustainable. A particular event pushed him over the edge.

Karl Wadensten: In 2001, I was at home, sick with bronchitis, which is very unusual for me—I normally go to work no matter what. So I got a call from Giovanni, one of our customer service reps, who said, "Karl, I have a grown man who's actually crying on the other end of the phone." The customer was a distributor who was supplying our vibrators for a large bridge project in Florida. You can't pour concrete without vibration, and this was the third Friday where we had missed the delivery date. He was afraid he was going to lose his job.

So I got out of bed and drove in. We have a shortened workday on Fridays, so I told people, "Call whoever you can and get them back to the factory. We need to get the facts and get an assessment of what's going on and how we can help this guy." Everybody came back; we worked like crazy on this order, actually held the UPS airplane for a half hour, and were able to ship the whole order.

When we did a postmortem, we found out that the sequencing of the order was all screwed up. Some departments had some things done; they were waiting on other departments that didn't have things done. The communication was a hodgepodge.

We had worked like crazy to complete this impossible task of getting the order shipped, but we couldn't really celebrate, because we had let the same guy down three times previously. As a company, we didn't understand the true voice of what the customer wanted and how important we were in the bigger scheme of things.

That Monday morning, when I drove into work, I had an epiphany and said, "Is this the kind of organization that I want to run? Is this the strategy that will make us a viable company for the long run? Am I serving my people and our customers with the respect that I would want?"

I think we weren't unlike most American corporations. We were fat and happy, and we kind of did things at our own pace. We would tout that we could do anything, but we really didn't know what *anything* meant, how much people valued our promise.

At first, I thought it was a production control problem. But on further reflection, I realized that the problem was our whole organization. All of us were rowing in the wrong direction. We didn't understand anything about anything.

I figured that if I hired a super-duper production system guy, he could figure it out. So I put in an ad and got a whole bunch of résumés, and they were so-so. So I asked a friend from a nearby factory who also had an ad and asked him how he had done. I remember the conversation. I was calling him at home from my kitchen.

"What did you do, Max?"

"I hired a Lean guy."

"What the heck is that?"

And Max went into this whole conversation about Lean at a basic high level. I realized this was exactly what I needed. As it happened, an associate of the guy Max had hired had also applied for that job, so I was able to get that individual to come to Vibco.

The key to Vibco's market is speed, and Wadensten knew that if he could establish better control over his processes, he could beat his overseas competitors on lead time and hold his own in the market. Because of Vibco's varied product line, maintaining inventory was not a viable option; the company would have to develop the ability to fulfill orders quickly on demand, and this was going to require extraordinary agility.

Wadensten cites two key stages in Vibco's Lean journey that helped achieve this: the initial creation of one-piece flow and the addition of Single-Minute Exchange of Dies (SMED), which allowed them to shrink batch sizes and manufacture to customer demand.

The Lean expert Wadensten had hired, Dan Donovan, began by gathering facts about Vibco's products and processes and breaking everything into small manageable components. Products were divided into families, and big batches were broken down.

The experience was daunting at first, but as the employees started to see improvement, Lean thinking caught on quickly.

Karl Wadensten: At the beginning, Dan was working on the idea of single-piece flow, and we were using the comparison with Snap-On Tools. I said, "We don't have the budget of Snap-On, we don't have the number of engineers that Snap-On has, we don't make the number of pieces they make. How's this going to work here?" That was the first no-no. If you start saying that, it's a self-fulfilling prophecy. You have to believe and then start chipping away at the future state piece by piece.

So Dan began breaking things down in families, gathering facts, and identifying the steps we could take to get standardization and predictability. For the first year, he held classes here and taught everybody, and we all started reading books, and we did *kaizens* all over in the shop. I attended every class and every *kaizen*. I could not get enough. Our people were firing on all cylinders.

I was so excited about all this that I had to temper myself down. I was out on the shop floor, crawling around, ripping things down. I realized that I had to step back to give everybody else a chance and do more listening and more supporting and let people break rules.

As batch production was replaced by single-piece flow, lead times started to improve and machine and employee hours were freed up. The introduction of SMED, however, allowed the most dramatic changes to take place.

Karl Wadensten: Before SMED, we were very inflexible in our machining area—we were very batch-oriented, we were very long setup time, all kinds of stupid things. I kept pounding on these guys before I knew about SMED, saying, "Guys, this isn't working. We have to do something different." I didn't know how to break down the problem, but they kept saying, "What do you want us to do?" I said, "I don't know, but this isn't working." We had an enemy of batches but did not know how to attack it.

SMED was a breakthrough for all of us, and we turned it into a huge collaborative effort. We didn't just involve the machine shop—we had office people, customer support reps, the front reception desk, assemblers, and shipping all involved in the SMEDs. What that gave us was that new set of eyes, that learning to see, that curiosity, that noninhibited ability to ask questions that might not normally be spoken in a meeting. We were questioning process everywhere in our organization.

Everybody could see the results. The machining area went from 40 or 50 jobs to 400 or 500. That's a 1,000 percent increase. It shocked us. Now all of a sudden it opened up everybody downstream to do more things, and everybody wanted to be a part of these teams.

The overall impact of the first two years of Vibco's Lean journey was dramatic. Setup time on automated machining centers was reduced from 2.5 hours to 10 minutes, productivity in selected work cells increased as much as 300 percent, and on-time delivery increased to 99 percent.

Encouraged by the improved capability, Wadensten introduced a new mantra: same day–next day. This means that it has become a companywide standard to build customer orders within 24 hours and ship within 48 hours. Everybody in the company understands and lives by this requirement.

Production results, however, are only part of the picture. As Linda Kleineberg, marketing and business strategist for Vibco, explains, Vibco had become a different kind of place to work:

> One of the key things that SMED did, more than any other Lean activity, was break down the internal silos here so that people from wherever in the building, whether it's front of the office, back of the office, machine shop assembly, reception, customer support, started talking to each other about process. The entire organization learned how to look at process together. All the silos disappeared. That was a really profound change.

For example, we would videotape a process in the machine shop, and then a cross-functional group would watch the videotape. People were collaborating in ways that I didn't think would ever happen. It's always been a family business where people know each other, but they hadn't worked together on process before.

That's now the heart of our Vibco Production System. Anyone can solve problems, find facts, and talk about process. That's our legacy.

Firm Leadership with a Questioning Attitude

The rapid progress of Lean at Vibco makes it all look easy in hindsight, but in some respects the challenges were just beginning. Lean is not a "set it and forget it" management system but one that requires constant and intensive maintenance.

Karl Wadensten: This is not for the weak of heart. This is so hard every single doggone day. Lean will surface all of your shortcomings and force you to deal with all the details.

To keep the energy and the excitement, the newness, the freshness, you have to commit to a very intensive role as leader. At the beginning, you can do all the *kaizens* you want on the floor and you can see some great results, but when you get deep into Lean, you're doing operational things behind the scenes that no one sees. That's where you need to be really persistent and show people how these points affect the outcome.

One of the most difficult aspects of this, says Wadensten, is that a large order or an unusual circumstance can throw the whole system out of whack and cause employees to get discouraged.

Karl Wadenstein: I often say that Lean flow is very fragile and everybody has to work hard to support the systems that make it possible. When our systems start to break down, things deteriorate very quickly. This happened to us six or eight weeks ago.

When we get out of balance, we all of a sudden watch our machine shop hours spike. Then assemblers are waiting for pieces, and then more yellows start showing up on the board, and people can't do the job they need to do. Then the call center starts asking about orders. "What happened? We were doing so well." Then everybody gets really, really frustrated.

It's as if you're at the top of a mountain, and then, all of a sudden, things change in the world and you're in a batting slump. It happens with professional ballplayers. They get in a batting slump. How do you get out of a batting slump? Do you stay there and your career is done? Or do you go back to your strengths?

This is why I'm out on the floor all the time, trying to help people play to the strengths that got us to where we are. We have a choir of people to support, challenge, and reflect with. I say, "In times of stress, look to your choir—people who call it like they see it constructively."

One of the toughest parts of being a coach, Wadensten says, is achieving a balance between constantly questioning and coming across as a confident leader:

Most leaders have to hold their questions, their doubts, their insecurities, and their feelings to themselves, because leaders feel that's an Achilles' heel that could potentially come back and bite them. You want to be open about admitting what you don't know, but at the same time, you don't want to show weakness.

So showing your human side to people and asking questions and not knowing the answers is a hard thing for any leader to do, because at the end of the day you're the one who has to be the last one in the lifeboat, you have to be the last one to leave, you have to be the Rock of Gibraltar for everyone. Balancing those two is really where true collaboration begins, and you're able to make great things happen.

Learning Is a Two-Way Street

Like many Lean CEOs, Wadensten has become a passionate advocate and role model for Lean. As an active member of the Young Presidents' Organization, Wadensten is in touch with hundreds of CEOs who have faced challenges similar to what he experienced at Vibco. He also sits on the Rhode Island Economic Development Corporation's (EDC) board of directors, hosts a radio show, and is a frequent speaker at events in the Lean community.

Perhaps most important, Wadensten frequently leads *gemba* walks in Vibco's plant. Companies, he says, eventually find themselves in a position where they need to change, as he did in 2001:

I think that every organization has a defining moment where what's working for it stops working. They typically go and pick up a book and start questioning the competency of their people. But it is their process that they should question. We've become pretty well known on account of our culture and the way that we work as a team, so lots of companies want to see what that's all about.

Getting to that tipping point, however, can take years. Ironically, the CEO who had introduced Wadensten to Lean abandoned his own Lean journey only to regret it eight years later. Another acted only when he got a very ominous warning while on a trip to China.

Karl Wadensten: He had made a trip to China to visit a company that he was outsourcing some work to, and he was given a tour of this huge factory—we're talking 1 million square feet—and they were going on and on about how they could make anything he wanted.

Then they brought him into a big showroom where they were displaying lines of his competitors' products, and they said, "We make all these products here. We can do the same for you." And then they opened up this secret curtain—sort of like a game show—and there was his complete product line.

"We can do all this cheaper and faster than you can," they said. "Why do you even need a factory?"

Can you imagine being in China, a CEO, and seeing this gargantuan factory and seeing your own product line behind the curtain? Of course, the unspoken part is that these guys could steal his market. That woke him up, but it still took him a long time to get the point where he was ready to make some major changes.

Wadensten now requires that all visiting companies bring their CEOs. Otherwise, he says, there will never be the commitment required for the level of hard work that Lean requires.

The company has hosted some 6,500 visitors in the last three years. Though demanding, the experience is also highly validating and energizing, and Wadensten is proud of the fact that his people aren't afraid to listen to and follow advice from visitors:

Our employees get enormously motivated by the tours. These are people they wouldn't normally interact with—we're talking public figures, presidents of companies, top level. Now these people are sitting and listening to every single word that they have to say. This creates validation for them and builds their curiosity and their confidence to question the status quo.

The learning is also a two-way street. Our visitors are encouraged to make suggestions, and our employees aren't afraid to jump on them. Sometimes when we're doing a debrief at the end of the visit, one of our employees from the shop floor will run into the room and say, "Come back out here; look what I did in the short time that you were gone. I really appreciated what you said; it was valuable, and look how we acted on it. It got me thinking."

Wadensten hopes that a growing Lean community will ultimately lead to a better quality of life for everybody:

I don't care if you're in North America or in India, Europe, or South America—there's enough business and enough opportunity for everybody to develop their people and achieve operational excellence. I can't imagine what the world would look like with everybody practicing operational excellence and respect for people. It could be a game changer for society and eliminate waste on a global scale. We may even find a new axis for the world to spin on.

Jumping to Five Times the Capacity

Sometimes the defining moment for needing a management system comes when the CEO takes the business to a new level. That was the case for Supremia Grup, a producer of food ingredients based in Alba Iulia, Romania.

The company, which was founded in 2000 by the current CEO, Hugo Levente Bara, grew rapidly in its first 10 years of operation to become Romania's largest food ingredient producer. Bara was involved in all aspects of the business, including the design of the plant and the equipment, day-to-day operations, and sales and marketing.

In 2011, Supremia opened a new facility to enable the company to establish a leadership role in the European Union. With seven times the floor space, a new generation of equipment, and double the number of employees, Bara began to look for a management system that reflected the values in which he believed.

Hugo Levente Bara: We were adopting new technology and preparing to build a new facility to give us five times the production capacity we had had previously. To help us make these changes, I was looking for a new management system to run the entire company.

Bara first saw Lean when he toured a nearby Bosch factory, followed by a presentation about the Bosch Production System, which is based on the Toyota Production System. After the visit, a colleague gave him a copy of Masaaki Imai's book *Gemba Kaizen*,[2] which convinced him that this was the management system he was looking for.

Hugo Levente Bara: This management system was very much a reflection of the things I believe in. Ideas like 5S, employee input, continuous improvement, standardization, and all these things. I practiced them before, but it was intuitive—I didn't have a professional management system to support this. So the book really felt right to me. It was not strange or unusual.

After several conversations, the company engaged Kaizen Institute Romania to help it launch its Lean transformation. Working with country manager Julien Bratu, the team employed a method called *kaizen* by harmony, which provides a holistic approach to unifying strategic and operational considerations and allows the development of both the individual and the organization.

The teams then moved on to a two-day *hoshin kanri* process that established key performance indicators and codified them into a system of *kaizen* scorecards. Then, through a combination of internal and external training exercises, basic Lean skills were rolled out to the entire workforce, covering areas such as 5S, the Seven Wastes, visual management, and standard work.

Work began immediately on improving equipment layouts to reduce walking and transport times, minimize interruptions, and improve safety. One hundred sixty-one work standards were created in this early stage, and most important, workers became aware of waste and how it can be removed from processes.

> *Hugo Levente Bara:* I think that the biggest change for workers was learning what is value and what is waste. When you move up or down, to the left or right, or you pick something up, you have to think, "Is this added value or is this waste?" After one and a half or two years, people become much more conscious of this—they actually become tired of waste, which has no value and doesn't do anybody any good.

With basic skills in place, the teams moved on to a series of value stream mapping exercises that provided a strategic framework for *kaizens*, and employee suggestions began to pour in. After six months, a company survey found that one idea per employee had been submitted over a three-month period.

> *Hugo Levente Bara:* The majority of our employees contribute ideas, and I am sure that soon it will be 100 percent. Also, the

number of suggestions doubled this year. We are also getting a lot of participation in our companywide meetings.

A lot of our suggestions are around reducing lead times or avoiding mistakes. One of the nice things that are happening is that people get together in the lunchroom and collaborate on ideas.

We have an award for best idea of the month, and from those, we choose the best idea of the year. We give prizes for these, and the whole exercise makes people feel that they are part of the system, not just robots.

Bara maintains a hands-on approach, maintaining a balance between leading and empowering:

I am the kind of person who has to know the process and see the process. I teach my managers to watch the processes and find improvements in every area. I participate every morning in the 9:00 meetings, where managers report on the activities of the previous day—quality problems and so on.

I am there, but in reserve—more like a peer. Of course in time, my management team will become more and more mature, and they will understand the whole thing better. It's very important for the management team to be able to lead the people.

The results on the shop floor were impressive. The lead time for ingredient preparation, a critical metric in the food industry, dropped 30 percent. The distance traveled by operators was cut in half. Unnecessary processes were eliminated.

As the company began to establish flow in the internal operations, Bara started to take action to involve his supply chain.

Hugo Levente Bara: At Supremia, we have three flows. We have an incoming flow from suppliers, we have internal flow, and we have external flow out to our customers. So we operate the company always looking at these three flows. They have to be interconnected.

Recently I had to fire a commercial manager who didn't think *kaizen* and flow had anything to do with him. Everybody in the company has to be part of this; otherwise you don't get the correct orders, and this upsets the production system. The timing has to be right. It's our job to teach our customers how to work with us as a team. Then you can build up the volume of orders. If you say you have nothing to do with this, then you are working at cross-purposes, and this is not good.

We now have the system up and running, and our customers and suppliers are coming on board and want to bring flow into their own processes. Every month we invite customers and suppliers to visit us, and people get very excited. This is similar to Toyota's approach.

So we are going to be able to build up a nice flow between our suppliers and our customers, and we see that happening over the next few years. This is going to give us a very stable position in the market.

Bara has been adamant that *kaizen* is for everybody in the company and all aspects of the operation. For example, there is now a companywide program in which departments are rated by how well they communicate with people in other departments.

Hugo Levente Bara: At Supremia, we've made it clear that everything in the company has to be improved. One example is that we measure the quality of our internal communications. We do this through a survey conducted twice a year by human resources. Everybody has to rate the communications of the departments he or she deals with. There are 50 questions that include quality, speed, and correctness of communications. There is a total rating for the whole company, and our goal is to improve it every year, which is a big challenge.

So our people have to be more careful how they communicate, including what they write, what they say on the phone, etc. I think we are the only company in Eastern Europe that is doing this. We built this system by ourselves. This came from our people.

The bottom line for Bara is that *kaizen* is not just a method but represents the values he wants to instill in the company. Lean creates a structure that allows everybody to contribute according to these values.

Hugo Levente Bara: I think it's very important in a company to teach values like trust, teamwork, and so on. This really helps people understand why they are coming to work in the morning. A lot of companies have these values, but they don't promote them, and I think that's a very big loss. This should be part of strategic management.

CHAPTER 12

SOLVING THE COST/QUALITY CONUNDRUM IN HEALTHCARE

America's health care system is neither healthy, caring, nor a system.

—*Walter Cronkite*

One of the most powerful aspects of Deming's "quality is made in the boardroom" principle is its universality. Whether a process involves the installation of a mirror on a truck, the approval of an insurance claim, or the preparation of a blood sample in a laboratory, the management system behind the process is what ultimately determines the outcome.

Applying management principles from an automaker to take on the challenges in healthcare is, therefore, no big leap. Healthcare, in fact, has suffered under the same flawed management systems that brought the American auto industry to its knees in the late 1970s. Here we see the silos, the poor coordination, the arcane structures, and a dictatorial management style that discourages feedback even in matters involving patient safety.

The result is a quality problem so severe that it is a leading cause of preventable deaths in the developed world. Dozens of studies bear this out. In an early eye-opener, the Agency for Healthcare Research and Quality (AHRQ), a U.S. government agency, reported in 2000 that medical errors are responsible for preventable injury in as many as 1 of 25 hospital patients and are the cause of as many as 98,000 deaths per year in the United States. Since that year, medical error has been established as the third largest cause of death in the United States, after heart disease and cancer.

The biggest headlines, however, are reserved for healthcare's rising costs. According to statistics from the Organization for Economic Cooperation and Development (OECD), per-capita spending on healthcare has doubled in the developed world in the last decade, as has health spending as a percentage of gross domestic product (GDP) since 1960. In the United States, that number has tripled to a whopping 17.7 percent.[1]

The one-two punch of rising costs and unacceptable quality puts healthcare CEOs in a bind. Traditional cuts, which have already run their course in most organizations, create unacceptable side effects such as crowded and undermaintained facilities, poor morale among care workers, antiquated equipment, and ultimately an increased risk of medical error. Yet costs continue to rise, and the resources to pay the bills are rapidly drying up. The industry began to look for solutions in the late 1980s, and many turned to Deming's methods. One of the key players was Donald Berwick, a pediatrician who founded the Institute for Healthcare Improvement (IHI), along with a group of colleagues who were, in the words of the IHI website, "committed to redesigning health care into a system without errors, waste, delay, and unsustainable costs." In the groundbreaking book *Curing Health Care*[2] Berwick and his coauthors, A. Blanton Godfrey and Jane Roessner, pulled no punches: mistakes were being made, and patients were dying.

Today the IHI promotes best practices in healthcare institutions through research, training, and dissemination of knowledge. One of the cornerstones is the Triple Aim Initiative, which sets out a framework for the simultaneous fulfillment of three goals:

- Improving patients' experience of care (including quality and satisfaction)
- Improving the health of populations
- Reducing the per-capita cost of healthcare

During the 1990s, healthcare institutions, often with the support of the IHI, began to develop competencies in quality improvement that were based on Deming's scientific methods and tools such as Six Sigma, but those improvements were small in comparison with the mammoth problem facing the industry.

The idea of Lean healthcare started to emerge around 2000 as Lean success at companies such as Wiremold started to attract attention. Reports that some manufacturing companies were approaching zero defects was a revelation for an industry that was struggling with defect rates that were by some accounts in the double digits.

Lean, furthermore, can address the cost issue. The chaotic redundant processes that are causing medical error are also highly inefficient, and they waste space, materials, equipment time, and human resources. The numbers add up: an Institute of Medicine (IOM) study released in 2012 pegs the waste in U.S. healthcare at $750 billion, roughly 30 percent of the total healthcare budget. Looked at through the lens of Lean, which classifies entities such as waiting rooms as *muda*, this figure would probably be much higher.

Consequently, Lean provides a golden opportunity to cut waste and its incumbent costs, improve throughput, and reduce defects simultaneously.

Applying the Toyota Production System to healthcare, however sounded not only improbable but crass. Do we really want doctors and nurses taking instruction from people who build cars? What was needed was somebody with a deep understanding of Lean who could connect the dots between the processes in a factory and those in a hospital. One of the first to step up to this task was George Koenigsaecker.

George Koenigsaecker: Healthcare is the largest industry, the most broken industry, and maybe the most important one. In my view of what Lean needed to do, it needed to help healthcare to culminate, if you will, what Lean should contribute to society.

I knew Lean would work in healthcare from 15 years of seeing it work everywhere. I'd helped Lean spread into admin work, product development, and all kinds of businesses, but I couldn't show anybody else who actually counted, like a healthcare CEO. By then I knew if you weren't a CEO you probably weren't going to be able to make it happen anyway. I had actually been looking for healthcare CEOs to mentor for a couple of years.

While Koenigsaecker was looking for a CEO to champion Lean healthcare, Dr. John Toussaint, chief medical officer of ThedaCare, a medium-size not-for-profit healthcare provider in Wisconsin, was looking for a better management system.

The organization, which consisted of two major hospitals and a network of smaller facilities, was performing well according to existing healthcare metrics, but Toussaint was deeply troubled by the incidence of medical error that was taking place under his watch.

John Toussaint: I went into healthcare to deliver a result for patients that was as perfect as possible. I took care of many patients in my career and then saw so many other problems as an administrator. It was very disappointing to me and frustrating that we were making mistakes and people were being injured by those mistakes, killed by those mistakes.

Like many of his colleagues, Toussaint had begun to experiment with the quality improvement tools that were available to hospitals. Although he could get results from his interventions, he found that none of those methods were creating real change:

> What I found is that we could, to use a metaphor, take a flashlight and shine it over into one corner and improve things there very nicely. But when we would take a flashlight and shine it over in the other corner, the improvement would go right back. We couldn't sustain anything.
>
> On the other hand, we knew that companies in some industries had their defects down to nearly zero. That led me to think, Is there a system or method that we're missing here? We'd tried TQM, quality circles, GE-style Six Sigma, and the traditional IHI improvement projects, but none of it produced sustainable results. But we figured that there had to be a system because some companies were getting these extraordinary results.

When Toussaint became the CEO of ThedaCare in 2000, his quest for a better management system went into high gear, and he began to look outside healthcare for answers. Interestingly, Toussaint had studied engineering before going into medicine:

> When I did become CEO, we spent the first six months sending some of our vice presidents to companies outside of healthcare to try to understand how they were delivering 3.4 defects per million quality on their widget making, whether it's furniture or batteries or whatever.

One of the facilities that the team decided to visit was the nearby Ariens Company. As it happened, George Koenigsaecker was on that company's board. Koenigsaecker had found his healthcare CEO, and Toussaint had found his management system. The gemba walk through the plant was an eye-opener.

> *John Toussaint:* What we saw was frontline workers who, rather than being on a line, were working in U-shaped cells with the snow blowers moving back and forth on carts. There was all kinds of communication going back and forth between the workers around any problems that weren't obvious. This was real teamwork, and the workers clearly cared about quality.
>
> What came to my mind was that there really wasn't that much difference between snow blowers on carts and patients on gurneys. Actually, the snow blowers were getting better attention and better care than our patients were. If we added caring and compassion to this process, we could deliver much better care.
>
> I also tell people that this was probably the only time in my tenure that our senior executive team agreed on anything, because we were all out there together. Whatever the heck they were doing out there was what we needed to do.

Dan Ariens, the CEO of Ariens, remembers the visit well:

> I think that what John was seeing is the attention we pay to what we call the presentation. If you're presenting the chassis or the major transmission to the assembler, you make sure that every component that the assembler needs for that process is right there in front of him. John called it care because it resembled the way that a patient is presented for the doctor just to go do what he needs to do.
>
> We present things on trays, like a lunch tray that a patient gets, with all the parts laid out on a cutout board. Whether it's a bolt or a set of bolts or a bracket, it's all presented to

you, and you know everything is there because visually you can see that every part is in its location. And you know that you put every part on, because they're all gone when you're done, and when the trays are done, they are placed on the cart in a slot below the workpiece—the patient, if you will—and they're put away nicely. They're brought in clean, and they're put away clean, and they move to the next station with some amount of care in a sequence, in an order, in a flow that's very synchronized. It's like a dance in some ways. It's choreographed, and everything has to flow through in a very thoughtful and precise manner. I think that's the kind of thing that John saw.

The idea of flow ties it all together. Just as the snow blower moves along an assembly line that requires a series of assembly steps, the patient moves through a care system that is composed of a series of steps aimed at resolving his or her problem. An emergency ward patient, for example, will progress from admitting, to triage, to a fracture clinic, to an operating room, to a bed.

The problem in healthcare is that the patient's journey through the system is at best haphazard. Each entity the patient encounters along the way is controlled by a separate department with a separate budget, and the presentation that was prevalent in the snow blower factory is typically absent. Often the patient arrives at the next stage of the process as a complete stranger.

The most ubiquitous symptom of this is waiting. Patients wait at admitting, wait at triage, wait to be examined, wait for a bed. Hospitals are full of waiting rooms.

Far more serious, however, is the impact on patient safety. Poor communication in patient handoffs is implicated in 80 percent of all preventable medical errors according to an analysis of over 4,800 sentinel events by the Joint Commission, a nonprofit American healthcare accreditation body.

Toussaint and coauthors Roger A. Gerard and Emily Adams were blunt about the issue in their book *On the Mend*, which chronicles the ThedaCare Lean transformation:

> Here is the ugly outcome of this silo working style: lack of communication and lack of focus on the patient, as a whole, results in misguided or contradicting orders and millions of incidents of medical harm every year.[3]

Healthcare's Secret Weapon

The encouraging flip side of this troubling scenario is that people care. The Lean flow in the Ariens factory is possible because of a fact of human nature: people would much rather go home after making a genuine contribution to building a quality product than leave work with the feeling that they had only gone through the motions.

If anything, this is even truer in healthcare. Those who choose the care professions are passionate about helping people and would much rather stop to help than ask a patient to sit in a waiting area, fill out yet another form, or go down the hall to another department. If given the choice, they would certainly prefer spending time with a patient to doing paperwork, searching for a missing file, or walking to another wing to find a piece of equipment.

Most care workers are weary of the arcane systems they are forced to work in and of seeing the same old problems recur over and over again. When given the opportunity to help improve their own processes, healthcare workers become energetic and innovative participants.

John Toussaint: I do think that those who have chosen to devote their lives to caring for patients believe deep down that the mistakes we make in healthcare are unacceptable. The problem is that leaders have not created the environment for them to be safe in identifying these problems and solving them. Which gets back to the management system. We have a fundamentally flawed leadership and management system in healthcare, which, if we don't fix it, is going to continue to deliver these lousy results.

The big challenge, says Toussaint, is leadership.

A New Model for Managing Healthcare

Having led a highly successful Lean journey that has transformed ThedaCare into a world-class facility, Toussaint is on a mission to ease the path for others. Now CEO emeritus of the ThedaCare medical facility, Toussaint is also the CEO of the ThedaCare Center for Healthcare Value, a not-for-profit dedicated to improving healthcare through Lean. Using ThedaCare as a model site, Toussaint personally hosts approximately 750 senior executives every year on three-day visits.

Toussaint believes that the task calls for a comprehensive management system, based on Lean principles, that enables the fulfillment of a patient-centric care model. Using the ThedaCare model as a base and employing feedback from hundreds of healthcare leaders, Toussaint is undertaking the construction of such a system:

I'm spending a lot of time documenting what companies need to do to be successful at this. This is what everyone is asking me for. So I'm spending a lot of time with senior executive teams and CEOs. I really need to get these concepts down, codify them, and create materials for the teams to study ahead of my spending two or three days with them.

This is much more prescriptive than I've ever been, but I think the industry is ready for that. And quite frankly, I think we are prepared, and I am prepared now, to actually recommend a series of strategies based on all the organizations I've studied and all the leaders I've interacted with. There are thousands of them at this point.

The center runs a four-month training program for executives—a sort of executive MBA in Lean healthcare management—that is based on the training that ThedaCare gives its new managers. It has been introduced to 13 hospitals in North America. The center also hosts a number of learning events that attract executives from a variety of industries, including manufacturing.

The program is not just about Lean techniques; it's about teaching people how to manage. Traditional management methods taught in business schools, Toussaint maintains, are fundamentally flawed and need to be replaced from the ground up:

> My conclusion is that we just don't have training systems in North America today that can actually help people understand what they need to do and how to do it. Typical MBA and other programs just aren't getting the job done. It's all based on traditional Sloan-style management that isn't working. We need to build a different kind of training system for most of the clinicians and for the administrators.

Toussaint draws from the lessons he learned from ThedaCare's journey. One of the most important of these occurred in 2007. As often happens with Lean journeys, ThedaCare had reached a crisis point whereby, despite numerous incremental successes, real transformation was not taking place.

The breakthrough came when Toussaint appointed a makeover team of doctors, nurses, patients, and outside participants to spend six months completely reinventing the inpatient care process. The outcome marked the beginning of collaborative care at ThedaCare.

Toussaint and his coauthors describe the effort:

The makeover team was determined to burn down the old hospital model—one of medicine's most sacred cows—in order to engage all staff directly with patients. They used Lean principles as a guide, but also redefined the model to become more patient-focused. This was in striking contrast to the traditional model of care in hospitals, where physicians control patient care, giving orders that are followed by all other caregivers who are not expected to provide input.[4]

As Toussaint explains, their management system had not supported the level of change they were trying to create:

I think what happened in our situation at ThedaCare is that we used the tools but didn't change the way we managed. We were still using the old autocracy style, expecting everybody else to identify and solve problems. There was just a lot of tension there that I think could have been avoided.

This is why I believe that using the management system principles and training these people up as we're starting to do with hospitals will turn out to be a better sequence for creating a Lean transformation. That's a hypothesis, and we're testing it in a number of hospitals.

Doctor, Nurse, Patient Roles Revisited

The Lean journey in healthcare brings some special challenges. First of all, healthcare is an emotionally exhausting environment that places workers in situations in which people's lives are on the line. Also, many facilities have been operating for years under severe budget constraints, and as a result, their doctors, nurses, and orderlies are working impossible shifts and coping with a lack of space and equipment as well as constantly hearing complaints from patients who are unhappy with the quality of care they are receiving.

In many facilities, workers have already been subjected to various flavors of the month in terms of improvement programs, and so skepticism is typically high when Lean or any other program is introduced.

Another difficulty is that Lean as a management system requires a thorough revisiting of physician autonomy, a principle that doctors hold sacred. Doctors are taught in medical school that they will call the shots and that their authority in patient issues will not be questioned. However, this kind of management by decree is anathema to building a broad culture of continuous improvement. As team members in a value stream, doctors must open their work processes to scrutiny.

The good news, Toussaint says, is that doctors are taught to think scientifically. What is needed is to turn that scientific eye not just on clinical situations but on the way they actually do their work. As Toussaint says:

Physicians are reasonably good at using scientific methods to take care of patients, clinical problems. We read the literature, we change the way we do things, whether it's procedures or prescriptions, based on what the science is telling us.

The problem is, we don't use the scientific method to improve the processes of care. And that's why we have so many mistakes. The doctor walks in and says, "I want you to do it this way," and he walks out of the room and expects that this autocratic system of management will work. We need to teach physicians to apply scientific thinking to the rest of the practice of medicine.

To overcome the many barriers that can be expected, Toussaint is adamant that the Lean transformation must be led from the top.

This means that the CEO must take an active role, backed by a board of directors that is completely on side.

> *John Toussaint:* We actually have a board training program that we've designed for this specific purpose. We spent about five hours with the board and actually take them to the *gemba*. We show them how many problems there are. We talk about non-value-added and value-added work. We talk about processes and waste. By the time we're done with the board, they at least have an understanding of what management is trying to accomplish by going down this path. So far, the boards that we've worked with have all said this is very valuable.
>
> The point is, the people leading these transformations really need to have their board behind them when things get difficult. Doctors don't like this when you get started, and many of the employees don't like it either because they think it's another flavor of the day. So you'll often see employee and physician satisfaction decline as you get going. What boards have to know is that this is not necessarily a bad thing. It needs to be addressed, of course, but when you're really trying to change the system, it's going to make people uncomfortable, and you're going to see signs of that. Then it's management's responsibility to build systems that fix those problems.

Patients must also be part of the conversation. Often their comments are surprising.

> *John Toussaint:* I was on a *kaizen* where we studied from the time a baby's born to the time the baby goes to the doctor for the first visit. We mapped out every single step in that process, and one of the steps was that the same nurse who delivered the baby would accompany the mother down to the car and teach her how to put the baby in the car seat. The

nurses felt this was very important—a sort of final bonding moment.

When we asked the patient, though, she said, "Don't bother. I would have been able to leave the hospital four hours earlier rather than wait for you, because you were delivering babies when I wanted to go home." The nurses were initially flabbergasted, but it was clear that this extra step wasn't worth it—any available nurse could show the mother how to use the car seat. If I had told this to the nurses, they would have blown me off, but it's hard to argue with the patient in this instance.

Can Healthcare Be Fixed?

Toussaint might be called an optimistic realist. Although he acknowledges that this is a long road, he is greatly encouraged by the feedback he is getting from the hospitals he is mentoring:

These principles and practices we've established are a way out from the cynicism, from the overworking, from the over-burden, from the massive waste that exists in the delivery of healthcare. As we expose managers, leaders, CEOs, and senior executives to this by having them come and actually see it in action, they absolutely get it, they absolutely say this is the way we should be working and this is what we should be doing.

But there's a long way to go. Most people today still think that the answer is to go to the hospital association meeting, hear a presentation on what a good leader is, and go back and apply that. Wrong. Leaders have to see for themselves that there is another way that is completely different from what they learned previously. That way, they can change first themselves and then their whole organization.

So we're setting up model cells and model hospitals so leaders can get have that "aha" moment, and as well, we're helping them acquire the resources and coaching to make the change happen. I have a number of hospitals working through that now.

A PRESCRIPTION FOR LARGE-SCALE CHANGE

Around the same time ThedaCare started its Lean journey, a newly appointed healthcare leader on the West Coast began a similar quest. When he became the CEO of Virginia Mason, a 6,000-employee organization in Seattle, Washington, in 2001, Dr. Gary Kaplan could see clearly that the organization needed to change.

Virginia Mason had a long history of using the quality improvement tools that were then common in the healthcare sector, but the organization was not seeing a major impact.

Gary Kaplan: We had been very early participants—in some ways leaders—in the quality improvement through TQM work in healthcare. We had teams as early as 1989 and 1990 going to work with the beginnings of the Institute for Healthcare Improvement. So we were well versed in quality improvement but realized that what we were doing wasn't working at the levels or the speed that it needed to.

Kaplan was under pressure to change the organization quickly. Virginia Mason had lost money for the first time in 1998 and again posted a loss in 1999. With stiff competition from other providers, he had little leeway. At an emotionally charged two-day retreat, Kaplan announced to his staff that the organization would either change or die.

Kaplan recognized that Virginia Mason, like other hospitals, had a physician-centric culture based on physician autonomy that would make major change very difficult. What was needed was a more collaborative model organized around the patient, and this required a new compact with the doctors. In late 2000, the organization began, with the help of consultant Jack Silversin, to draft and perfect the Virginia Mason Medical Center Physician Compact. This process was led by frontline clinicians, and the resulting document clearly delineated what physicians could expect from the organization and what the organization could expect from physicians.

Kaplan also realized that there was no precedent in healthcare for where he needed to take the organization and that the answers he was seeking probably would have to come from outside the industry. Then, through a chance encounter, he and his colleagues became acquainted with John Black, a consultant who had brought Lean methods to nearby Boeing. Black introduced Kaplan and his team to the Lean community.

Gary Kaplan: As members of the business community in Washington State, we kind of stumbled on what the Boeing Company had been doing with Lean. Nobody had really done this in a significant, substantive way in healthcare. For us, Lean was very visual, and it was really focused on continuous improvement and respect for people. The more we learned about it, the more this seemed to have direct applicability to healthcare.

So our role models were outside of our industry. Some of our earliest conversations were conference calls with Art Byrne and Orry Fiume of Wiremold. They were giants in applying TPS to manufacturing and really intrigued us with what they were sharing. In November 2001, I led our entire executive team to Wiremold.

The Wiremold tour, led by Art Byrne himself, made a powerful impression. Byrne describes what the physicians saw in his book *The Lean Turnaround*:

When Gary Kaplan, CEO of Virginia Mason Medical Center (VMMC) in Seattle, Washington, started his Lean journey, he flew 30 of his key managers and doctors from Seattle to Hartford, Connecticut, to spend a couple of days with Wiremold. The main thrust of this visit was to see if they could understand what we did in a manufacturing environment that was similar to what they did and could therefore be transferred back to Virginia Mason.

We started them out with a simple concept. We explained that in our business, we began with a piece of steel or plastic (our raw material). We then moved it through a series of processes where we drilled holes in it, attached things to it, wrapped it up, put it in a box, and sold it to a customer. Their business, we explained, was exactly the same. They started with a human body (the raw material), moved it through various processes where they drilled holes in it, attached things to it, bandaged it up, put it in a car (no box, please), and sent it home. They got a few laughs out of this analogy, but at the same time they understood that this was basically true. What we did and what they did were fundamentally the same.

We spent the rest of our time together showing them how we moved our raw material through the shop. We explained how our gains came from removing the waste—all the time that our parts spent lying around waiting—and letting the raw material flow directly into the box. They could easily relate this to their own situation, where their patients (i.e., the raw material) spent endless hours waiting and being moved around so that value could be added to improve their condition sufficiently that they could finally get in the car and go home.

This was a great visit. We all had fun, and we learned a lot from each other. Virginia Mason had brought its A-team, so when they went home, they were all on the same page.[5]

With his senior management team on board, Kaplan was ready to make a major commitment. He recognized that the resistance to what he was about to do would be enormous and believed that he needed his management team not only on the right side but firmly immersed in Lean thinking.

Consequently, Kaplan made the dramatic step of taking the entire senior management team to Japan for a two-week immersion experience. Resistance to the idea was enormous, especially because of Virginia Mason's financial situation, but Kaplan had the support of his board and was ready to bet the store on Lean.

The trip "blew our minds," says Kaplan. During their visit to the Toyota plant in Nagoya, the team saw "symphony like" synchronization, workers collaborating to make improvements, clear communication on the shop floor replete with visual cues, and enormous care going into building a quality product. Team members also got the opportunity to participate in *kaizens* and worked as operators on the Hitachi air-conditioner assembly line.

Kaplan and his colleagues took special note of a particular incident that they observed on the shop floor. A worker was having a problem on the line and reached up and pulled the *andon* rope. A minute later he pulled it again, and the entire line stopped. Kaplan and his team were fascinated that every worker in the plant had the power to stop the entire line if there was a quality problem. The idea that you don't send poor quality down the line was not just a slogan: employees lived by it. Yet this power did not exist in the healthcare system, even in life-threatening situations.

When they returned from Japan, the Virginia Mason leadership team put their own *andon* system in place, the Patient Safety Alert (PSA) policy. This gives all staff the authority and the duty to stop a process if there is a concern about patient safety, even if this means overruling a doctor. Furthermore, in a safety alert situation, all staff members can connect with leadership at all levels and, if necessary, directly to Kaplan and other senior leaders.

Building a Strong Executive Team

Kaplan now had a team that was not only sold but deeply committed to Lean. He also had another important weapon: Carolyn Corvi, a senior VP from Boeing who was a staunch Lean advocate, joined the board in 2002.

Gary Kaplan: One of the key things to understand about our journey is that we decided early on that we weren't going to be able to pull this off in healthcare without changing the culture. Healthcare is dominated by a professional culture with high value placed on autonomy, and that was a major issue. However, we had been confronting these issues with our physician compact and other things, which I think set us up in a good way for continuing the journey with the new management method.

While our senior executive team works hard to avoid groupthink, we decided that in order to truly make the transition, we had to be of one mind on the need to change the culture. We said, "We have to change the minds of leadership before we can think about having these conversations at a deeper level with our physicians and staff." That's why the entire executive team went on that first trip to Wiremold. That's why the first trip to Japan was a requirement. If you were an executive leader, you had to go.

The resolve of the leadership team gave me tremendous fortitude in the one-on-one or small group conversations that needed to occur as we were moving things forward. It was much more than just a series of conversations. It was a series of experiential learning opportunities. What John Kotter calls "see, feel, and change" was probably most powerful in helping people come along.

Dr. John Kotter's see, feel, change paradigm fits well with the experiential aspect of Lean: the fact that people don't really get Lean unless they see it and interact with the people who are practicing it. Furthermore, Lean requires that all participants adopt a set of beliefs that support continuous improvement. In the introduction to *The Heart of Change*, Kotter and his coauthor, Dan Cohen, explain how this works:

> Changing behavior is less a matter of giving people analysis to influence their thoughts than helping them to see a truth to influence their feelings. Both thinking and feeling are essential, and both are found in successful organizations, but the heart of change is in the emotions.[6]

Kaplan is also a collaborator with and close personal friend of management guru Edgar Schein, whose ideas about organizational culture are highly relevant to the Lean transformation in healthcare. Schein's model of organizational culture, which dates back to the 1980s, looks at the relationships between the behavior we see in organizations and the belief systems that support them.

In spite of his preeminence in the field, Schein continues to reevaluate his ideas and to be an active participant in the Lean healthcare leadership conversation, Kaplan said:

> Ed understands things much better than he even did a year or two ago about healthcare. He's done a lot of work in high-reliability industries. He's somewhat aghast at where healthcare was and some of our cultural backwardness, so to speak.
>
> Ed really understands clearly the role of healthcare leaders in setting the culture and that leaders' behaviors are the single most important determinant of evolving a culture. That's one of the things we talk about.

Recent books by Schein provide direct insight into the idea of humble leadership, another key aspect of Lean leadership.

Gary Kaplan: I believe relationships are critically important, and that's one of the things that as a leader I focus on. That's helped me understand that I can't be in a one-up position if I want to build strong, meaningful, sincere relationships. That helps, particularly in tough times.

Relationships at the board level are also critical, and Kaplan sets up a number of activities to ensure that every member of the board is thoroughly immersed in the Lean philosophy.

Gary Kaplan: Alignment is critically important—from the boardroom to the front lines of patient care. Every public board member who is in his or her first three-year term at Virginia Mason has to spend two weeks on a *Gemba Kaizen* trip to Japan. What that does is, it builds the kinds of relationships, glue, and content expertise that keep the board fully engaged, committed, and supportive of this work, which at times is very hard work. Going and seeing for yourself is a huge part of how we act as leaders here.

Structuring the Organization Around the Patient

Kaplan, like Toussaint, decided to create a management system that was based on Lean tools but would provide a complete structure for managing a healthcare organization. Working with John Black, Kaplan's team developed the Virginia Mason Production System

(VMPS), which is modeled on the Toyota Production System. Kaplan does not like to call it Lean, though:

> One of the reasons I don't use the word *Lean* is that I think a lot of people think of it as a tool kit. It's a set of tools that are very effective and instrumental in improvement work, but in healthcare it's just a tool set within the context of large-scale change.
>
> By contrast, the Virginia Mason Production System, which is based on Lean, is about a lot more than that. The building blocks are a set of tools and workshops, but it's really about shared urgency for change, a shared vision to know where we're going, and defining and aligning expectations. It's also about leaders leading in new and different ways.
>
> VMPS has three basic components:

- *Management by policy:* setting goals and tactics according to strategic plan
- *Cross-functional management:* delivering value across traditional silos through the value streams
- *Daily management:* the responsibility at the front line of care for every staff member and every supervisor or manager

> *Gary Kaplan:* That together integrates into a management system that defines how we do everything here. Strategic planning, process improvement, performance management and development, that's how we think of it—not just as building blocks but as a system within which we function and do our jobs.
>
> So the Virginia Mason Production System is about all of our work, including my own. I lead many events, including the Tuesday morning stand-up meeting weekly as well as the quarterly stand-up review. I attend report-outs whenever I am in town, and if not, our COO is there. I also lead our two-week

trip to Japan every summer. This is a very different way to spend my time than I would in a more traditional setting.

Lessons from a Tragedy

A tragic event occurred at Virginia Mason that galvanized the will of Kaplan and his team to further accelerate their work on patient safety. A patient who was a beloved member of the local community known for her charity work had been diagnosed with a brain aneurysm and had come to the medical center for a radiology procedure. After the procedure, she suddenly began to show unexplainable symptoms. The situation worsened, and the patient died a few days later.

An investigation revealed that the patient had been mistakenly injected with chlorhexidine, a powerful antiseptic. The staff was devastated. Never had the outcome of a medical error hit so directly.

Although it was common practice in healthcare to keep medical errors under wraps, Kaplan decided to go public immediately:

> She came to us for a tertiary procedure, one that we do pretty often, and we failed her. We had already been engaged with VMPS for three years, and we knew that we had no choice but to tell the truth. Up until that time only one or two times did that really happen across the country.

Telling the truth was both morally correct and absolutely necessary for building a culture of continuous improvement that would prevent errors like this from ever happening again. This was not a time for blaming: the team knew that it was not people but the process that had failed, and the process belonged to everybody. A Patient Safety Alert (PSA) had, in fact, been filed when the error was identified, but this was not enough to save the patient.

What was needed was a series of safeguards that would make mistakes like this impossible. In a comprehensive initiative, all procedures were examined for possible weaknesses that could lead to error, and mistake-proofing steps were added wherever there was danger. Sometimes the interventions involved 5S: shadow boards were used to determine the location of bowls, syringes, swabs, and scalpels on carts so that nobody conducting an emergency procedure at 3 a.m. had to rely on his or her memory.

Management also took action to strengthen the PSA process and promote a culture that relentlessly pursued patient safety. While Virginia Mason had made huge strides with the PSA system, there was still confusion around it, and there needed to be a stronger commitment to making improvements in processes when systemic errors were uncovered. Consequently, communication was improved, procedures were clarified, and organizational goals were aligned with patient safety. In 2007, the board of directors formed a committee to review critical PSA incidents.

These changes put Virginia Mason's safety initiative in high gear, and helped embed patient safety in its culture. Thousands of incidents have been reported since the 2005 tragedy, and in many cases, these incidents have led to significant improvements in patient safety. In addition, the data from the incident reports has become a valuable tool for spotting overall trends.

Today, the hospital's safety record is exemplary. In 2010, the Virginia Mason Medical Center was one of two U.S. hospitals to receive the Top Hospital of the Decade award from Leapfrog, an advocacy group that promotes safety and transparency in healthcare.

Hopeful Signs for Healthcare

Virginia Mason has become a model for Lean healthcare transformation and is visited each year by hundreds of leaders from healthcare and other industries. Through the Virginia Mason Institute, the organization is sharing knowledge with other organizations, such as the province of Saskatchewan, which is modeling its provincial healthcare system on the Virginia Mason Production System.

Kaplan is optimistic that Lean healthcare is going to get health-care out of its current crisis:

> We've worked on many things here over the past several years on improving the patient experience, capturing the true emotional content of what patients feel during their care experiences, and then using that as impetus to further evolve as caregivers, care delivery teams. I think the future is bright, I think the patients are going to get a level of care they've never had before.
>
> For healthcare workers, this is about engaging people and giving them hope. They are the ones who know the challenges and problems most clearly, because they are experiencing them every day. They're also the ones who, using VMPS methods and tools, have the best opportunity to create improvements. This will improve the care we are able to deliver to patients, and it will reduce the burden of work for those working in health-care so they aren't spinning their wheels and wasting their time.
>
> Lean is one of the most advanced people systems in the world for getting people to realize their capabilities in terms of coming to work every day to do their jobs and to improve their jobs.

A Campaign to Eliminate Variation

Bob Brody is another CEO who has led a successful Lean transfor-mation. Like the others, Franciscan St. Francis Health began experi-menting with Deming's quality principles in the early 1990s with the encouragement of its then-CEO, Kevin Leahy.

What this work created, says Brody, was a strong management culture that featured inquiry and quality improvement:

> It began with book clubs where people would meet and discuss Deming's 14 points and other ideas. When I was elevated into

his position about 17 years ago, I was able to carry on the mentality that we're here to continually improve our own performance and that the more scientifically we arrive at those opportunities for process improvement, the more effective we can be.

Brody was introduced to Lean when the staff began taking courses in TQM at nearby IUPUI, a joint effort between Indiana University and Purdue University in Indianapolis. Through the program, he was introduced to Lean expert Joe Swartz, who began doing consulting work for Franciscan St. Francis and who was eventually hired in 2006 as director of business transformation. Swartz has coauthored a Shingo Prize–winning book, *Healthcare Kaizen*, with Mark Graban that highlights the successes at Franciscan St. Francis.

For Brody the transformation has always been about continuing the work with Deming's principles that began over two decades ago:

I think that the long and the short answer to how we've changed the organization is that we're doing our best to eliminate variation across the board. And that's in response to the pressure that we're dealing with across the industry.

Seventeen years ago, we very deliberately started to think more like a healthcare delivery system and look for more opportunities to standardize and centralize support services. This forced us to focus on eliminating variation and identifying best practice. Over time, that proved very productive for us, and as the industry has changed, we've begun very deliberately striving to ensure that our evidence-based clinical practice is the standard across the organization.

Lean has given workers and management the tools to fulfill this vision. The turning point in the spread of Lean thinking in the organization, Brody says, was the establishment of an ongoing learning program for his 300-member management team:

> These events take place roughly three times a year—participants spend a day in an educational setting or forum. I think this made an incredible impression on employees, because the workshops simplified to so many what Lean is all about, what our *kaizen* program was all about, and where we were headed in terms of a culture where everyone is encouraged to offer thought around how we might better please the patient, reduce costs, and operate more efficiently. All this was presented in a very appealing way for the audience.

In parallel with the training for managers, employees at all levels were trained so that anybody could initiate a *kaizen* improvement event.

> *Joe Swartz:* Our *kaizen* program began with a series of pilot projects. So in the first year or so, we were able to influence maybe 100 staff members. When it came to bringing Lean to the other 4,000 employees, we started with a kickoff meeting for 200 of our leaders—that was in the spring of 2007. As part of that rollout, we started teaching all staff about basic Lean concepts like the Seven Wastes, 5S, and the Five Whys—real basic Lean tools we would teach to anybody who came to these open sessions that we held many different times. So we'd teach them how to think this way and ask them to go out and implement an individual *kaizen* or a small-group *kaizen* that uses these ideas.
>
> We soon started getting lots of *kaizens* turned in with these things. We also started to standardize some of our learning events. I think that's permeated the organization fairly well. Last year we had 36 percent of our employees turn in a *kaizen*—over 4,000 were turned in last year. So I think that

through the *kaizen* program, we are seeing nurses think differently. Thinking about value and waste and ways they can simplify the daily work that they do and the work environment that they're in.

Brody, however, sees himself not as a direct leader of Lean activity but as an enabler:

From a leadership perspective, I'm not well versed in process. My job is to enable our people to realize their potential. We always emphasize here that all of our work is the result of a team effort, and these concepts play very well into that message. So my job is to help people do their best in whatever their capacity is.

"We Had Patients Waiting Far Too Long"

As the Lean journey progressed, the improvement teams began to look more deeply at the underlying processes. When they confronted the situation at the emergency department, it was clear that the entire process for handling patients needed to be reconsidered.

Bob Brody: We had patients waiting far too long—they were stacking up in the corridors while they awaited bed assignments on the floors. We had patients walking out on us out of frustration.

So we very deliberately attacked that whole enterprise and took it apart and put it back together in ways that we think really responded to the needs of various customers. Not only patients but the physicians and the nursing staff and the folks who made the bed assignments and the folks on the units that received the patients.

As the improvement process unfolded, the teams were directly confronted with the issue of physician autonomy.

Joe Swartz: When we started to redesign our ER processes, we were really struggling. We had made improvements over a few years all around the doctors. The doctors wouldn't let us change anything, so we improved all the processes with the nursing staff.

When we finally had to address the doctors, we had the data, and we understood the metrics that we needed them to be accountable for. Eventually, they dramatically redesigned how they work in the ER. It was a big culture change for them. But the fact that Bob had hung with them for three or four years made this relatively painless.

Brody, like Toussaint, offered the observation that doctors are trained to think like scientists, and once you have the data, they will respond to it.

Bob Brody: Physicians are scientists, and they respond to depth. If you make a strong case based on evidence that you've assembled and present it in a rational manner, then they are not only scientists, they are very competitive and for the most part perfectionists. If you show them how to do something better and can prove it, they'll respond.

However, as accountable care becomes a reality under the Affordable Care Act, Brody cautions that he may not have the luxury of being so accommodating:

The pace is picking up, and I don't think we can afford to be as patient as we've been before. We're coming as a system at our entire enterprise very directly around the need to reduce costs like most organizations around the country. And that is impacting every dimension of the enterprise here, including physician behaviors and performance.

Also, we are working with the physicians who historically have been independent practitioners but now are employed in many cases. The present circumstances give us a pretty good case for asking them to do things differently. And this philosophy—this methodology and practice—allows us to do that pretty effectively.

The emergency department transformation ultimately produced stunning results. Swartz reports that time to see a doctor was reduced from 45 to 11 minutes and the average stay dropped 40 percent; customer satisfaction, once in the 13th percentile, is now in the 70th and climbing.

Fulfilling the Accountable Care Mandate

In the United States, the Affordable Care Act is changing the rules for healthcare providers. Franciscan St. Francis was one of the early adopters of accountable care.

Bob Brody: We are strapped like a rocket ship that needs a new fuel source. And as we move off of our traditional payment platform into a value-based reimbursement system, we are absolutely required to arrive at every efficiency that we can identify. And for the first time we're much more accountable for quality and for price than ever before.

So this is a matter of survival in our mind. And it's absolutely appropriate. It's about time that we produce services in a way that is fiscally accountable. It's about time in terms of meeting our responsibilities as citizens to manage this portion of the economy appropriately.

Brody credits the organization's longtime culture of scientific approach for the success of Franciscan St. Francis's Lean transformation:

One thing we've been able to do here is embrace change. When you're part of an organization that's 135 years old, there's a mindset that suggests that we're going to adapt as necessary to survive, and that mission is the essence of the organization and why we exist. If the world is changing, we're going to figure it out. And Lean has given us a set of tools and a mindset that we think has allowed us to prosper at a time when a lot of organizations are flustered and failing.

Organizations such as ThedaCare Medical Center, Virginia Mason Medical Center, and Franciscan St. Francis Health have become living, breathing examples of what medical facilities can be. Transforming our healthcare systems is a long, difficult journey, but the road has already been built.

❖

CHAPTER 13

DEFINING AND DELIVERING VALUE IN GOVERNMENT

There is good government when those who are near are made happy, and when those who are afar are attracted.

—*Confucius*, The Wisdom of Confucius

The frequent association of the words "government" and "bureaucracy" reflects the popular notion that governments are slow, inept, unresponsive, wasteful, and, yes, bureaucratic.

From a Lean perspective, governments have a value problem in the eyes of the public they serve, and the classic signs of *muda* are hard to miss. Who would willingly pay to fill out a lengthy form for renewing a driver's license, for a complex yearlong approval process to acquire a building permit, or for a contractor to tear up a local street twice in a year: once to upgrade a water main and again to install new gas lines?

Our strained relationship with government has become increasingly politicized as officials cope with tight budgets and impatient electorates. Politicians at all levels campaign on promises to cut spending, remove red tape, and make governments more accountable. Many governments have undergone significant rebranding to try to establish themselves as customer-oriented service providers.

The idea of using Lean to deliver on these promises is relatively recent. Although not all characterizations of waste in government are fair and valid, Lean, through its ability to deliver more with less, presents an unparalleled opportunity to satisfy the calls for more efficient government.

Cutting waste, however, is hard work, as the private sector has proven for over half a century, and contrary to what many politicians promise, there are no quick fixes. The good news is that waste in government can be eliminated just as it can in the private sector through a long-term program of continuous improvement that utilizes scientific method and the knowledge of those who participate in the processes on a day-by-day basis. Of course, Lean thinking represents a radical departure from the common practice of bringing in outside consultants to do expensive studies and then attempting to apply the cuts they recommend.

The special challenge for governments is that it is not always clear what constitutes customer value; in some cases, it is not even clear who the customer is. If the government provides a school for your child or sends a squad to your house to put out a fire, the matter is pretty straightforward. But what if a cop gives you a speeding ticket? What if your factory has to undergo an environmental assessment? Government deals with many multistakeholder scenarios that place customer value in a gray area.

In spite of these complexities, the Lean government movement is gaining momentum. In the United States, substantial Lean programs can be found in 15 states, the U.S. Environmental Protection

Agency, and the U.S. Army. Interest is picking up in Europe, especially in the United Kingdom and Sweden, and several provinces in Canada have programs as well.

A HELPING HAND FROM THE PRIVATE SECTOR

One of the most ambitious and all-encompassing efforts at Lean government is being undertaken by the state of Washington. Lean initiatives there began under the previous administration with the help of a partnership with the Seattle-based aircraft giant Boeing. In the Lean tradition, that company agreed to share its Lean expertise at no charge. Darrell Damron, who today is the senior Lean consultant for the state, explains how it all began:

> We didn't have millions to throw at this, so we needed to find another way. This idea of partnership started with a conversation between Boeing Co. and our governor at the time, Christine Gregoire. When Boeing suggested that the government should be using Lean, our governor said, "That's a great idea, but we don't have money to go hire fancy folks to help us, so why don't you help us?" The Boeing Co. said, "In fact, we would be happy to do that."
>
> So we had the privilege of spending time with two of Boeing's internal Lean consultants, who helped us in many ways. They spent a lot of time envisioning what a Lean journey could be for our enterprise state government, and they did everything from helping with this strategic thinking about the future to providing some developmental training for some of our leaders. They even did some value stream mapping process improvement work to demonstrate the kinds of things that work.

When Governor Gregoire signed an executive order in December 2011 that established the state's commitment to Lean,

Damron began to look for other companies that might be willing to help:

> *Darrell Damron:* We had a hypothesis that said if one company is willing to help us, maybe there are others out there. So we started asking, and we heard a lot of yeses. In fact, we've engaged a total of 189 Lean experts from 84 different organizations who have given us advice or training or coaching or let us go on tours of their organizations for our state government.

In the 2012 gubernatorial elections, both opposing candidates had Lean in their campaign platforms. The winner, the Democrat Jay Inslee, had taken his Lean mandate to heart:

> *Jay Inslee:* Before becoming governor, I was aware of—and impressed by—the improvement gains at places like Boeing and Virginia Mason Medical Center. Washington's state government had started using Lean, but not in a large-scale way. Lean requires a commitment to continuous improvement throughout the entire enterprise, and that's what I want to see in our state government.

In September 2013, Governor Inslee signed an executive order that established Results Washington, a body that would bring Lean to the entire state government. The document contains the following preamble:

> Washington state and its public servants are committed to the continuous improvement of services, outcomes and performance of state government, to realize a safe, beautiful and healthy place to live and work. In order to achieve these aims, "Results Washington," an innovative, data-driven, performance management initiative, will drive the operations of state government through Lean thinking. This initiative will

aid state leaders in fact-based decision-making, enhancing the breadth of understanding, focus and commitment to our customers—all Washingtonians.[1]

Structuring a Statewide Transformation

Results Washington is run out of the office of the governor. Its charter is a strategic framework with five goal categories:

- World-class education
- Prosperous economy
- Sustainable energy and a clean environment
- Healthy and safe communities
- Efficient, effective, and accountable government

The categories are further broken down into 53 task areas, each represented by a goal council consisting of agency directors, representatives from the governor's budget and policy office, and members of the Results Washington team, who act as facilitators.

Often the work needed to improve against these targets crosses the lines of two or more agencies. The goal councils are responsible for bringing the agencies together. As Results Washington's director, Wendy Korthuis-Smith, explains, the current model was based on successful cross-agency work done during the previous administration:

> One early example of getting agencies together on common goals was an initiative called Target Zero, which was about reaching zero traffic fatalities by 2030. That was a joint goal with joint strategies between our Department of Licensing, our Department of Transportation, our Washington State Patrol, and our Traffic Safety Commission. We saw that as a great model that we wanted to replicate in this administration.

That's where we really set up the structure with the five goal areas that are composed of 53 goal councils. By having them focus on goals and measures that cross their areas, we're asking everyone to get in the game and have accountability and ownership of these pieces.

And so you'll have a goal council that's part of the Prosperous Economy category, for example, where you've got the Commerce Department talking about the gross business income in maritime, and you've got the Employment Security Department talking about the job related to that particular sector. The question is, How do they work together with strategy to make sure that we're making a real difference in those areas?

Measurement of results is a key priority of the team. Goals are reinforced by a hierarchy of targets and subtargets, and the results are posted on the Results Washington website. For example, under the category Sustainable Energy and a Clean Environment, there is a subgoal titled Clean Transportation that entails reducing transportation-related greenhouse gas emissions from the 2011 figure of 42.2 million metric tons per year to 37.5 metric tons per year by 2020. This is supported by subgoals to reduce vehicle greenhouse gas emissions, improve vehicle fuel efficiency, and increase the number of plug-in electric vehicles registered in the state.

To build momentum and help promote a Lean culture at the grassroots level, Results Washington has also established a best practice community that allows participants in different projects to share expertise. The initiative involves approximately 630 nonmanagerial state employees who represent 40 state agencies. Approximately 100 of them come together for a monthly meeting in Olympia, the state capital, and they communicate on an ongoing basis via a listserv group.

Darrell Damron: The whole point of this practice is breaking down the agency silos and giving people not only permission but the expectation of talking to each other about what's working well and what's not working well as we're going on this transformation journey as an enterprise. For some people, this is the first time they've ever been able to go meet with folks from another agency without being looked at like they are starting something illegal. We're giving them permission for that. It's working amazingly well in terms of the connections that our employees are making with each other.

According to Inslee, willingness to step outside the box is central to the culture he is trying to promote with Results Washington:

> Government is not known for embracing risk. But Lean requires a willingness to try improvements, see how they work, and refine them. You have to be willing to make mistakes. That can be a challenge for agencies and management that are comfortable with long-established processes and systems.
>
> It easy to fall back on "We've always done it this way," but that runs a risk in itself: the risk of institutionalizing under-performance, inefficient processes, and unhappy customers.

The Value of Speeding Tickets

With private business, customer value is relatively clear: customers tell companies what they're willing to pay for, and if the companies don't deliver, they vote with their feet. With government, it gets a lot more complicated; sometimes it is not even clear who the customer is.

> *Darrell Damron:* Let's say one of our state troopers on the road catches someone exceeding the speed limit, pulls them over, and gives them a ticket. Let's assume the driver is a Washingtonian. That Washingtonian is the direct recipient of a government product and service, in this case, a ticket for speeding being issued.
>
> But of course we don't design the process with just that customer, or the direct recipient of the product and service,

in mind. Because if we were to think of just asking that customer what they value, they'd say they value getting out of the ticket. So we have to design that process also in light of Washingtonians as stakeholders, and generally Washingtonians want troopers to be on the road helping people change their behavior in terms of speeding by issuing those tickets.

So the customer conversation is one we have all the time at every level throughout our government, because we are striving for that clarity of who it is we serve in any given process and whom we should be designing the value in this particular process for. How do we balance the needs of those who are interested from a stakeholder standpoint and those who are the direct recipients of the product and service? That conversation happens all the time.

Hollie Jensen, an enterprise Lean consultant who recently joined Results Washington from Starbucks, reflected on some of the differences between the public and private sectors:

Coming from the private sector, I found that the definition of the customer was one of the biggest things that I had to wrap my head around. At Starbucks, our mission was much simpler. Here we have the education, healthcare, and social health services, so this mission is pretty broad. State government impacts everyone, and because of that we have to be transparent about what we do, which puts our work in the public view and scrutiny in a very different way than what we see in the private sector.

"A Lasting Legacy of Continuous Improvement"

In a July 2014 report to the state legislature, Results Washington, not yet a year old, was able to report on 115 projects across 33 agencies.

The Department of Labor cut the average time for processing employer requests for reconsideration of audit findings from 441 days to 67, the Department of Health cut the wait time for handling complaints from four weeks to one, and the Department of Transportation cut the time to fulfill public disclosure requests by 55 percent.

The emphasis, however, is on moving steadily toward the larger long-term goals. Progress is tracked with a dashboardlike display on Results Washington's data site, which clearly spells out areas that need improvement as well as those that are on schedule. Employment numbers, economic growth, carbon emissions, student test scores, and customer satisfaction with government services are all on the radar.

Progress on these goals will take an army of Lean practitioners, and basic training is under way. According to the report, 22,000 of the state's 55,000 employees have attended at least one training event, 9,300 have received managerial training, and 735 have been trained as facilitators.

In fall 2013, Results Washington held a Lean convention that drew 2,300 attendees, making it one of the largest Lean events in the United States. The event featured a keynote speech from the governor and 40 presentations by Lean experts from the private sector.

The hope is that there will soon be enough momentum to create sustainable change that can survive the many uncertainties of politics.

> *Jay Inslee:* My hope is that we build a lasting legacy of continuous improvement. Many organizations approach Lean improvements as a project. They hire an outside expert, hold a daylong seminar, and make some changes. And study after study shows that those sorts of improvements are rarely sustained.
>
> We're taking a different approach. This isn't a once-and-done improvement project. This is an ongoing commitment to everyone focusing on improvement all the time.

LEAN AS GOVERNMENT POLICY

Another jurisdiction with a comprehensive, officially sanctioned Lean government program is the state of Connecticut.

Conversations related to Lean concepts began there in the 1990s. At that time, Connecticut was one of several states, including Iowa and Ohio, that experimented with TQM, quality circles, and other methods that had been taught by W. Edwards Deming and his followers. In 2000, Connecticut's department of labor began to develop core competencies around Lean tools and provide Lean training and assistance to other agencies. The departments of energy and environmental protection and transportation were among the pioneers.

Jodi Rell, who served as the state's governor from 2004 to 2010, endorsed those efforts and asked state agencies to become familiar with Lean and use it to become more efficient. There was, however, no legislation in place to support it. That changed in 2011 when Rell's successor, Dannel P. Malloy, enacted a statute mandating the application of Lean practices and principles to the permitting and enforcement processes of five agencies, to be administered by the Office of Policy and Management (OPM).

Together with the OPM, the five agencies formed a steering committee to oversee the implementation of the Lean statute. In September 2012, the governor released a report titled "Changing How Connecticut State Government Does Business" that highlighted a number of improvements that the five agencies had realized, including the following:

- The Department of Revenue Services reorganized its operations, leading to $8.25 million in operational savings.
- The Department of Motor Vehicles shortened title issuance processing from 145 days to 22 days.
- Department of Transportation process improvements reduced steps by 45 percent and saved 1,200 staff hours.

In March 2013, Governor Malloy expanded the directive to include the rest of the state. "Lean is one of the best ways we can continue to improve service delivery even in the face of a tough budget and a challenging economy," he said in the press release. "By getting routine activities to function smoothly and consistently, staff time is freed up to focus on higher value tasks that are more directly linked to meeting customer needs."

Later that year, the state set up a program called LeanCT, which runs as part of OPM. Headed by Alison Newman Fisher, who moved over from the budget office to take on the role of director in November, 2013, the group supports and monitors continuous improvement on a statewide basis by providing assistance in contracting Lean resources, establishing standards, and providing strategic guidance on key projects. Working with the steering committee, LeanCT also collects data on improvement efforts and reports to the governor.

The expanded mandate has brought in a flurry of Lean activity across the state. Over 40 agency heads have assigned Lean coordinators, and over 2,000 employees have been trained to use Lean tools and principles. There have been hundreds of *kaizens*, spanning all functions of government, that have led to measurable performance improvements ranging from 10 percent to 80 percent.

An important feature of these improvement projects has been senior management presence. Although care is taken to empower employees to take the initiative, the visibility of *kaizens* is very high.

Alison Newman Fisher: In many of these cases, teams will be asked to report directly to a commissioner on their progress at certain points—quarterly, annually, or whatever. After the event is over and we do a final report-out on the Friday afternoon, there are always commissioners, deputy commissioners, high-level managers every time.

We definitely have that commitment and that interest, so that makes it a lot easier to build a system around that.

That's one of the reasons we've gotten so many people into training—because they don't have to ask for approval.

Bringing the Methods to the Workers

The creation of LeanCT, along with the steering committee, has allowed Connecticut's transformation to Lean government to move forward on a statewide, as opposed to a departmental, basis. One aspect has been the standardization of Lean training and services. Five outside vendors are on contract to provide a variety of courses and consulting services, and competency levels are tracked for each agency. Training is coordinated so that an employee gets to participate in a *kaizen* shortly after completing a course.

LeanCT, however, is not just about Lean. The steering committee is looking at a broader range of competencies that include change management, critical thinking, and strategic planning. Accordingly, LeanCT tracks and supports many projects that employ non-Lean disciplines.

> *Alison Newman Fisher:* Ultimately what we're doing is changing our culture and moving to a more critical thinking/ continuous improvement type of environment. So what we're trying to do is bridge everything and not say Lean is the only answer. It's all part of a greater effort to move toward a continuous improvement culture.

There's also concern about moving beyond projects and changing everyday attitudes in the workplace. Employee engagement therefore is a major part of LeanCT's work, and this means thinking beyond numerical results.

> *Alison Newman Fisher:* Measuring results isn't incredibly interesting to most people. So how do you engage them while

you're making them report on what they do? It's tough to do this with 50,000 people.

Part of the challenge, Newman Fisher says, is that past management practices in government have discouraged the kind of participation that continuous improvement calls for. Therefore, in some respects, LeanCT is about changing the way people are managed.

Alison Newman Fisher: Previous theories of motivation are why government has been trapped for so long. We've as an institution been throwing up our hands and saying, "Well, we can't pay people more, so I guess there's nothing we can do."

But what about empowerment? What about making people proud to go to work? In government we do one of the most prideful jobs in the world. Direct service—it doesn't get better than that. Just framing this in a way where people understand the impact they make and tapping into why people became public servants in the first place is, I think, one of the most important tools we have to motivate. But I think people don't have those conversations.

One of the keys to extending the conversation, Newman Fisher says, is aligning the message with the way people are thinking and feeling in the workplace and avoiding unnecessary jargon or technical information:

We try to message this in a very basic way. A lot of what we try to say is that we're just trying to do the best we can with what we've got, because that's essentially what this is about.

So we've made posters and flyers that just say, "Do you feel frustrated? Would you like your job to be easier? Does it take too much time to process paperwork? If you've answered 'yes' to any of these questions, please come to this information session." Stuff like that. So we don't actually use the terminology to get people in the room. We just try to answer the questions that we know they have and respond to the comments we've heard indirectly.

LeanCT, like Results Washington, also plays a significant role in bringing together agencies with responsibilities that often overlap. For example, the Department of Children and Families may need to collaborate with the Department of Education to help disadvantaged children. Traditionally, there might have been little interaction between these groups.

Alison Newman Fisher: Getting different agencies together has happened really quickly here, and now we're really capitalizing on that. That's been one of my primary focuses since I took this position, to build more and more cross-agency projects. That's where we're going to get the most success.

The challenge is not getting people to the table but establishing accountability once the project is implemented. This is where having a centralized authority is essential.

Alison Newman Fisher: The agencies have always been willing to work together. The challenge is about who pays and who's responsible when the *kaizen* is finished and you come back to work on Monday. So we struggle with that, and that's why OPM has taken a central role on helping sort through these issues.

Another interesting collaboration has been with the state's information technology group. Connecticut is currently engaged in an open data project that involves a great deal of interaction with stakeholder groups. LeanCT is helping the group use value stream mapping to facilitate the conversation.

Alison Newman Fisher: IT has the same issue that Lean does— speaking a language that nobody understands. So we've started to use Lean events to bring IT and users together. When you look at a software project on a value stream map, you've got everybody speaking the same language, because the process flow is right there. So people are able to have a conversation about what needs to happen—that's one of the biggest changes we've seen. This is sort of an intangible result. So it's just as important as taking 50 days off of a process.

LeanCT is also beginning to interact with other jurisdictions. Newman Fisher recently presented at a five-state event in Portland, Maine, that also featured a presentation by Washington's Hollie Jensen, and Connecticut has joined a national community of practice that involves 14 other states. This will allow governments to share best practices and seek advice on some of the tougher problems facing them.

Alison Newman Fisher: Lean affords us the opportunity to solve issues that we need to solve because government is constrained. We have limited revenue and expanding expenditures every day, and we need to figure out a way to do things more efficiently because people will be requesting our services until the end of time—that's kind of the nature of our business.

"IT'S REALLY ABOUT UNIFICATION"

In much of the world, including Canada, many if not all healthcare services are delivered by governments. In 1947, Saskatchewan, a prairie province, introduced a health insurance plan for all its residents, and this became the model for the Canada Health Act, which establishes healthcare as a basic right for all Canadians.

Since then, the cost/quality conundrum facing healthcare has become a hot political issue in Canada, with frequent calls to bring spending and wait times under control. In 2008, Dan Florizone, then a regional CEO within Saskatchewan's health system, visited the Virginia Mason Medical Center in Seattle to learn how that institution had used Lean to bring itself out of the same crisis.

After an intensive week that included *gemba* walks, presentations by staff and patients, and participation in improvement events, Florizone came home a Lean convert.

Florizone was soon promoted to deputy minister of health, becoming the highest-ranked civil servant in the province's healthcare system. In that role, he sponsored hundreds of Lean improvement initiatives, attacking problems such as wait times, errors, inefficiencies, and systemic error; those efforts often led to double-digit improvements in performance.

In 2012, the province signed a major contract with Seattle-based consultant John Black Associates, a key architect of the Virginia Mason Production System, to roll out Lean to the entire provincial healthcare system. Valued at $40 million Canadian over a four-year period, the contract includes a comprehensive program of training, planning, mentoring, facilitating, and visits to Lean facilities, including Virginia Mason.

In 2013, Florizone assumed a double portfolio: he became deputy minister of education and deputy minister for Lean, a newly established role with the mandate to bring Lean to the entire province.

Florizone reflected on his broad mandate:

Lean government is, first and foremost, about culture. We've had a great history in this province and across the country of pride in the civil service, but the difficulty for us and other governments is that we lose sight of who we serve. It's very easy to suggest that we're here for the public interest, but that becomes far too nebulous.

So first of all, we have to be able to identify who the customer is in the context of the service we are delivering, whether that customer be a citizen, a patient, a student, or a business.

Second, we must be able to measure value and waste from the customer's perspective. Again, there's a huge cultural component to that. A lot of what we did in the past was in the realm of cost cutting as opposed to waste reduction and value creation, so this represents a big shift.

Third is the ability to actually see through the eyes of people who interact with customers in order to generate positive ideas for change right on the floor. In government, we may not be directly involved in service delivery but may be part of the chain as funder, policy developer, or decision maker. Therefore, we need to actually look to the ground in order to understand what impact our policies have, and we also need to engage our 9,000 or so civil servants plus our 23,000 staff in the education sector and our 43,000 staff in the health sector so that they understand their role.

Finally, we need to create an environment that supports incremental improvement—small tests of change with targets and time frames that lead us strategically in directions we want to go. This allows us to progress and improve day in and day out so that tomorrow is better than today.

So overall, I would suggest that government needs a major cultural shift. On one hand, that cultural shift is not dissimilar to what a manufacturer would need or a service industry player would need. On the other hand, there isn't a profit motive in government, so value and eliminating waste become our reason for being.

Florizone is currently implementing an extensive strategic planning process across the province. Using the Production Preparation Process (3P) that is commonly used to design Lean processes, managers, workers, and customers participate in strategic planning exercises that cross the jurisdictions of different ministries and define the issues of delivery in the context of the customer within the value stream.

The status quo is that governments are used to optimizing their own functional areas, such as their department within the Ministry of Transportation. The planning process is designed to instill a very different kind of thinking.

Dan Florizone: Lean gives us the tools to put our customer— for example, the patient or the student—together as a whole. Currently, we've got our customers sliced and diced every which way. What Lean allows us to do is look at the person as a whole, create value streams, and articulate how it feels on the receiving end of a myriad of services.

In health, for example, you have mental health clients who are also clients of social services. So as you're developing an initiative, you want to take a look at the individual's entire journey. This means examining all the touch points that cover not only health and social services but education, justice, and all the agencies that the individual might come in contact with.

So it's really about unification. Rather than just focus in on, say, acute care for an individual, we are looking upstream and saying, "What can we do to prevent a patient from becoming a patient in the first place?" We can then make investments in the proper places, and this is where education comes in. If we can get students to graduate and successfully integrate into the economy, we can break the cycle of poverty.

When you start to look at these grand value streams and look at the person as a whole and their journey throughout those value streams, we can pick our points that have the greatest impact. Otherwise, what will happen is that we'll simply build more hospitals and more jails and provide for more social benefits and services without really figuring out what we can do to intervene.

Unifying a myriad of government services around the customer requires in-depth conversations about what that customer needs and expects from government, and a unique planning process that is a radical departure from the prototyping that is normally practiced in planning government services.

The approach Florizone is using is to create a value stream that represents a single individual, and then scale it up. For example, they might start with the requirements of a special-needs student and then consider a group of five who share those needs. The model is scaled up in increments of five until it represents the needs of an entire identifiable group across the province.

Dan Florizone: This is very different from traditional piloting, where you come up with a theory and test it in the field. In that case, you are really looking at policy at large through the unidentifiable and the statistical. Usually in government, pilots start and then die a slow death because somebody has forgotten what they are there for.

What we're talking about in terms of prototyping is going into a particular area or multiple areas, focusing our energy on modifying for local context, and then moving to spread. A prototype means that although we're going everywhere, you just can't do it all at once.

Driving Major Policy Decisions

The planning process is causing some major rethinking at senior management levels in the province. One of the key issues is that when costs are assessed across the value stream, a very different picture emerges.

Dan Florizone: Let's take the example of paying a $15 pre-
mium to get an immediate medical test result, as opposed to
having the patient wait three days. If you're thinking like a
director of laboratory services, you're going to try to get that
sample into a centralized process where the economies of scale
get you down to pennies a test. The mantra here is that central is better and economies-of-scale efficiency is always better
when it's centralized.

However, if you look at this through the Lean lens, spending an extra $15 to get an immediate result might be a great
investment, especially given that with our geography, people
sometimes have to travel considerably to get to a doctor
appointment. In fact, why don't we have small labs and quick
point-of-care testing in every medical clinic so that you have
the results in hand when you see the physician as opposed
to getting a requisition, then going out, providing, and then
coming back for a repeat visit with a physician?

Of course, the redundant doctor appointment with the old
system costs the province a lot more than the $15 laboratory test.
With doctor time in short supply, particularly in rural areas, the
change could be a triple win: the patient gets better service, wait
times for doctors decrease, and costs are reduced.

Utilization of facilities and related assets is another key. Looking
at the utilization of resources in terms of where they fit in the value
stream could lead to major changes in the province's school systems.

Dan Florizone: In education, we spend probably 10 percent
of our budget just transporting children to and from school.
That's over $120 million for us. We've got thousands of
kilometers that we're putting on a day on buses. Now a Lean
sensei might look at this and say, "You guys are batching;
you've got big buses. Maybe what you should do is look at

smaller vehicles and do smaller milk runs more often. This would mean lower capital costs, better fuel economy, and a better outcome for students who want to minimize their time on the bus."

Along similar lines, can we deliver better value if we use staggered start times or evening classes to increase the capacity of existing facilities? And why aren't we running our schools year-round? That's a controversial idea, but we know that the learning drop-off from the summer hiatus is significant. We also know that the biggest risks for the students, much as in health care, are all in the transition—their pass rate in high school is connected clearly to how many moves they've made in-year between schools. So how can we improve that?

When we look at these questions through the Lean lens, we consider all the personnel in addition to the teacher who share the responsibility for the student's success. This includes everyone from counselors to math coaches to speech language pathologists, not to mention occupational therapists, nurses, and corrections workers. As well, there's a whole myriad of background services, ranging from something as simple as getting a transcript to as complex as figuring out how we work with addiction and mental health in the health sector to make sure that a child who comes from a family at risk has the supports that are necessary.

Another big change is the way governments look at data. Like private companies that have used Lean accounting as a dashboard, Florizone is calling for the use of real-time data:

A lot of the data that we get is through research, as opposed to real-time reporting. This means that by the time we get the data, it's a year old. That's an improvement from when it used to be three years old, but we can't continue to operate this way.

The point is, if we get too hung up on precision, we wind up losing the benefit. I'll take a figure reported at 92 percent versus 92.4539 percent for timeliness any day. We need to get those quick and dirty measures that are more of a reflection of what's happening now as opposed to what's happening last year so we can get away from this rearview mirror look at the world.

The Will to Serve the Public

As with any culture change, the people component is essential. Florizone is confident that Lean will engage public servants because it provides a delivery mechanism for them to do things that they have been trying to do for years:

What's exciting about this is that we're really getting to the heart of why we do what we do in the public service. Whether you are a teacher, an occupational therapist, a bus driver, or a healthcare provider, you don't want these processes around you that are fundamentally broken. Nobody wants to be doing confusing and repetitive paperwork and wondering what this is all about. So we actually get, from the front line, a lot of support for this work. They're the ones coming up with the ideas.

CHAPTER 14

◆

CONCLUSIONS

The Lean CEOs have spoken.

Their Lean journeys were, to paraphrase Taiichi Ohno, born of necessity, but that necessity took many forms. The CEOs may have been compelled by collapsing market prices, economic downturn, defecting customers, low productivity, or dying patients. They turned to Lean because they saw that conventional methods couldn't support the real change that their organizations needed.

The decision to adopt Lean was never an easy one, and it often led to painful choices. The CEOs faced resisters, detractors, and lots of well-presented arguments why Lean could never work "in our organization." In many cases, there were false starts where the organizations dabbled with Lean methods before taking Lean to the enterprise. Some CEOs were confronted with personal doubts years into the transformation.

These were journeys of discovery. Each organization found its own way to train employees, apply the Lean tools, practice *kaizen* and other participative processes, and spread a Lean culture throughout the organization. Often, CEOs brought in other disciplines, such as John Kotter's change management process or Edgar Schein's methods of creating a corporate culture.

Even the Lean tools themselves were adapted, combined, and renamed to suit the culture and business realities of the environment, as Kevin Meyer observed in Chapter 9:

I think the best Lean companies get really good at understanding the value and treat the tool set as just ideas that you use to create your own tools. There are a lot of things we did at Specialty Silicone that I couldn't really put into 5S or TPM or any of those buckets. But they optimized customer value.

There is, however, nothing vague about Lean. The hallmarks—employee engagement, continuous flow, elimination of waste, a focus on customer value—are tangible and universal, as are the challenges that organizations face in pursuing these objectives. Thus, a snow blower factory can give hospital managers a better understanding of patient care, and a farm equipment manufacturer can provide guidance for streamlining government processes.

As Lean Enterprise Institute CEO John Shook explained, it's important to look beyond the Lean methods to what the organizations are pursuing, and how they are involving their people in that pursuit.

John Shook: Lean happens in a lot of different ways, and we have to be very practical. . . . When I go into an organization, I don't look for the tools much. I don't look for the jargon. I look to see employees engaged in some type of PDCA occurring in service of the customer—defining gaps and continuously working through, and then, especially then, there's the focusing mechanism of the aim of achieving flow. If that's there, then I'm happy to call that Lean.

Lean is also intrinsically holistic, and the Lean CEOs broadened the horizons significantly as their Lean journeys progressed. Tom Everill at the Northwest Center adopted Lean to create fulfilling work for people with diverse abilities. After three years, he not only achieved that but increased revenues 500 percent and turned his company into a competitive force with a stunning quality record. Dan Ariens started using Lean to bring his company out of a financial crisis and created such a collaborative work environment that his plant became a teaching model for healthcare.

All this is difficult to codify, and Lean clearly has to be seen to be understood. The definitive bible for Lean, therefore, is not a textbook, but the living, breathing examples that inform the Lean community. Toyota represents the pinnacle, and its discipline in following Lean principles for over half a century and its generosity in sharing its knowledge have given it the well-earned reputation of being the undisputed leader of the Lean movement.

HOW THE LEAN CEOs LEAD

Lean sets the bar high for CEO accountability, and many Lean CEOs were vocal critics of the negative behaviors that are often associated with corporate executives. The Lean CEOs did not mislead their employees; engage in short-term, self-serving strategies; play factions against one another; or mislead customers and shareholders.

It's easy to see why a self-serving leader would never survive in a Lean environment. Lean makes above-average demands on all employees. Lean environments, furthermore, are transparent and exposed; with problems posted in plain view and employees speaking out and pulling the *andon*, there is nowhere to hide. Hypocritical self-serving behavior on the part of the CEO would be immediately obvious, and would quickly destroy any effort to create a Lean culture.

Beyond these table stakes, there was a clear set of common leadership practices that characterize Lean CEOs.

In brief, Lean CEOs

- Are active on the front lines
- Are stewards of a companywide transformation

- Create a culture of trust and empowerment
- Exercise discipline and constancy of purpose

Lean CEOs Are Active on the Front Lines

The leadership practice of being present on the front lines, which was dubbed management by wandering around by Tom Peters and Robert Waterman in *In Search of Excellence*, was universally followed by the Lean CEOs profiled in this book, although *wandering* is a poor descriptor of the purposeful manner in which they approached the workplace. Regardless of their educational background and experience, the Lean CEOs showed a deep respect for the work in *gemba*.

Their approaches varied. Some got their hands on the equipment to get a feel for what the workers were doing. Some participated in or led *kaizens*. Many personally led tours. All shared a skepticism about computerized reports and showed an urge to see "the real thing." There were no "Silent Sloans" managing from behind the scenes.

Presence in the workplace was accompanied by genuine curiosity and intellectual honesty: a willingness to accept that when we go and see, we don't always see what we expected. Lean CEOs are comfortable being told the plain truth about problems in the workplace and willing to learn from workers who live and breathe the value-creating processes that account for the organization's existence.

Lean CEOs Are Stewards of a Companywide Transformation

The Lean CEOs pursued a long-term vision, and recognized that the Lean transformation must take on a life of its own. Often, their stories were not about their own actions, but about how the transformation unfolded. They spoke about how fragile a culture of continuous improvement is and how leaders need to step back and allow its magic to take root.

Thus, the transformation's progress became their dashboard. They spent less time looking at financial reports, and more time observing how the Lean transformation was taking hold. Were employees taking initiative to make improvements? Are the results from the *kaizens* sticking? Were managers learning to coach and support their workers?

The Lean CEOs took the leap of faith that if the transformation goes well, the bottom line will follow. And as we can see from their stories, they were often empowered and motivated by revelations that a sustainable culture was taking root: something that would survive their tenure.

Lean CEOs Create a Culture of Trust and Empowerment

The Lean CEOs all believed in their employees, and understood of the dynamics of empowerment. They applied this awareness to their own interactions and instilled this kind of behavior in their managers. Much of this was about learning to listen and teaching their managers to listen as well.

The Lean CEOs also showed they could get very impatient with managers who didn't get it when it came to respecting and empowering workers. Their actions reflected that Lean environments call for sensitivity toward people, but at the same time, constant vigilance and a willingness to give and accept criticism.

Lean CEOs Exercise Discipline and Constancy of Purpose

Lean involves the pursuit of aggressive targets and engagement of the entire organization in a comprehensive change process with no completion date. Lean processes are easily derailed, and setbacks are common and discouraging. Even in mature Lean organizations, new problems arise that can threaten the hard-earned gains from the transformation.

All this requires incredible singularity of purpose on the part of the CEO. There will always be problems, naysayers, and hundreds of reasons to put the journey on hold. Lean CEOs have what it takes to lead not just for the next quarter but year after year.

WHY LEAN ORGANIZATIONS OUTPERFORM NON-LEAN ORGANIZATIONS

There are many ways of explaining why Lean organizations achieve extraordinary results. Within the context of the Lean journeys described in this book, I believe that two primary reasons for Lean success stood out: (1) Lean brings out the best in people, and (2) Lean gets leaders in touch with reality.

Lean Brings Out the Best in People

Organizations are ultimately collections of individuals, and all else being equal, a group of people who enthusiastically use their talents to further the purpose of their organization are bound to outperform a group of people who are otherwise inclined.

Lean provides an environment where employees can achieve real, tangible results and be recognized accordingly. This helps workers become valuable to the organization and the organization's customers and experience the satisfaction that can arise only from providing real benefits to others. In that respect, Lean accomplishes what incentives, leadership training, career counseling, and other HR interventions cannot.

Teamwork plays a major role here. Lean environments are designed so that there is no incentive for workers to pass defects on to their coworkers or throw problems over the wall for others to fix. The manager of the machining department does not fight with the manager of the welding department over overhead allocation; instead, both managers share their best people so that they can succeed as a team.

Lean provides the antidote for the common complaint "I love my work, but I can't stand all the other stuff that goes on." Lean sees that "other stuff" as waste, and any employee who feels that frustration can lead the charge to get rid of that waste.

Lean also recognizes and systematically harvests the tacit knowledge of people in the workplace and converts it to explicit knowledge through continuous improvement and standard work. Workers know best how to improve their processes, and that knowledge again and again was the key to shortening lead times, reducing defects, eliminating waste, and meeting customer delivery times. Processes perpetually get better when workers are empowered to improve them. To put it another way, Lean companies succeed because they listen and learn.

Finally, Lean leads to cooperation between workers and management, higher morale, and lower turnover and helps companies attract and retain the best people. This is a virtuous cycle.

One can conclude that Lean reflects the widely accepted holistic view of human motivation presented by Abraham Maslow and others. This makes for a far more realistic approach to managing people.

Lean Gets Leaders in Touch with Reality

When W. Edwards Deming criticized American industry for being out of touch with reality, he knew that the problem was not a lack of information. Senior managers all had a plethora of figures about every minute cost in their organizations. The problem was, to quote Deming, that "information is not knowledge."

Real knowledge, Deming argued, has to be contextual. This means that people looking at the data must have a prior understanding of how all the parts in the system interact. Without context within a system that has a clear, common purpose, the data are meaningless.

The de facto system used by companies to provide context is the pyramid-shaped organizational chart model. This provides a hierarchical structure for the various entities in the corporation, showing the path of accountability from each one to the CEO.

The pyramid organizational chart serves an important function: it helps simplify a complex collection of employees, equipment, facilities, information systems, intellectual property, and a host of other entities on a single sheet of paper. The fixed organizational model aligns with the balance sheet, tells shareholders what they own, and serves as a suitable model for GAAP accounting.

The problem is that although the pyramid chart shows what the organization is, it does not describe what it *does*. Nowhere is there a description of how the entities work together to create the product or service the customer is paying for, as Deming adeptly pointed out:

> The pyramid only shows who reports to whom. Information flows from the top. A pyramid does not describe a system of production. It doesn't tell anybody what his job is. It does not tell anybody how his work fits in with the work of other people in the system. If the pyramid conveys a message, it is that anybody should, first and foremost, try to satisfy his boss (get a good rating). A pyramid, as an organization chart, thus destroys the system.[1]

CEOs who work exclusively with this model are essentially managers of fixed entities. They invest or divest in business components, outsource, consolidate divisions, or acquire new technology or facilities. Instead of engaging in a continuous improvement program, the traditional CEO is more inclined to initiate a massive restructuring.

The limitations of this approach are often disastrous. Entities within the company are managed as if they were separate businesses, and the resulting functional silos prevent cooperation and cause distrust. Inventory and work in process fall into the cracks between the functional areas and are allowed to build up, cluttering factories and leading to huge storage, transportation, and deterioration costs.

In healthcare, hospital managers manage the various entities—doctors, nurses, equipment, labs, facilities—with little idea of how a patient flows through the system, resulting in long wait times, miscommunication, and medical errors.

In Lean organizations, decision makers focus on what the organization does and use value streams as a tool to understand that. Here we simplify not the entities in the company but the thousands of events that make up production: the flow of materials and information and the work of everybody in the organization. The value stream is a dynamic model that reflects the activity for which customers are paying.

The value stream therefore provides the context for observing real circumstances in the workplace. Metrics such as lead time, customer service percentage, and employee engagement, which might never find their way into a financial report, are front and center in Lean organizations. These are the metrics that make the difference for customers and are where the future of the company lies.

Lean does not hide problems from decision makers. Production delays are posted in red throughout the plant, and with no inventory to hide inconsistency, every imaginable production problem is out in the open. In healthcare, the elimination of waiting rooms forces clinics to run on schedule. A defect does not have to travel through multiple layers of management to get to the CEO: one pull of the *andon* in a factory or a hospital will bring it right out into the open.

The value stream, finally, provides the context for seeing waste. There's no point noticing inventory building up between processes if there is no system in place that identifies it as waste and shows the value of eliminating it. Lean as a business model truly values *genchi genbutsu* and unleashes its power.

Throughout the journeys, we saw evidence of leaders who were connected with reality. They acted early when they saw quality starting to slip or sensed that the drive to continuously improve was losing momentum. They planned carefully to weather the downturn of 2009 and emerged more quickly than their competitors did. Time and time again they acquired the know-how to replicate their success in acquired companies, in other divisions, or with their suppliers and business partners.

WHY DON'T MORE CEOs EMBRACE LEAN?

CEO adoption is a perpetual question in the Lean community. In light of the documented success of Lean companies, why do so few CEOs make the leap?

Ignorance appears to be a major factor. Many people still think that becoming Lean means running a company with a skeleton staff and outsourcing everything in sight. Even in a manufacturing environment where Lean practices are widely known, a CEO who suggests looking at Lean to a plant manager is likely to hear, "Oh, we're doing that," based on having completed a 5S exercise or having built a few U-shaped cells to streamline production. When one mentions Lean casually, the typical response is, "Oh, you mean Lean manufacturing."

Similarly, the old rules of management are deeply entrenched. Those who have made it to the top have adapted very well to an existing culture. In asking them to change, we are asking them to forsake a system that has made them and their friends very prosperous. Together, they mutually reinforce the beliefs that define the status quo.

Lean is not an easy course even for those who believe in it. As we saw, Lean calls for extraordinary persistence and dedication, and there's no end to the journey. By their own admission, even the exceptional CEOs profiled in this book would not have adopted Lean without the pressing needs they described at the beginning of their journeys.

It appears likely, however, that more organizations will be facing burning platforms in the near future. Energy and other natural resources are getting harder to find and process, climate change is threatening the world's food supply, and the healthcare crisis is deepening. Waste that was tolerable in the past will simply become unaffordable. Wider Lean adoption is probably not a question of if but of when.

LOOKING OUTWARD

At a certain point in their journeys, the organizations in this book began to look beyond their walls and share what they had learned with the outside world. Spreading best practices is not unusual in the business world, but the intensity here certainly is. Lean companies not only open their doors but allow visitors to discuss manufacturing techniques with operators, give feedback, or sit in on *kaizen* events.

The activity often gets more extensive. Lean companies routinely second their best Lean people to their suppliers or dealers, host study sessions for managers, or open up their Lean courses to business partners, government personnel, and nonprofits. It's no wonder that when Washington State went knocking on doors, it was able to enlist free assistance from 84 Lean companies. Jon Miller, a Lean authority and also a Washington State resident, commented on this:

> I have been watching the development of a community of Lean practice in Washington State for over a decade with great interest, helping where I can. This truly remarkable public-private partnership is becoming a model for other regions. The leadership and initiative that we have now at the state government level gives me great optimism for the future that Lean can bring people together to solve even what seem like our most intractable problems.

The knowledge Lean companies share has real substance. This is not about endless slide presentations and philosophical overviews. We're talking about real methods and real results, coaching and mentoring, and a surprising level of candor and generosity. One rarely sees Lean advocates saying, "This is what you must do." Instead, they will say, "Tell me what you're trying to do and let me see if I can help you."

This is not about public relations. Lean companies have found that teaching is the best way to reinforce knowledge, and workers are enormously empowered by the satisfaction that comes from seeing others derive value from what they know. As Matt Long said in Chapter 5,

> I often apologize to our people for the time these visits take from their normal jobs. The answer I get back from them so often is, "Don't apologize. By me having to explain it to other people, I really have to think about my own system. And there's a level of accountability that I have to have that I might not have otherwise. So it helps me to stay on the journey."

When Lean companies help their suppliers and dealers create flow, those companies become better business partners. This is a win-win in a very real sense.

The sharing of Lean practices, however, goes beyond the company's business community; there was a certain public spirit shown by the many of the CEOs. Mary Andringa, who sits on numerous advisory committees, advocates for Lean government at every opportunity on the municipal, state, and federal levels. Bob Chapman is working with the Association for Manufacturing Excellence to make respect for people one of its pillars. John Toussaint works tirelessly to try to fix the healthcare crisis in the United States.

Lean brings people together like no other management system, and the openness and discussion that characterize Lean have the potential to rally people around the problems we all share as a community. As organizations face the burning platforms inherent in a global economy, the community-building aspects of Lean may prove to be even more important than Lean's utility at cutting waste.

In the end, Lean is about people. As the Lean CEOs have told us, once people get behind a purpose, there is no limit to what they can do.

NOTES

Preface

1. Taiichi Ohno, *The Toyota Production System.* New York: Productivity Press, 1988, p. 14.

Chapter 1

1. Bernard Beaudreau, *Mass Production, the Stock Market Crash, and the Great Depression: The Macroeconomics of Electrification.* Lincoln, NE: Author's Choice Press, 2004, p. 10.
2. Charles Sorensen, *My Forty Years with Ford.* New York: Norton, 1956, p. 116.
3. Ibid., p. 117.
4. Henry Ford, *Today and Tomorrow.* New York: Doubleday, 1926, p. 100.
5. Ibid., p. 101.
6. Ibid., p. 91.
7. Ibid., p. 230.
8. Alfred P. Sloan, Jr., *My Years with General Motors.* New York: Doubleday, 1963, p. 175.
9. Ibid., p. 187.
10. Ibid., pp. 139–140.
11. H. Thomas Johnson and Robert S. Kaplan, *Relevance Lost: The Rise and Fall of Management Accounting.* Cambridge, MA: Harvard Business School Press, 1987, pp. 1–2.

12. Peter Drucker, *Concept of the Corporation*. New York: John Day, 1946, p. 179.
13. Ibid., p. 183.
14. Ibid., p. 192.
15. Claire Crawford-Mason, "Made in Japan Is No Joke Now, Thanks to Edwards Deming: His New Problem Is 'Made in U.S.A.'" *People* magazine, vol. 14, no. 10, September 8, 1980.
16. NBC News documentary: *If Japan Can, Why Can't We?* June 10, 1980.

Chapter 2

1. Taiichi Ohno, *Toyota Production System: Beyond Large-Scale Production*. New York: Productivity Press, 1988, p. 3.
2. Ibid., p. 4.
3. Ibid., p. 19.
4. Ibid., p. 5.
5. Ibid., p. 11.
6. Ibid., p. 17.
7. W. Edwards Deming, *The Essential Deming*, ed. *Joyce Nilsson Orsini*. New York: McGraw-Hill, 2013, p. 296.
8. Masaaki Imai, *Kaizen: The Key to Japan's Competitive Success*. New York: McGraw-Hill, 1986, p. 43.
9. Union of Japanese Scientists and Engineers, main website, www.juse.or.jp.
10. Deming, op cit., p. 305.
11. Imai, op cit., p. 37.
12. Kaizen Institute website, www.kaizen.com.
13. Jon Miller, Mike Wroblewski, and Jaime Villafuerte, *Creating a Kaizen Culture: Align the Organization, Achieve Breakthrough Results, and Sustain the Gains*. New York: McGraw-Hill, 2014, e-book location 939.
14. Eiji Toyoda, from presentation "The Path to TQC Implementation," September 1965, Toyota Motor Corporation website.
15. "A Forty-Year History of Toyota," p. 254, Toyota Motor Corporation, Toyota website.
16. Satoshi Hino, *Inside the Mind of Toyota: Management Principles for Enduring Growth*. New York: Productivity Press, 2006, e-book location 1393.

Chapter 3

1. Masaaki Imai, *Kaizen: The Key to Japan's Competitive Success.* New York: McGraw-Hill, 1986.
2. Masaaki Imai, *Gemba Kaizen: A Commonsense Approach to a Continuous Improvement Strategy,* 2nd ed. New York, McGraw-Hill, 2012, p. 198.

Chapter 4

1. Jean E. Cunningham and Orest J. Fiume with Emily Adams, *Real Numbers.* Durham, NC: Managing Times Press, 2003.
2. James Womack and Daniel Jones, *Lean Thinking: Banish Waste and Create Wealth in Your Corporation.* New York: Free Press, 2003.
3. Ibid.

Chapter 6

1. Frederick Herzberg, "One More Time: How Do You Motivate Employees?" *Harvard Business Review,* January 1968, vol. 46, no. 1, pp. 53–62.

Chapter 9

1. Peter Senge, *The Leader's New Work: Building Learning Organizations.* MIT Sloan Management Review, October 15, 1990, pp. 7–23.
2. W. Edwards Deming, *The New Economics for Industry, Government, Education.* Cambridge, MA: MIT Center for Advanced Educational Services, 1994, p. 123.
3. Eric Ries, *The Lean Startup.* New York: Crown, 2011, p. 38.
4. Taiichi Ohno, *Toyota Production System: Beyond Large-Scale Production.* New York: Productivity Press, 1988.
5. James Womack and Daniel Jones, *Lean Thinking: Banish Waste and Create Wealth in Your Corporation.* New York: Free Press, 2003.
6. James Womack, *The Lean Post* (blog), February 25, 2014.

Chapter 11

1. Michael E. Gerber, *The E-Myth Re-Visited.* New York: HarperCollins, 1995.
2. Masaaki Imai, *Gemba Kaizen: A Commonsense Approach to a Continuous Improvement Strategy.* New York: McGraw-Hill, 2012.

Chapter 12

1. OECD Health Care Statistics 2013, OECD website, http://stats.oecd .org/Index.aspx?DataSetCode=SHA.
2. Donald Berwick, A. Blanton Godfrey, and Jane Roessner, *Curing Healthcare: New Strategies for Quality Improvement*. San Francisco: Wiley, 1990.
3. John Toussaint, MD, Roger A. Gerard, PhD, Emily Adams, *On the Mend: Revolutionizing Healthcare to Save Lives and Transform the Industry*. Cambridge, MA: Lean Enterprise Institute, 2010, e-book location 315.
4. Ibid., e-book location 337.
5. Art Byrne, *The Lean Turnaround*. New York: McGraw-Hill, 2013, p. 165.
6. John P. Kotter and Dan S. Cohen, *The Heart of Change*. Cambridge, MA: Harvard Business Review Press, 2002, p. 2.

Chapter 13

1. Executive Order 13-04, Office of the Governor, State of Washington, September 10, 2013.

Chapter 14

1. W. Edwards Deming, *The Essential Deming: Leadership Principles from the Father of Quality*, ed. Joyce Nilsson Orsini. New York: McGraw-Hill, 2013, pp. 153–154.

READING LIST

The purpose of this list is to suggest additional reading for those unfamiliar with Lean who want to get a better understanding of the methods used in the Lean transformations featured in this book. The following is a small selection from the many excellent books that have been written on the subject.

Byrne, Art, *The Lean Turnaround: How Business Leaders Use Lean Principles to Create Value and Transform Their Company*. New York: McGraw-Hill, 2013.

Cunningham, Jean, and Orest Fiume, with Emily Adams, *Real Numbers: Management Accounting in a Lean Organization*. Durham, NC: Managing Times Press, 2003.

Imai, Masaaki, *Gemba Kaizen: A Commonsense Approach to a Continuous Improvement Strategy*, 2d ed. New York: McGraw-Hill, 2012.

Liker, Jeffrey K., *The Toyota Way: 14 Management Principles from the World's Greatest Manufacturer*. New York, McGraw-Hill, 2004.

Martin, Karen, and Mike Osterling, *Value Stream Mapping: How to Visualize Work and Align Leadership for Organizational Transformation*. New York: McGraw-Hill, 2014.

Miller, Jon, Mike Wroblewski, and Jaime Villafuerte, *Creating a Kaizen Culture: Align the Organization, Achieve Breakthrough Results, and Sustain the Gains*. New York: McGraw-Hill, 2014.

Ohno, Taiichi, *Toyota Production System: Beyond Large-Scale Production.* Portland, OR: Productivity Press, 1988.

Rother, Mike, and John Shook, *Learning to See: Value Stream Mapping to Add Value and Eliminate Muda.* Brookline, MA: Lean Enterprise Institute, 1999.

Toussaint, John, Roger A. Gerard, Emily Adams, *On the Mend: Revolutionizing Healthcare to Save Lives and Transform the Industy.* Brookline, MA: Lean Enterprise Institute, 2010.

Womack, James, and Daniel T. Jones, *Lean Thinking: Banish Waste and Create Wealth in Your Corporation*, rev ed. New York: Free Press, 2003.

INDEX

Abegglen, Jim, 50
Absorption, 12
Accountability, 151–152
Accountability culture, 144
Accountable care, 279, 280
Accounting reports, 72–74
Acqua Minerale San Benedetto, 135–140
Adams, Emily, 258
Agile software development, 206
Alexander, Dan, 213
Alignment, 271
All Toyota Quality Control Conference, 43
Aluminum Trailer Company (ALC), 88–96
American Motors, 17
Andon, 29, 44, 268
Andringa, Mary, 108–116, 316
Antioch University Center for Creative Change, 173
Appleton Papers, 196, 199
Appvion, 196–205
Ariens, Dan, 78–88, 256, 307
Ariens, Henry, 79
Ariens Company, 78–88, 255
Assertiveness and empowerment, 193
"Asset-light" business model, 108

Association for Manufacturing Excellence (AME), 171
Autonomous maintenance, 29, 44

Bara, Hugo Levente, 245–250
Barry-Wehmiller, 160–172
Barry-Wehmiller University, 168
Beaudreau, Bernard C., 5
Berwick, Donald, 252
Best idea of the month, 248
Best practice community, 288
Bevan, Chris, 211
Black, John, 266, 271
Boeing, 285
Bottom-up approach, 136
Bradford, Bob, 81
Bratu, Julien, 247
Brenneman, Steve, 88–96
Brody, Bob, 275–281
Byczynski, Ed, 152–157
Byrne, Art, 56–69, 96, 110, 266
Byrne's Lean metrics, 61

Caetano Bus, 129–135
Cahill, Kevin Edwards, 19
Capacity, 107–125
    "asset-light" business model, 108
    demand forecasting, 107–108

Capacity (*Continued*)
  Herman Miller, 115–125
  traditional capacity planning
    exercises, 107
  Vermeer Corporation, 108–115
Cash flow, 101, 102
Cell, 44
Changing behavior, 270
"Changing How Connecticut State
    Government Does
    Business," 292
Chapman, Bob, 160–172, 316
Chief executive officer (CEO).
    See Lean CEO
Chief financial officer (CFO)
  fiduciary duty to shareholders, 201
  flow/cash flow, 101
  minute merchant, 101
Chrysler, 17
Clean Transportation, 288
Cohen, Dan, 270
Collins, Jim, 195
Concept of the Corporation
    (Drucker), 14–16
Confronting managers who oppose
    Lean, 194
Confucius, 283
Connecticut, 292–297
Continuous deployment, 206
Continuous flow, 44
Continuous improvement, 38, 39
Continuous improvement director, 200
Conway, William E., 19
Corvi, Carolyn, 269
Cost accounting, 12–13
Crawford-Mason, Clare, 17–19
Creative idea suggestion system, 28
Crisis situation. *See* Financial crisis
Criticism, 309
Cronkite, Walter, 251
Cross-functional cooperation, 152.
    See also Management teams
Cross-functional management, 272
Cunningham, Jean, 72–75, 154

Curing Health Care
    (Berwick et al.), 252
Current-state value stream map, 34
Customer service percentage, 61, 62

Daily management, 272
Damron, Darrell, 285, 288–290
Danaher Corporation, 52, 56–58
Demand forecasting, 107–108
Deming, W. Edwards, 17–19, 20,
    35–39, 71, 173, 188, 251, 311, 312
Deming Prize, 36–37, 40
Detransactionalize, 103
Direct-based accounting, 201–202
Disabled employees
  Goodwill Industries, 181–185
  Northwest Center, 173–181
Diversified corporation, 217–234
  goal deployment process, 223
  inch wide-mile deep, 224
  Ingersoll Rand, 217–234
  just do its (JDIs), 224
  leading by example, 233–234
  metrics, 221
  Operational Excellence, 221
  problem solving, 228
  respect for people, 229–230
  servant leadership, 227–229
  team leader development
    program, 230
  value streams, 224–227, 233
Division of labor, 11
Dobyn, Lloyd, 19, 20
Donovan, Dan, 238
Drucker, Peter, 14–16, 141

E-Leather, 211–216
E-Myth Revisited, The (Gerber), 235
Eames, Charles and Ray, 115
Earl, Harley, 9
Economic slowdown (1970s), 16–17
Economies of scale, 25, 26
Edison Illuminating Company, 4
Employee engagement, 169, 226, 294

Employee-owned company
    (Appvion), 196–205
Employee suggestions, 247–248
Employees. *See also* Putting people first
    accountability, 151–152
    disabled, 173–185
    empowerment, 309, 311
    mistakes, 149–150
    motivation. *See* Worker motivation
Empowerment, 309, 311
Endnotes (notes), 317–320
Everill, Tom, 173–181, 306

Ferree, Tom, 201
Fiefdoms, 152. *See also* Functional
    silos; Silos
Fifth Discipline, The (Senge), 188
Financial crisis, 71–105
    Aluminum Trailer Company
        (ALC), 88–96
    Ariens Company, 78–88
    "cut and hope" approach, 72
    Lantech, 75–78
    Steffes Corporation, 96–105
    traditional accounting, 72–74
Firefighting duties, 142
Fiume, Orest, 58–59, 66, 72
Five-day *kaizen* event, 40. *See also*
    Kaizen event
Five whys, 31, 44
5S, 30, 44, 274
Flattening the organization, 215
Florizone, Dan, 298–304
Flow, 24, 27, 44
Ford, Henry, 4–8
Ford Motor Company, 4–8, 17
Franciscan St. Francis Health, 275–281
Functional silos, 13, 312

Gemba, 2–3, 44
Gemba Kaizen (Imai), 246
Gemba walk, 229, 233, 243
General Motors, 8–10, 14–16, 17, 107
Genshi genbutsu, 44

Gerard, Roger A., 258
Gerber, Michael, 235
Giannattasio, Frank, 89
Go and *see* imperative, 110–111
Goal councils, 287
Goal deployment process, 223
Godfrey, A. Blanton, 252
Good to Great (Collins), 195
Goodwill Industries, 182–185
Government, 283–304
    best practice community, 288
    Clean Transportation, 288
    Connecticut, 292–297
    goal councils, 287
    LeanCT, 293–297
    Production Preparation Process (3P),
        299–300
    public/private sector, contrasted, 290
    real-time data, 303–304
    Results Washington, 286–288, 291
    Saskatchewan, 297–304
    speeding tickets, 289–290
    unification, 300, 301
    Washington State, 285–291
GPL. *See* Guiding Principles of
    Leadership (GPL)
Graban, Mark, 276
Gregoire, Christine, 285
Guiding Principles of Leadership
    (GPL), 163–165, 168

Healthcare, 251–281
    accountable care, 279, 280
    alignment, 271
    flow, 257
    Franciscan St. Francis Health,
        275–281
    IHI, 252, 253
    medical errors, 252, 254, 257, 273
    patient handoffs, 257
    patient input, 264
    Patient Safety Alert (PSA),
        268, 273, 274
    physician autonomy, 262, 279

Healthcare (*Continued*)
　rising costs, 252
　see, feel, change paradigm, 269, 270
　skepticism, 262
　ThedaCare Medical Center,
　　254–265
　Triple Aim Initiative, 253
　Virginia Mason, 265–275
　waiting, 257, 278
　waste, 253
Healthcare Kaizen (Swartz/Graban), 276
Heart of Changes (Kotter/Cohen), 270
Herman Miller, 115–125
Heroic workarounds, 199
Herzberg, Frederick, 127–128
Herzberg's two-factor theory, 128
Hicks, Ron, 76
Hiding problems, 148
Hierarchical organization chart, 11–12
Historical overview
　economic slowdown (1970s), 16–17
　Ford and the moving assembly
　　line, 4–8
　management by numbers, 12–14
　mechanistic view of people, 14–16
　quality movement, 20
　scientific management
　　(Taylorism), 10–12
　Sloan and General Motors, 8–10
　Toyota. *See* Toyota Motor Company
　"work smarter, not harder," 17–19
Hoffman, Keith, 197
Hoshin kanri, 41, 44, 223, 224, 247
Humor, 148
Hyatt Roller Bearing, 8
Hygiene factors, 128

Iacocca, Lee, 19
If Japan Can, Why Can't We (TV), 17–19
Imai, Masaaki, 37, 39, 47–49, 69, 246
In Search of Excellence
　(Waterman/Peters), 308
Inch wide-mile deep, 224
Ingersoll, Simon, 217

Inslee, Jay, 286, 289, 291
Institute for Healthcare Improvement
　(IHI), 252, 253
Internal value streams, 103
Inventory turns, 61, 62
Ishikawa, Ichiro, 35
ISO 9000, 20
Iwata, Yoshiki, 48, 49, 53, 56

Jacob's Chuck, 56
Jacob's Vehicle Equipment Company
　(Jake Brake), 49, 52–56
JDIs. *See* Just do its (JDIs)
Jensen, Hollie, 290, 297
Jidoka, 29, 44
JIT. *See* Just-in-time (JIT)
John Black Associates, 298
Johnson, Thomas, 14
Johnson Controls Inc. (JCI), 218
Jones, Daniel T., 77
Juran, Joseph, 36
JUSE. *See* Union of Japanese Scientists
　and Engineers (JUSE)
Just do its (JDIs), 224
Just-in-time (JIT), 22, 24, 28, 32, 44

Kaizen, 39, 45
*Kaizen: The Key to Japan's Competitive
　Success* (Imai), 37, 48
Kaizen blitz, 40
Kaizen by harmony, 247
Kaizen Culture (Miller et al.), 40
Kaizen event
　Aluminum Trailer Company,
　　89, 90, 94
　Ariens Company, 81
　E-Leather, 214
　five-day kaizen, 40
　Franciscan St. Francis Health, 277
　Herman Miller, 118
　Jake Brake, 56
　PLZ Aeroscience, 154–156
　President's Kaizens, 57
　teaching others, 315

Kaizen improvement approach, 78
Kaizen Institute, 48, 213, 246
Kaizen newspaper, 78
Kanban, 30, 45
Kaplan, Gary, 265–275
Kaplan, Robert, 14
Kearns, David, 19
Key performance indicators (KPIs), 139
Kleineberg, Linda, 240
Koenigsaecker, George, 49–57, 224, 254, 255
Korean War, 27
Korthuis-Smith, Wendy, 287
Kotter, John, 269, 270, 305
KPIs. *See* Key performance indicators (KPIs)

L3 (Living Legacy of Leadership), 167, 168
Lack of knowledge, 142
Lamach, Mike, 217–222, 225–234
Lancaster, Jim, 78, 142–152
Lancaster, Pat, 74–78
Lantech
  financial crisis, 74, 75–78
  management teams, 142–152
Leahy, Kevin, 275
Lean
  above-average demands on employees, 307
  building capacity, 108
  constant and intensive maintenance, 241
  criticism, 309
  culture of trust and empowerment, 309
  disciplined structure, 235
  extraordinary persistence and dedication, 314
  getting people to change their thinking, 155
  hallmarks, 306
  importance of, in future, 314–315
  intrinsically holistic, 306
  long-term view, 139–140
  metrics, 61, 313
  paradigm shift in way organization is run, 142
  perpetual change requires constant adjustment, 114, 121
  prerequisites for successful Lean adoption, 100
  seeing is understanding (living, breathing examples), 307
  speak-up, listen-up kind of environment, 205
  spreading best practices (sharing information), 315–316
  teaching, 316
  teamwork/cooperation, 310–311
  TPS and TQC, 43
  transparency, 307
  value stream, 313
  why not adopted by more CEOs, 314
Lean accounting, 201–202
Lean CEO
  balance between questioning and coming across a confident leader, 242–243
  confronting managers who oppose Lean, 194
  constancy of purpose, 309–310
  humble leadership, 271
  leading by example, 233–234
  management by wandering around, 308
  most important person in getting Lean journey going, 87
  provide vision of whole picture from beginning to end, 123
  reality "check"/real knowledge, 311–314
  steward of companywide transformation, 67–68, 308–309
Lean grow-up, 210
Lean start-up, 205–216
Lean Startup, The (Ries), 205, 206
Lean Startup Circle, 210

Lean Thinking (Womack/Jones),
    77, 89, 207
Lean Turnaround, The (Byrne), 266
LeanCT, 293–297
Learning organization, 187–216
    Appvion, 196–205
    assertiveness and empowerment, 193
    continuous improvement
        director, 200
    defined, 187–188
    E-Leather, 211–216
    relevant Lean practices, 189
    senior management, 204–205,
        209, 215
    sharing knowledge, 209
    Specialty Silicone Fabricators (SSF),
        189–196
    start-ups, 205–216
    uncertainty, 189, 214
Learning to See (Rother/Shook), 33
Lewis, Charles, 5
Lifetime employment, 22, 23
Living Legacy of Leadership (L3),
    167, 168
Long, Matt, 116, 120, 125, 316

MacArthur, Douglas, 35
Malcolm Baldridge Award, 20
Malloy, Dannel P., 292, 293
Management by numbers, 12–14
Management by policy, 272
Management by wandering around, 308
Management teams, 141–157
    cross-functional cooperation, 152
    Lantech, 142–152
    PLZ Aeroscience, 152–157
    shop floor experiences, 146–147
Manager
    barriers to success, 142
    essential skills, 141
    information, 150
    mistakes, 150
    participation on a team, 156
    shop floor experiences, 146–147
    worker like his/her peers, 141–142

Manufacturing capacity. *See* Capacity
Market collapse. *See* Financial crisis
Marquip Ward United, 164
Martin, Jim, 182–185
Maskell, Brian, 99
Maslow, Abraham, 159
Material resource planning (MRP), 74
Matrix management structure, 41
McBean, Chris, 212–216
McDonnell, Dan, 222–224, 228–230
Mechanistic view of people, 14–16
"Merger of the Guiding Principles of
    Leadership and Lean Enterprise,
    The," 167
Meyer, Kevin, 189–196, 306
Miller, Ed, 89
Miller, Jon, 40, 315
Minimum viable product (MVP), 206
Mistakes, 149–150
Model AA, 22
Model T, 4, 8
Morgan, Bob, 144
Motivating workers. *See* Worker
    motivation
Motivation-hygiene theory (two-factor
    theory), 128
Moving assembly line, 5
MRP. *See* Material resource
    planning (MRP)
Muda, 24, 45
My 40 Years with Ford (Sorensen), 5
My Years with GM (Sloan), 10

Nakao, Chihiro, 49, 53
Nashua Corporation, 19
Nelson, George, 115
Newman Fisher, Alison, 293–297
Nissan, 40
Northwest Center, 173–181, 306

Ohno, Taiichi, 23–27, 29–32, 48, 114,
    187, 207
Ohno circle, 31, 55
OMCD. *See* Operations Management
    Consulting Division (OMCD)

On the Mend (Toussaint et al.),
258, 261
"One More Time: How Do You
Motivate Employees?"
(Herzberg), 127
One-piece flow, 44, 238, 239
OPEC oil embargo (1973), 17
Operational Excellence, 221
Operations Management Consulting
Division (OMCD), 43
Order spikes, 104, 112
"Order to cash" value stream, 120
Overhead, 12
Overprocessing, 25
Overproduction, 25
Owner-operator CEO, 235

Paperwork, 142
Paradigm shift, 142
Patient Safety Alert (PSA),
268, 273, 274
PDCA (plan-do-check-act), 37, 38, 45
Pentland, Bob, 52, 53
Peters, Tom, 308
Peterson, Donald, 19
Physician autonomy, 262, 279
Piece rate incentive system, 84
Pinto, Jorge, 128–135
PLZ Aeroscience, 152–157
President's Kaizen, 57
Problem-solving skills, 228
Problems, make them visible, 148
Production Preparation Process (3P),
299–300
Productivity (Byrne's Lean metric), 61
Pull, 26, 45
Putting people first, 159–185. *See also*
Employees
Barry-Wehmiller, 160–172
disabled employees, 173–185
Goodwill Industries, 182–185
Guiding Principles of Leadership
(GPL), 163–165, 168
Ingersoll Rand (diversified
company), 229–230

L3 (Living Legacy of Leadership),
167, 168
Northwest Center, 173–181
Pyramid organizational chart, 311–312

Quality (Byrne's Lean metric), 61
Quality control circle (QC circle),
37–39
"Quality is made in the boardroom"
principle, 251
Quality movement, 20
Quarterly reports, 72
Quinn, Mike, 175–177

Ratto, Carlo, 138
Re-industrialization, 18
Real experience, 146–147
Real Numbers (Cunningham/Fiume), 72
Real-time data, 303–304
Reducing batch size, 207–208
*Relevance Lost: The Rise and Fall of
Management Accounting*
(Johnson/Kaplan), 14
Rell, Jodi, 292
Results Washington, 286–288, 291
Retrenchment, 104
Richards, Mark, 196–205
Ries, Eric, 205–210
Rockwell International, 50–52
Rocssner, Jane, 252
Rother, Mike, 33
Rothschiller, Joe, 97–105
Ryan, Dick, 166, 167, 169

Sales
helping dealers improve their own
processes, 112–113
order spikes, 104–105, 112
Same day—next day, 240
San Benedetto. *See* Acqua Minerale
San Benedetto
Sarasohn, Homer, 35
Saskatchewan, 297–304
Scaling down production to meet
demand, 79–80

Scaling expenses to correspond with
    immediate demand, 102
Schein, Edgar, 270, 271, 305
Schulist, Jason, 202–204
Scientific management
    (Taylorism), 10–12
See, feel, change paradigm, 269, 270
Self-audit, 200
Senge, Peter M., 188
Servant leadership, 227–229
Seven wastes, 25
Sharing knowledge, 209
Sharma, Anand, 76
Shewhart, Walter, 37
Shingijutsu, 48, 49, 56, 57
Shingo, Shigeo, 32
Shook, John, 33, 306
Shop floor experiences, 146–147
"Silent Sloan," 10
Silos, 142, 152, 209, 240. See also
    Functional silos
Silversin, Jack, 266
Simpler, 223
Single-minute exchange of dies
    (SMED), 32, 45, 238–240
Single-piece flow, 44, 238, 239
Six Sigma, 20
Sloan, Alfred, 8–10, 16
SMED. See Single-minute exchange
    of dies (SMED)
Smith, Adam, 11
Software development, 206
Solomon, Jerry, 164
Sorenson, Charles E., 5
Specialty Silicone Fabricators (SSF),
    189–196
Speeding tickets, 289–290
Spike orders, 104, 112
Standard cost accounting, 59, 73, 142
Standards, 28
Start-ups, 205–216
Steffes, Paul, 97–98, 105
Steffes Corporation, 96–105
Strategic finance, 212

Streiner, Herbert, 18
Stretch goals, 64
Supremia Grup, 245–250
Sustainable businesses, 215
Swartz, Joe, 276, 277, 279, 280
Systemic barriers to success, 142

Takenaka, Akira, 49, 53
Takt time, 28, 45
Taylor, Frederick, 10–11, 127
Taylorism, 10–12
Team-building exercise, 194
Team leader development
    program, 230
ThedaCare Center for HealthCare
    Value, 259, 260
ThedaCare Medical Center, 254–265
3P. See Production Preparation
    Process (3P)
Thrift store (Goodwill Industries),
    181–185
Time and motion studies
    (Taylor), 10
Time on hand (waiting), 25
Today and Tomorrow (Ford), 6
Tosato, Pierluigi, 135–140
Total Productive Maintenance
    (TPM), 29
Total quality control (TQC),
    36–37, 41–43, 45
Total quality management
    (TQM), 20, 45
Toussaint, John, 254–265, 316
Toyoda, Eiji, 27, 40
Toyoda, Kiichiro, 21–23, 189
Toyoda, Sakicki, 21
Toyoda, Shoichiro, 42, 48
Toyoda Loom Works, 21, 23
Toyota Motor Company
    All Toyota Quality Control
        Conference, 43
    andon, 29
    autonomous maintenance, 29
    Corolla introduced, 42

creative idea suggestion
system, 28
Crown introduced, 40
five whys, 31
hoshin kanri, 41
jidoka, 29
kanban, 30
layoff of 1600 employees, 23
leader of Lean movement, 307
lifetime employment, 22, 23
matrix management structure, 41
Model AA, 22
Operations Management Consulting
Division (OMCD), 43
origin, 22
SMED, 32
"symphony like" synchronization, 268
takt time, 28
Training Within Industry
(TWI), 28
U.S. Army's ordering of
trucks, 27
value stream, 32–33
winner of Japan Quality Control
Prize (1970), 42
Toyota Production System (TPS),
25, 29, 30, 33, 43
Toyota Production System,
The (Ohno), 207
Toyota Quality Control Award, 43
TPM. *See* Total Productive
Maintenance (TPM)
TPS. *See* Toyota Production
System (TPS)
TQC. *See* Total quality
control (TQC)
TQM. *See* Total quality
management (TQM)
Traditional accounting, 72–74
Training Within Industry (TWI),
15, 16, 28, 45–46
Trane, 218, 219
Trial-and-error approach to
implementation, 192

Trust, 85–86
TWI. *See* Training Within
Industry (TWI)
Two-factor theory, 128

Uncertainty, 189, 214
Unification, 300, 301
Union of Japanese Scientists and
Engineers (JUSE), 36
United Motors Company, 8
Us versus them environment, 127

Validated learning, 205
Valmont Industries, 196, 197
Value stream
align expenses with demand and
customer value, 101
Aluminum Trailer Company, 91
commitment to bring Lean to entire
organization, 100
defined, 46
diversified corporation,
224–227, 233
dynamic model/activity for which
customers are paying, 313
Herman Miller, 120
Steffes Corporation, 103
Toyota, 32–33
Value stream manager, 102
Value stream mapping (VSM), 33, 34,
46, 213, 214, 247
Values, 250
Variances, 13
Vermeer, Gary, 108
Vermeer Corporation, 108–115
Vibco Vibrators, 236–245
Vietnam War, 17
Virginia Mason Institute, 274
Virginia Mason Medical Center,
265–275
Virginia Mason Production System
(VMPS), 271–272, 275
Virtuous cycle, 232
Visual control, 61

Visual information, 29–31
VSM. *See* Value stream
    mapping (VSM)

Wadensten, Karl, 236–245
Walker, Brian, 117–125
Washington State, 285–291, 315
Waste, 2, 24, 25, 247, 314
Waste removal, 2
Wasteful activities, 142
Waterman, Robert, 308
Wealth of Nations (Smith), 11
*What Ever Happened to Good Old
    Yankee Ingenuity,* 18
"What Happened in Japan?"
    (Deming), 36

Wiremold, 58–67
Womack, James P., 77, 211
"Work smarter, not harder," 17–19
Worker motivation, 127–140
    Acqua Minerale San Benedetto,
        135–140
    Caetano Bus, 129–135
    caveats, 128–129
    common HR motivators, 128
    Herzberg's two-factor theory, 128
    Lean motivators, 128
    motivators intrinsic to work
        itself, 128
Wyman, Todd, 221

Yanmar Diesel, 49, 53